Photo credit: Nicole Jones

Fiona McAnena grew up in Northern Ireland during the Troubles, graduated from Cambridge University, and worked in brand management and marketing strategy in multinational businesses. In 2018, she became concerned at how trans demands were eroding women's rights and got involved in the resistance. She spent five years as a volunteer with Fair Play For Women, working across its campaigns and directing its successful work in sport. She joined Sex Matters in early 2024 as director of campaigns.

I devoured this essential history of the people and campaigns that turned Britain into *Terf Island* in a single sitting. Packed with sharp insights and telling details, this is social history written with the thrill and verve of a whodunnit.

—Helen Joyce, author of *Trans: Gender Identity and the New Battle for Women's Rights*

When historians chronicle this period of insanity, due honour will go to the four heroic women whose stories are told in this engaging and important book. It's easy to talk sense now that the tide has turned, but it took real courage in the days when you could lose your job, suffer savage bullying and almost universal ostracism, even physical violence, simply for stating a scientific fact.

—Richard Dawkins FRS, Emeritus Professor of the Public Understanding of Science, University of Oxford

A bracing account of the battle for sanity in a society that fancies itself so modern but has actually gone medieval. The gutsy women in this compelling book have risked everything to defend the reality of unalterable biological sex.

—Lionel Shriver, author of *We Need to Talk About Kevin* and *Mania*

A fascinating book about brave key figures in the UK sex-realist movement, told grippingly by another brave key figure. These women deserve to have their stories widely heard.

—Kathleen Stock, author of *Material Girls: Why Reality Matters for Feminism*

I love this book. It's calm and authoritative, a reminder of what women can achieve when faced with an overtly misogynist ideology. Anyone who's heard the phrase 'toxic on both sides' should read it, and marvel at the patience and persistence of the inspiring women McAnena has written about.

—Joan Smith, author of *Misogynies*

History is mostly written by men, about men. This vastly entertaining and informative book is different; about a handful of women whose efforts changed the UK for everyone, including incisive portraits of heroines from Kellie-Jay Keen to Maya Forstater.

—Julie Burchill, journalist, polemicist, novelist; the TV adaptation of her YA novel *Sugar Rush* won an International Emmy

While much of the world has capitulated to gender identity ideology and its regressive impact on women's rights, the UK has taken a different path. If you want to know how – and who made that happen – this is the book for you.

—Andrew Doyle, writer and broadcaster, author of *The New Puritans* and *The End of Woke*

One day the world will look back on this insane period of biology denial and the wilful mutilation of vulnerable children with true horror. All those in this book from Terf Island can say they did their very best to stop it. Feisty women, every one. I'm proud to be amongst them. Fiona tells the story in brilliant detail of just how hard it was to get facts, science, statistics and even simple respectful debate out into the public domain. All these women are modern day super-heroes.

—Sharron Davies MBE, legendary British Olympian, Olympic silver medallist and campaigner

Proud to have been an outspoken Terf Islander although I came to the protest a little later than the women in this book. Defending the rights of women and children was a tough, dangerous and painful battle. These women never gave up. We must all thank them for saving our sex.

—Dame Jenni Murray, writer and broadcaster

TERF ISLAND

HOW THE UK RESISTED TRANS IDEOLOGY

FIONA McANENA

SPINIFEX

We respectfully acknowledge the wisdom of Aboriginal and Torres Strait Islander peoples and their custodianship of the lands and waterways. The Countries on which Spinifex offices are situated are Djiru, Bunurong and Wurundjeri, Wadawurrung, Gundungarra and Noongar.

First published by Spinifex Press, 2025

Spinifex Press Pty Ltd
PO Box 200, Little River, VIC 3211, Australia
PO Box 105, Mission Beach, QLD 4852, Australia

women@spinifexpress.com.au
www.spinifexpress.com.au

Edited by Pauline Hopkins, Renate Klein and Susan Hawthorne
Index by Belinda Nemec
Cover design by Deb Snibson
Typesetting by Helen Christie, Blue Wren Books
Typeset in Arno Pro
Printed in the USA

NATIONAL LIBRARY OF AUSTRALIA

A catalogue record for this book is available from the National Library of Australia

ISBN: 9781922964267 (paperback)
ISBN: 9781922964274 (ebook)

For everyone who found their voice,
and for everyone who needs help to find theirs.

Courage calls to courage everywhere.

Each time a woman stands up for herself, without knowing it possibly, without claiming it, she stands up for all women.

—MAYA ANGELOU

Never doubt that a small group of thoughtful, committed citizens can change the world; indeed, it's the only thing that ever has.

—MARGARET MEAD

CONTENTS

INTRODUCTION

Welcome to Terf Island

LONG BEFORE TERF ISLAND HAD ITS NAME THERE WERE women who spotted the risks. English journalists Julie Bindel and Suzanne Moore were vilified years ago for writing about it. Julie expressed concerns about transgender ideology and its impact on women's rights as early as 2004, writing for *The Guardian*, an English national newspaper with impeccably left-wing credentials. That made her a target for activists, who called her a transphobe and a bigot. A few years later, she was nominated for a Stonewall award for her work promoting gay rights. Yes, *that* Stonewall, the UK charity promoting equality for gay, lesbian and bisexual people. No mention of trans. Back then, their focus was LGB, without the T. But she didn't get the award, despite winning the public vote, because of protests by pro-trans activists. Suzanne first got into trouble in 2013 for writing that women were expected to look like "Brazilian transsexuals."

Feminist academics talked and wrote about the issue too, long before Stonewall even acknowledged it as a cause. Sheila Jeffreys and Julia Long, both lesbian feminist academics, resisted attempts by trans-identifying men to stop them from speaking and to close down their events. Germaine Greer was one of the first women to be cancelled from speaking at a UK university for denying that transwomen are women. "I'm not saying that people should not be allowed to go through that procedure," she explained in 2015. "All I'm saying is that it doesn't make them a woman." Being Germaine, she went much further, saying in a radio interview:

> Just because you lop off your dick and then wear a dress doesn't make you a fucking woman. I've asked my doctor to give me long ears and liver spots and I'm going to wear a brown coat but that won't turn me into a fucking cocker spaniel.

It must have been hard, being one of those early lonely voices and being sanctioned for it. And then what bittersweet relief to see, as the threat grew, a gradual dawning of understanding that there was a problem, and other people finally speaking out.

The work done by the women in this book to draw attention to the UK government's *Gender Recognition Act* (GRA) proposals played a big part in the sharp increase in awareness in 2018. It may also have been a big year for transgender publicity, if the pro-trans crowd wanted to normalise trans ahead of their hoped-for change to self-ID in the GRA. The first trigger I remember was the gender-fluid banker, Pips Bunce, who was also a catalyst for Maya Forstater getting into trouble. That was in June before the government's consultation opened.

Many people have had a hand in the making of *Terf Island*.[1] It would be impossible to give credit to them all, especially since some of them remain anonymous. In this book I track the campaigns, and the women who led them, which created public awareness and mobilised resistance in the UK at that critical time. Without their readiness, it seems likely there would not have been sufficient pushback on self-ID. It may have been passed into law without much public awareness at all, as happened in Ireland.

---

1 'In late March 2022, an American journalist wondered on Twitter why the "UK elite" contains more "Terfs" (trans-exclusionary radical feminists) than those of the US or Canada. "The answer is Mumsnet, I believe," the *New York Times* columnist Ross Douthat responded.' As reported in <https://www.newstatesman.com/politics/media/2022/05/mumsnet-founder-justine-roberts-interview>.

Instead, a few brave women took on the fight.

The first one I saw was Kellie-Jay Keen on *Sky News* in autumn 2018. Soon after, I ventured to my first in-person meeting, a Rad Fem 101 event in a church in central London. Both Kellie-Jay and Stephanie Davies-Arai were in the audience. I approached each of them in turn to thank them for what they were doing. Sheila Jeffreys, Julie Bindel and Julia Long were speakers, along with a Scottish woman whose name I didn't catch. She kept breaking into a half-song half-chant of "she burrrns" which I found quite unnerving. Baby terf that I was, I didn't get the reference. Terfs[2] are evil witches, you see, or their modern incarnation. Linda Bellos and Venice Allan also spoke briefly (see Chapter 3).

A month later, after emailing to offer my time as a volunteer for Fair Play For Women, I met Nicola Williams. Maya Forstater was still in her job then. We didn't meet until the spring of 2019 when she was asked to give her first talk at a Woman's Place UK meeting which Nicola and I attended together.

These are the women I saw putting themselves out there when there was no cover. They weren't the first, but they succeeded in making the issue mainstream, and they did it when it mattered most. Their impact, directly and in encouraging others to join the fight, was monumental. In telling their stories, I have mentioned some others who made important contributions too. There were many more. Other campaign groups have come and gone; new ones have emerged. Scotland has its own groups which started in the critical period from late 2017 to 2018 to fight self-ID laws and which are still fighting important battles. Their stories are told in the important book edited by Susan Dalgety and Lucy Hunter Blackburn, *The Women Who Wouldn't Wheesht* (2024).

2 In November 2019, Mr Justice Julian Knowles, in the case of Harry Miller against Humberside Police and the College of Policing, said in the UK High Court, "I have become familiar with the term 'terf'. It is a derogatory term used by those who seek to de-platform those who hold different views."

We can be proud that in this period of women's rights under attack, when transgender ideology is harming children and vulnerable adults, both straight and gay, we have earned the nickname, 'Terf Island'. Campaigners around the world look to us in the UK, on Terf Island, for inspiration, courage and hope.

Linda Bellos and Venice Allan at the Rad Fem 101 event in a London church in November 2018

Photo courtesy of Venice Allan

Author's Note

In researching this book, I have found that memories vary. There have been instances where two people remembered the same events differently. It follows that this account is not perfect. I hope it does justice to the people whose stories it tells.

I have used quoted speech where I am quoting someone's exact words, usually from my interviews with them. Where I report the gist of what was said but not the precise words, I have reported speech without using quotation marks.

I have quoted Tribunal Tweets' posts on Maya's various court hearings. These are real-time posts so cannot be taken as perfectly accurate. I've also tidied up a few of them where there were obvious typos.

I've referred to Twitter, not X, because that was its name at the time. The habit of calling posts 'tweets' is hard to break.

1

Stephanie Davies-Arai

STEPHANIE DAVIES-ARAI RAISED THE ALARM ABOUT THE risks of transgender ideology for children. No one has done more to protect children from the harm of unnecessary medical treatments that claim to change their sex. Her work led ultimately to a court case which was reported worldwide; a major review by the UK's National Health Service; the closure of the UK's child gender treatment centre, the Gender Identity Development Service at the Tavistock Clinic in London; and the ending of the use of puberty-blocking drugs on healthy children in the UK in 2024.

As children, Stephanie and her twin Helen were tomboys. They wore clothes from the boys' catalogue, played football, climbed trees and hated girly stuff. As Stephanie remembers, "We called each other Mike and Bill and we modelled ourselves on Just William. When we were about six, my parents bought us toy prams for our birthday. We turned them into tanks and terrorised the neighbours."

It's no surprise that puberty hit them hard. They both developed eating disorders. Stephanie told feminist blogger Lily Maynard:

> I grew up in the era of Page 3. Pan's People were on Top of the Pops. Family entertainment was Benny Hill: older men lusting after schoolgirls and trying to escape their nagging wives. There were strippers in the local pub in Leicester at lunchtime. It was constantly in your face how a woman 'should' be. It was only

> looking back that I realised I'd imbibed all that and I had a deep internal misogyny. I had a real contempt for anything that was feminine.

Maybe they were lucky that they grew up in the punk era, when rejecting femininity was acceptable.

After art college, Stephanie became a successful sculptor. Her sculptures are organic, curvaceous, semi-abstract female forms, ranging from something you could hold in the palm of your hand – and you want to, because they're so tactile – to life-size pieces cast in bronze or carved in marble. A few years after graduation, a Japanese gallery wanted to buy some of her work, and she decided it would be an adventure to deliver the work herself. She did well in Japan, winning prizes and commissions. She learned to speak and write Japanese. After five years, she came back with a Japanese husband and a six-month-old son, settling in the south of England.

During her pregnancy, the eating issues had faded away. They had three more children. While the children were small, Stephanie co-founded a private primary school, Lewes New School, and was a parent-governor. She volunteered there, supporting the head teacher and working with the children. She studied parenting theory and parent effectiveness training from the USA, but felt it was too child-centred. She believed it should be informed by how children develop, but not *led* by them – because they are children, with immature brains and limited understanding. As a parent and a school governor, she saw how children perceived and understood things differently, and that meant they couldn't be put in charge. She saw that children believe what adults tell them, often taking things literally. She developed her own training programme to help Lewes New School teachers and parents to understand this and to communicate more effectively with children.

Word spread and teachers from other schools started asking Stephanie to run training days for them. She also worked one-on-one with parents. Communicating with Kids became a business,

Stephanie's main source of income, and eventually a book which she published in 2015. By then she was amicably divorced, her children were in high school, and she was no longer involved in Lewes New School. Alongside Communicating with Kids, she developed a programme called Communicating with Teens, but by then the transgender issue was starting to take over her working life. Communicating with Teens only ever got one airing before Stephanie parked it indefinitely. She felt there was a more pressing problem to tackle.

As part of Communicating with Kids, she wrote a light-hearted weekly blog about parenting. This led to occasional articles for media sites like the *Huffington Post* and for Mumsnet. Naturally she read about children too, and around 2013 she started seeing stuff about the idea that children could be transgender. It was usually about a child being 'born in the wrong body', and how the parents and sometimes teachers had to adapt to enable this child to be 'their true self'. The 'trans child' was celebrated, with no questioning of what being trans meant, how it had occurred, or what it might mean in the future. Everyone in the child's life was expected to accept the 'transgender child' as truly being the other sex. Siblings were usually in the know, but as far as possible no one else would be told that this was a male child presenting as a girl or vice versa. When a child was socially transitioned very young, before starting school, other children at school were generally not told the child's real sex. Changing schools was another way that a 'trans kid' could start afresh with their new identity.

None of this seemed to Stephanie like a good way to treat a child. She felt that the children – the 'trans kid', their siblings bearing this family secret, and any school mates who knew the truth – were all made to carry an adult burden in juvenile minds. School friends who didn't know were deceived by parents and teachers as well as by other children. It didn't sit right with everything she knew about child development and especially children's understanding. She could see how these so-called 'trans kids' did not conform to sex stereotypes, just like she and her sister had been as children, but she couldn't see how any child could be born in the wrong body. It sounded almost religious, like a soul, another thing she didn't believe in. She and Helen started talking about this growing phenomenon, collecting and sharing articles and noticing how there was more and more coverage, all of it enthusing about the 'transgender child'.

At that time, Stephanie was part of a campaign to stop the daily publication of topless images of women in national newspapers in the UK. The biggest paper, *The Sun*, was the worst offender, with a topless model on page three every day. Other papers sometimes had topless women on the front page. In 2012, a woman called Lucy-Anne Holmes started an online petition called 'No More Page 3', asking *The Sun* to stop. They tried to get media and political interest in the problems caused by sexualised images of women being everywhere. The following year, *Woman's Hour* on BBC Radio 4 had a phone-in on the issue. Stephanie called in and talked about 'No More Page 3'. Shortly afterwards, through her Communicating With Kids website, she got a message from the campaign founder saying, We heard you on *Woman's Hour*. We thought you were amazing. Would you like to join us on the campaign?

Stephanie rapidly became central to the team. She usually did the social media and most of the radio interviews because she worked from home. She spoke at the annual general meetings of the UK's largest retailers, Tesco and Sainsburys, and went to meetings at Tesco's head office. This commercial pressure, rather than moral or political pressure, was probably the catalyst for *The Sun* to drop Page 3 in January 2015.

But if you read the history of the campaign published by another of the core group years later, you won't find Stephanie. You'll read about things she did, like enlisting Mumsnet and the involvement of the big supermarkets that was so key to the campaign's success. But Stephanie is not there. She thinks this is because the 'No More Page 3' campaigners want to distance themselves from her because of her later work. It's a retrospective cancellation.

The 'No More Page 3' campaign was coordinated through a private Facebook group they called HQ. As the main tweeter, if Stephanie wasn't clear whether to retweet something, she'd put it in HQ for discussion. They didn't agree on everything but the single-minded focus on Page 3 meant they didn't have to thrash out a position or take sides on pornography, prostitution, or any other issue. One day there was a query from another team member on Twitter duty about whether to retweet a post promoting a women-only event. Other people in the team said they shouldn't retweet it because it was non-inclusive. It didn't include trans women (the term they used). Stephanie said, "Well, if you have it as inclusive of trans women, then the most vulnerable women that this group is intended for, the ones who actually need women-only space, won't come. So you'll end up excluding them." The subject was dropped.

At the peak of the 'No More Page 3' campaign in 2014, the feminist writer and campaigner Caroline Criado Perez wrote a blog about 'cis', the term being used to mean 'not trans', and why saying 'cis woman, trans woman' wasn't just like saying 'black woman'. This was also discussed in a HQ chat and Stephanie tried to explain how offensive this could be to black women and disabled women: that they're being talked about as if being black or disabled is the same as somebody who's male. Again the group let it drop so as to focus on the main goal.

When a campaign has a single aim, it's clear when the work is done. After their victory in early 2015, the 'No More Page 3' campaign was over but the crew stayed in their private Facebook group. They had worked so closely, been in daily contact for three years, and achieved something huge in the face of great scepticism and sometimes abuse. They'd really bonded.

A few weeks after their victory, Stephanie saw something in the *Huffington Post* that tipped her over the edge. It was yet another piece about a young child being transitioned, and she sat down and furiously wrote about it for her Communicating with Kids weekly blog. Her post was called, 'Is my child transgender?' She'd done her research, and she was in no doubt about the answer. The blog post, which links to nine different articles and research studies, starts like this:

> 'Is my child trans?' Research says probably not. It is not abnormal or unusual for a child to like playing with toys and wearing clothes which are associated with the opposite sex. It is also not uncommon for such children to insist that they actually are the opposite sex. The research shows clearly that the overwhelming majority of children outgrow identification with the opposite sex during puberty and that by far the most likely outcome is that these children will turn out to be gay or lesbian, as these research studies show.

About that time, one of the 'No More Page 3' team had set up a service for women who'd been sexually abused to have healthcare like cervical smears done by women in a women-only space. She'd made it trans-inclusive. Stephanie didn't comment at first on the trans-inclusive women's healthcare service but suddenly in HQ, she was "descended on," she thinks in response to her blog post questioning trans identity. An argument broke out, with Stephanie saying, "But look, the most vulnerable women won't come if they can't be sure that it's female-only." The others disagreed, insisting that being trans-inclusive was the only way to be.

"I'm not sure if I was outright called a bigot," Stephanie says, "but I was certainly treated as if I was a terrible person." This was devastating. After three intense years of work, did they not know her?

> We were such a tight team. We'd been through so much together on that campaign. Suddenly, everybody was against me. I ended up just saying, Look, I think I'm causing problems in this group and making it uncomfortable for others. I'm going to leave. I'll stay here for the rest of the day so that you can all say nice things about me. And then I'll quietly leave at the end of the day, which I did.
>
> It was really really horrible. These were women I'd been close to, some I'd helped and supported when they had problems. I was thinking, These people know me, they know I'm not a bigot.

> What's going on? We can't just have a discussion about it? People were angry.

This was Stephanie's first experience of how divisive this issue can be. It's the first, and closest, friendship group she lost. She says the others are still a tight-knit group. But to them it's as if she didn't exist.

From 'No More Page 3' to 'Transgender Trend'

So here she was in early 2015, finished with 'No More Page 3', full of pent-up anxiety, rage even, about the transitioning of children. She could see it was a rapidly-growing trend which was being promoted as wholly positive. "I was desperate to write about it. I was desperately worried about children and what was happening."

She collected all the evidence she could find, looking at the work of Dr Ken Zucker, the world-renowned Canadian expert on transgender identity, and at published studies from the Dutch clinic where the puberty-blocking protocol began. She was hearing about clusters of girls transitioning – her 15-year-old daughter told her that there were three girls in her year who were all planning double mastectomies. But no one mentioned social contagion, in which attitudes, emotions, or behaviours can spread subconsciously within friendship groups, especially teenage girls.

Meanwhile in the press, it was mostly about little children being transitioned in primary schools. Stephanie felt that this was child abuse:

> I consider treating a child as an adult to be child abuse. I think that's emotional abuse. Because a child has no way of understanding that this is an ideology, no way of understanding that you are affirming their gender identity. You're just telling a boy he's a girl. Children trust what adults tell them, particularly adults in positions of authority like parents and teachers. They can only respond to the reality that they're given, initially by parents and then the rest of society. It takes maturity and growing up before you start questioning the messages that your society gave you as a child.

By then, TV programmes promoting being transgender as a good thing had gone mainstream. In 2014, the BBC children's channel, CBBC, aired a documentary called *I Am Leo* about a transitioning girl, aimed at six to 12-year-olds. It presented medical transition as benign. It featured Dr Polly Carmichael, a clinical psychologist from the Gender Identity Development Service, known as GIDS. It was the only specialist gender clinic for children in England and Wales, part of the Tavistock and Portman NHS Trust. They received referrals from all over the UK. In the documentary, Dr Carmichael looks and sounds the very picture of a confident, caring medical practitioner when she explains gently that the puberty blockers Leo would take were just "a pause button" – complete with a graphic on the screen like pausing a video – and if you stopped them everything would resume and get back to normal. The logic was that it gave unhappy children time to work out their 'true' identity, male or female, before they went through puberty.

After puberty, the human body is so obviously male or female in so many ways that medical intervention after that is much less effective in helping someone to 'pass' as the other sex, especially for men who want to look like women. It's not just the sex organs, it's the shape of the face and forehead, getting an Adam's apple, a lower voice, a beard. A boy whose puberty is blocked will not develop those distinctive male characteristics. So if he tries to 'feminise' his appearance later, it will be easier and more convincing. This was the core logic of the Dutch protocol – the approach developed by the clinic in the Netherlands which pioneered the routine use of puberty blockers for children who said they were trans.

If you believe that children can be born in the wrong body and need medical help to change their body to match their inner feeling, then it makes sense to interrupt the 'wrong' puberty of those children. In 2014, Dr Carmichael was reported in a newspaper article as saying the results from their puberty blockers trial had been good and they were rolling it out – not treating it as a trial or a research study, just adopting it as routine treatment. The 2010 study protocol had stated that the project would run for about six years, starting in 2011 and recruiting participants for the first three years. By 2014, they had only just finished recruiting children into the study and no results had been published.

Six months after *I Am Leo*, the popular documentary-maker Louis Theroux made a programme called *Transgender Kids* which went out on primetime TV. "That's when I knew it was mainstream, it would explode," says Stephanie. "The programme wasn't called 'children with gender dysphoria', it was 'transgender kids'." As if they were born that way. Referrals to the GIDS clinic doubled that year. In the programme, no one asks what it means to be a boy or a girl, or why these children believe they are the other sex. One boy clearly does not believe it but his mother does. They seem to associate boy and girl with certain characteristics: boys always have short hair, girls never. If these are the external signifiers of some inner sense, what is that sense? Or could the external stuff be all there is? It matters because the implications of medical transition are far from trivial.

Stephanie was scared when she posted that first 'Is your child transgender?' blog in March 2015. She already knew this was an area you weren't allowed to talk about. But she got lots of responses to the post from parents expressing their relief that finally somebody had written about this. Several were worried about their own child. They wanted to know where to get information and advice they could trust. A typical email might say, "My daughter says she's trans, she says she's a boy, and I don't know what to do." Stephanie searched online to see what sort of information those parents would find. It all seemed totally one-sided. A child's declaration of feeling transgender was being treated the same as an adult declaring they were gay: accept, affirm, celebrate.

But there is a huge difference between saying you are gay and saying you are transgender, especially for a child. Being gay doesn't involve medication or surgery. No one refers a gay person to the doctor. But children were being referred to a clinic if they said they felt they were meant to be the other sex, and some were put on powerful medication that stopped their natural development. What if they changed their mind? Stephanie's concern was that they were only children. How could they know for sure that they needed to change their bodies in order to be happy? If under 18s are not allowed to get a tattoo, or trusted to drink alcohol, how could they be allowed to commit to this? Why would their parents be expected to take the child's declaration at face value?

Affirmation was being presented as good for children's mental health. Stephanie disagrees:

> I think it's terrible for children's mental health to be affirmed as something they're not. But because of the constraints that have been placed on us regarding language, it's very difficult to say that without sounding like you're a real bigot. And you can't say, is it kind to reinforce a delusion? These are children who are confused and suffering and unhappy with the sex they were born. Is it really kind to say you're right to hate that person? That's what affirmation means. You are affirming that girl's self-rejection or body hatred. You are affirming that child's sense of being wrong. You are agreeing that that girl is worthless and that the girl in front of you is right to want to kill off that girl and replace her with a boy. And she's right because we welcome that boy, we celebrate the boy, and we'll forget all about the girl.

That first post, 'Is your child transgender?', was found by an American woman, Denise, who had started her website, 4th Wave Now, a couple of months earlier. She invited Stephanie to join her group of concerned parents. For a while they considered making a single international site, but there was too much to cover. Just keeping up with all the different policies and laws across the US states would be overwhelming. It was valuable learning but Stephanie decided she had to focus on the UK and go it alone. Nonetheless, Stephanie and Denise developed a close friendship and finally met in person at the 2023 Genspect conference in Denver. Stephanie says:

> Denise has always been a huge support to me; whenever horrible stuff was happening I could give her a call, knowing she would

Denise and Stephanie first met in person at the Genspect conference in 2023
Photo courtesy of Pamela Garfield-Jaeger

> understand. We are very close, doing similar work in the US and the UK. Denise is my best mate across the ocean.

At first, she thought the transgender issue was just one aspect of parenting that she could cover on her website but it quickly took over. She found it was all she wanted to write about, and she wanted to talk about it, too.

> I wanted the media to contact me because there were no questioning voices in the media. For that to happen, I had to be an organisation. And it worked. I put out a press release and the requests from journalists for comments on 'trans kids' stories started coming in regularly.

She planned a website separate from Communicating with Kids, to be an online resource that gave clear information, evidence and facts, an alternative to the groups saying you must affirm.

> What struck me was that nothing existed for parents, no evidence-based resources. I researched parenting books and websites, parent coaches and children's charities. Other than ordinary mothers starting to ask questions on the Mumsnet website's feminism board, I found nothing. Usually when there is a new childhood theory or approach, people will be openly discussing it, questioning it. But in this area: nothing. Radio silence. I realised that it had to be me.

After months spent gathering information, reading and researching, she was ready to launch the new website in November 2015. She called it 'Transgender Trend' because that was a search term that parents would use when they looked for help online. She saw it as a trend but she didn't see herself as an activist. It was different from the 'No More Page 3' campaign with its clear goal. This was giving information and providing balance given that everything else seemed to be promoting transgender identities and transition. She'd looked for the evidence to support affirmation, social and medical transition and the use of puberty blockers in children, and she couldn't find it. She felt a responsibility to make sure parents who were worried about their children had access to the facts. She wanted parents to be able to separate out what was evidence-based and what was ideological or coming from activist groups with an agenda.

Why Don't You Just Stop?!

As she threw herself into Transgender Trend, she became more and more alarmed at the lack of evidence and at the rapid growth in trans identification among young people, especially girls. Parents who contacted her formed a working group. One came to the rescue when Stephanie first published the website and couldn't get it to display properly. That mother and her husband became Transgender Trend's web and resources designers. "She's also an ace detective, finding obscure resources on the net," says Stephanie.

It was the BBC that reported a shocking statistic about the growth in referrals to GIDS, which were published annually. The year to

March 2016 showed a 100% increase. The old pattern of mostly boys had changed, too. For the first time, it was more girls than boys. Since the medical interventions were all happening in this one national clinic, Stephanie decided she needed to get to know them:

> I knew they had connections with the transactivist group Mermaids and I thought, I will establish a relationship with them too. My role will be as a 'critical friend'. Maybe they would listen to me as an organisation for parents of these children. I think I was quite naïve in retrospect.

Her first chance came when she heard about a seminar in Cambridge called 'Gender Non-Conforming Children: Treatment Dilemmas in Puberty Suppression'. It was presented by Dr Bernadette Wren, Head of Psychology at the GIDS clinic. Stephanie didn't see herself as an antagonist or a protester. She felt she had legitimate concerns that people working in the clinic would want to hear, so she registered and went along. Her report of the event on the Transgender Trend website shows that the GIDS approach was relatively cautious back then. Dr Wren reported that 18% of their referred patients were autistic compared with 1% of the population. She said that most children desisted, that is, they stopped thinking they were the other sex, but that they couldn't tell which children would persist in believing they were trans and which would desist. She mentioned that desistance was a lot lower among those children referred to the gender clinic. Dr Wren did not, in her talk, address the question that seemed obvious to Stephanie: whether this meant they were somehow the 'right' candidates for transition, or whether being affirmed as trans, and perhaps being put on puberty blockers, might solidify their belief that they were in the wrong body?

There was much musing about what was going on, admitting that they did not know what the long-term health effects of puberty blockers might be. But still, Bernadette Wren talked in a matter-of-fact way about puberty blockers and cross-sex hormones as if blocking a child's puberty was as normal as treating a migraine. She reported tension between her team and some pro-trans advocacy groups, especially in their use of the "suicide narrative, scaring children and parents into demanding puberty blockers." She said those groups were pushing for treatment-on-demand based on self-identification. Meaning that if a child says they are 'trans', they should be able to go to the clinic and get puberty blockers, and later, cross-sex hormones, just on their say-so. It was all there, in 2016.

Stephanie stood up and asked Dr Wren what evidence they had that puberty blocking was the best approach, and how they could determine which children would persist and which would simply grow out of their belief and be happy with their birth sex. The answers gave her no assurance. They just did not appear to know. It wasn't hostile but it was a bit uncomfortable, everyone squirming a little because the lovely supportive atmosphere of the event was suddenly spoiled. Stephanie knew that asking the question would create that discomfort but she felt it was essential that the audience got to hear the questions and the lack of answers. Afterwards, she approached Bernadette Wren to speak to her. Another person, who said they were the parent of an adult trans son, was asking questions and Stephanie listened to Dr Wren's answers. It was a sobering moment. "I came away from that seminar thinking, Why don't you just stop then? If you don't know what the outcomes are, why don't you just stop!"

She'd heard from the supposed experts but had still seen no evidence to support either the idea that some children were transgender or that blocking their puberty would help them. She felt so strongly that it was wrong. But it looked like no one was going to stop these doctors.

Transwash in the Media

Stephanie watched the growing media coverage with horror. It was all completely uncritical. *Woman's Hour* on BBC Radio 4 covered the rise in female referrals. So did BBC Radio's flagship news programme, *Today*. A journalist called Victoria Derbyshire with her own news and current affairs show on BBC TV talked about children being transgender without questioning what it meant, though it sounded like it meant not conforming to sex stereotypes. But the tenor of these reports was all sympathy and acceptance. No one else seemed to be wondering whether telling children they could change sex, and in some cases blocking their puberty, was in their best interests. Stephanie knew from her online reading and from attending seminars that even the doctors doing it did not know its long-term effects.

A serious BBC radio programme called *Analysis* had an episode in 2016 called 'Beyond Binary' in which there was no analysis at all, just celebration of people who felt gender fluid or non-binary. One such was Pips Bunce, a male banker who is known on his man days as Philip. "Today Pips has long blonde hair and is dressed in a smart lacy frock, tights and court shoes," said the presenter, "a beacon of immaculate corporate femininity."

Then an American academic called Jen Jack (because 'non-binary') Gieseking reported on 'their' research into Tumblr, where Jen Jack had collected more than a million posts with a trans hashtag. Jen Jack described the role of Tumblr in influencing people to adopt a trans identity and then to seek medical intervention. "There really isn't a trans person I've met under the age of 30 who hasn't been on Tumblr and hasn't been significantly affected by the kind of images they've seen there. They are sharing a lot of medical knowledge, where should I go, what surgeon should I go to, what does your surgery look like, like everyone shares surgery pictures ..."

Dr Carmichael from GIDS popped up, saying, "I think it would be fair to say that this is a developing language, the non-binary language, we're all learning along the way." Stephanie thought, Seriously? You're blocking these children's puberty and you're 'learning along the way'? Again she was thinking, how can medical professionals be doing this? How can they justify it to themselves, never mind the parents and the children?

Stephanie shared all this through the Transgender Trend website and on Twitter and raised it in the media whenever she could. She thought that if she could point out its flimsy foundations, something would change. Her blog posts encouraged people to complain to the media if they saw reporting that was biased or ill-informed. She wrote about what was going on in schools, and about a court case where Mermaids, the leading charity advocating for 'transgender children', was ordered to stay away from the family of a six-year-old because of its role in transitioning him.

One of Stephanie's first media appearances was on Mariella Frostrup's programme *Bringing Up Britain* on BBC Radio 4 in July 2016. She was on a panel with a psychiatrist from the Sandyford Clinic, the Scottish version of GIDS. He didn't say much while they were recording the programme but afterwards he said that they were seeing exactly the same at the Sandyford. She felt that he agreed with her position. The other guest was an actor whose daughter was a 'transman'. The woman talked about how it was such a relief when her trans-identifying daughter got her double mastectomy. Apparently the daughter said "I can breathe again," because she'd been wearing a binder. The mother declared herself to be relieved and delighted.

It was hard to be the nay-sayer implying that this young woman and her mother might have made a mistake. Stephanie had a go, carefully, saying, "I'm not here to judge. I'm here to ask some questions." That was her first experience of doing a pre-recorded interview. She felt it went brilliantly and she got to say everything she wanted to. She was buzzing when she came out.

When it was broadcast, she was gutted at what she heard. "They'd included all my rambling about the children's toy industry promoting stereotypes," and left out what for her was the really important stuff, the trans stuff. Stephanie was shocked at how different it was from what she'd expected, and it taught her an important lesson about pre-recorded interviews – the editing is everything.

Years later, someone told her that hearing her speak on *Bringing Up Britain* had saved her child from medical transition. This woman's daughter had started identifying as a boy. One of the mother's friends had heard the programme and suggested she have a listen. The mother thought this Stephanie woman sounded sensible so she contacted her for support, instead of going to Mermaids as she had intended. Talking to Stephanie and reading the Transgender Trend website changed the woman's approach. Instead of affirming her daughter as a boy, which could have led onto a medical pathway, she avoided the gender clinic and waited it out. In time, the girl desisted. Since she'd had no medical interventions, there was no lasting effect. But that was later. At the time, Stephanie felt like she had blown a big chance.

"You're Cancelled, Best Wishes, Susie Green"

Around that time, the cancellation started. A reputable British charity, the National Society for the Prevention of Cruelty to Children, known as the NSPCC, had planned an event called 'Is Society Letting Down Trans Children?' as part of its 'Dare to Debate' series on serious issues facing children. After advertising the event, they cancelled it, citing concerns from 'the trans community'. You might think that those are the very people who might want to explore the question in the seminar's title. Their concerns were that the person who was to chair the debate, a journalist called Sarah Ditum, was supposedly transphobic, because she had researched and published an article exploring the development of the idea of 'innate gender identity'. In fact, the NSPCC had approached Stephanie months earlier to chair the debate. She'd replied saying she would do it but never heard from them again. Maybe someone warned them off her before it even got as far as being made public. They went to Sarah Ditum instead, but ended up dropping the whole thing.

The same week, Stephanie was blocked from attending a conference in London hosted by Mermaids called 'New Perspectives on Healthcare Provision for Transgender Youth'. Mermaids' position was that some children were born trans and should be affirmed and medicated to change their bodies as soon as possible. Its then-chief executive, Susie Green, had a 'trans child' of her own. Stephanie had signed up for this because the keynote speaker was Dr Norman Spack, the US doctor who had prescribed puberty blockers to Susie Green's 12-year-old. Stephanie had registered and paid for her ticket weeks in advance. Two days before the event, she got a reminder email. But later that same day she got an email from Susie Green. It was short though not very sweet: "Unfortunately due to oversubscription, your tickets have been cancelled for this event. You will not be able to gain admittance on the day, we apologise for any inconvenience, Best wishes, Susie Green."

Stephanie knew of others who also got this message and she suspected that Mermaids had combed the list of registered ticket holders and removed those with opposing views. This was perhaps the first clear example of what was to come, a pattern of blocking any discussion, exploration or research. Only total affirmation would do.

In November 2016, Stephanie was invited onto *BBC Newsnight* along with Susie Green. That was the first and last time they were on the same programme. Susie Green went first, talking about her 'daughter', who was born male. She said the child was different from about 18 months of age and that she, the mother, thought she had a sensitive little boy who would probably grow up to be gay. But at the age of four, Susie said, the child had told his mother he was meant to be a girl and had never doubted or regretted it.

The presenter, Evan Davis, turned to Stephanie saying, "That seems like a straightforward story, and why wouldn't you just accept the child?" Stephanie said she didn't comment on individual cases, but she questioned the use of puberty blockers on unhappy children, saying there was good evidence that 80% desisted if they were not medicated. Susie Green insisted that desistance was extremely rare and that outcomes were better among those children given puberty blockers. Stephanie said there were no long-term studies to show the outcomes. Evan Davis pointed out that these were factual questions that should have an answer. But he didn't seem curious about which might be the right one, where the data came from, or indeed what it meant to be transgender. Someone who knew nothing about the issue would just see two opposing camps, each claiming to have the truth. Although Stephanie didn't claim to have the truth. Her point was that the medics didn't either. Somehow this basic point was not landing. The requirement to be empathetic towards the 'transgender child' seemed to get in the way.

Transwash in the House

The Transgender Trend website was for parents and others who needed information like the media. But Stephanie wanted to register her concerns with the people and organisations who made the rules. She needed to get to politicians and policy-makers.

It became apparent that pro-trans groups were already working to get the UK parliament on board with their demands. In the UK, there are parliamentary committees made up of members of Parliament from all sides, each committee with its own focus. These committees run inquiries into areas of interest to them. Anyone can submit written evidence through the parliamentary website and expert witnesses are invited to speak to the committee. The Women and Equalities Select Committee (WESC) had launched what it called its 'trans inquiry' in 2015, but hardly anyone knew about it. The push had come from a trans campaign group called Press for Change. One of its founders, Dr Stephen Whittle, born female but long transitioned, was the key adviser to the committee on the trans inquiry. The committee was considering making recommendations to change the law to make it easy for anyone to change the sex registered on their birth certificate.

Women who knew about the inquiry submitted their concerns, including Julia Long, a feminist academic and campaigner whom Stephanie had met when she was doing 'No More Page 3', and Stephanie's sister Helen Saxby. Stephanie's submission[3] addressed the problems of this self-ID proposal. How could single-sex services or spaces be maintained if any man could declare himself a woman? She also pointed out how a purely affirmative approach to transgender identification could be harmful to confused or distressed children, encouraging them to believe they could change sex, and promoting serious medical interventions in pursuit of this impossible goal. She assumed that setting out the issues in a rational way would make a difference. In those early days, Stephanie's approach was "sort of innocent," as she remembers it now. She said what she felt needed saying, in plain English. She had no idea no one would listen.

After the written submissions, the committee selected people to speak to them in person about how to enable trans equality. No one really defined what trans meant or what inequality they were facing. Susie Green was invited as chief executive of Mermaids, sitting alongside two trans-identifying adults and Dr Bernadette Wren of GIDS. One of the trans people, Jay Stewart, born female but now a transman, was co-founder of a charity called Gendered Intelligence. The other, a student called Anna Lee, was one of four trans-identifying men invited to give evidence. The tension between Susie Green and Dr Wren was clear. Dr Wren more or less said they were always being pushed by campaign groups to make puberty blockers available for younger children. She spoke of uncertainty at GIDS, saying, "We, in our small way, are trying really to support individual children but not to get swept along in something that we simply do not understand at this point."

The trans-identifying witnesses to the committee, along with Susie Green, said it was humiliating and dehumanising to be asked to prove their gender identity in order to 'correct' their birth certificate.

3 <https://committees.parliament.uk/writtenevidence/57322/html/>.

They said being trans was not a mental illness so the requirement for two doctors to sign it off was wholly inappropriate. This overlooked the fact that the justification for the *2004 Gender Recognition Act* was that some people were so distressed by their birth sex that they needed to live in stealth as the other sex. It certainly sounded like a mental health condition. It was because of these exceptional circumstances which, it was argued in parliament, would affect only a few thousand people in the UK at most, that the extraordinary right to change their birth certificate had been granted. Bear in mind, too, that Mermaids and other activist groups constantly raise the threat of suicide, saying children and young people who aren't affirmed or who go through the 'wrong puberty' may kill themselves. But the committee was being told it's not a mental illness and no doctors should be involved in signing off on the right to change their registered sex. No women who had submitted evidence on the potential impact on women's rights and child safeguarding were invited to give oral evidence. The recording and transcript of these hearings are still available on the UK parliamentary website.[4]

The WESC trans inquiry report had a long list of recommendations to the UK government, including that people should have the legal right to change the sex stated on their birth certificate on demand, with no need for medical approval or any justification at all. This was self-identification or self-ID. It doesn't mean being allowed to dress how you like and call yourself whatever you like. That's already protected in the *Equality Act*. It means being allowed to change the sex on your birth certificate on your word alone, so that someone born male can produce a legal document 'proving' he was born female.

In September 2016, the Women and Equalities Select Committee hosted a debate on transgender equality at Westminster. Its goal was to amend the *2004 Gender Recognition Act* and update the

4 <https://committees.parliament.uk/event/8510/formal-meeting-oral-evidence-session/>.

Equality Act – with "utmost urgency," as they put it. This marked the start of the process of trying to change the law in the UK to allow self-ID. Stephanie posted on the Transgender Trend website encouraging people to contact their member of Parliament asking them to consider the implications, with pointers on what to say. Only transgender people were invited to speak at the Westminster debate, but those who had made submissions to the inquiry were invited as audience members. This was a chance for Stephanie to speak directly to the Committee chair, an MP called Maria Miller, and give her a Transgender Trend information flyer.

A few academics got in touch, worried about what they saw as misinformation being circulated to promote medical transition as the only safe option for children who thought they were trans. It wasn't just Mermaids. Another campaign group called GIRES, the Gender Identity Research and Education Society, was pushing for it too. Susie Green claimed that a survey of more than 2000 trans people in the UK showed that 48% of 'trans youth' attempted suicide. Transgender Trend published an analysis of this figure by a scientist friend. She dug into the survey that was supposed to have shown this and found that it was a survey of LGBT people, mostly gay or bisexual, not trans. How many trans people answered the questions on suicidal ideation? Twenty seven. So this 48% was actually 13 people out of a sample of 27. Not more than 2000, as Susie Green said. We can't tell how many of those 13 made a serious suicide attempt, if any. We do know that none of those 13 succeeded, since they were all there to answer the survey.

This did not stop transactivists from conjuring up the terrifying spectre of suicide to justify moving unquestioningly to medical transition, with variations on the theme "Better to have a live daughter than a dead son." Stephanie pointed out in her posts that specialist charities like The Samaritans say that speculation about the cause of a suicide can oversimplify the issue and should be avoided. They also say that young people are more susceptible to suicide contagion. But they said nothing about how it featured in the pro-transition narrative. Stephanie's view was that the approach preferred by Susie Green and Mermaids seemed to terrify young people rather than to provide reassurance or reliable information; for parents, it could feel like emotional blackmail.

In the year since Stephanie had started Transgender Trend, that trend had ramped right up. Being trans, especially for children, was promoted as something to celebrate. Trusted media like the BBC seemed to report on it monthly. Now self-ID was being pushed by the parliamentary committee with 'Women' in its name as if it was the most reasonable thing in the world, with no thought for the possible impact on anyone else.

Trying to Get the Truth Out

To evaluate the role of the media in fuelling the trend, Stephanie called for volunteers to analyse media coverage of so-called 'trans' kids, categorising it by topic and sentiment. Someone she'd met through a feminist group on Facebook, Dr Nicola Williams (later of Fair Play For Women), led a team of volunteers and crunched the numbers. The report was called 'Is It Surprising that Referrals of Children to the Tavistock Clinic Continue to Soar?' It showed overwhelmingly positive coverage, never questioning the reasons for gender dysphoria or the implications of being affirmed as the other sex. Stephanie's concern was for children being put on a medical pathway based on false expectations and also for those around them being expected to go along with it. In schools, this was at the expense of their own privacy. The media report showed how the coverage was all about how 'trans kids' conformed to the stereotypes of the other sex. Later that year, after this report had been published, Stephanie started to notice media coverage that was a bit more sceptical, albeit only by a few journalists.

The Transgender Trend website reviewed TV and radio programmes showcasing 'trans kids' and analysed the dodgy suicide stats they cited. It followed parliamentary activity on the issue, with suggestions for people to respond to consultations or write to their MP. It reported on meetings attended and conference presentations. There was also personal testimony from parents of trans-identifying young people, always anonymous to protect those involved. Stephanie spent much of her time on the phone to desperate parents. They would tell her that people thought they were bigots for wanting to protect their own child. This was intense and exhausting work but she could understand their desperation. They had nobody else to talk to.

In parallel, Stephanie responded to public consultations and wrote to healthcare professional bodies trying to draw attention to the lack of evidence for puberty blockers, along with the strong evidence that most gender-confused children would grow out of these feelings and most likely become gay adults. She says: "Watchful waiting is the most progressive approach we have for children with gender dysphoria because it allows for any outcome. The most likely outcome is homosexuality." This is why Stephanie sees the affirmation of children who claim to be the other sex as potentially homophobic. She knows, too, the shameful origins of gender transition in trying to cure homosexuality.

Transwash in the Therapy World

Stephanie hoped to reach professionals working in the field – psychotherapists, clinical psychologists, counsellors – people who provided talking therapy to distressed patients. The first therapist to contact her didn't give his real name. He wanted to tell her about a proposed change to the Memorandum of Understanding on Conversion Therapy (MoU), a policy document for counsellors and therapists. The original MoU, published in 2015, was a protection against gay conversion therapy. It was signed by all the major counselling bodies and colleges along with NHS England and the Royal College of Psychiatrists.

Now the UK Council for Psychotherapy (UKCP), the psychotherapy regulator, was co-ordinating a review, and activists within the profession were campaigning to add 'gender identity' to the MoU. He saw that it could easily lead to "affirmation by the back door," because it prohibited any questioning of what may have led to a client's identification with a cross-sex gender identity and so potentially outlaw exploration with patients what being trans meant to them, or why they felt that way. In effect, they'd have to affirm clients of all ages as whatever 'gender' they said they were. A therapist who tried to explore why a teenage girl might think she was a boy could be in trouble for malpractice. If what they did was labelled conversion therapy, they could be sanctioned and removed from the register.

This would mean that no one could help someone work out why they thought they were in the wrong body. It would have to be accepted as fact. The risk of someone, especially a young person – the group growing fastest at gender clinics – having medical treatments and surgery they may later regret, would be exponentially increased. These proposals would tie up the whole UK therapy sector. He said that UKCP officers were talking to politicians about using the MoU as the basis of a law against conversion therapy for 'gender identity'. To explore and question could then become a criminal offence – the police in the therapy room.

He'd heard of Stephanie and her work from another therapist, Bob Withers, and he thought she could help. After a few long phone conversations, they began to trust each other and he revealed his real name, James Caspian. In time they became good friends.

Stephanie tried to raise the alarm. She wrote to the junior health minister warning that adding gender identity to the MoU would mean children who were confused or distressed about being boys or girls would not get therapy. Worse, affirmation might instead set them on a harmful medical pathway. She copied the letter to all the counselling and therapy professional bodies that were signatories to the MoU. No one responded to her, and the change was duly adopted. She heard that her letter was read out at a meeting where representatives from all the professional counselling and therapy groups were discussing the proposed change. But, she was told, no one expressed agreement with her concerns, or opposed the addition of gender identity to the MoU.

This tip-off led to a painful run-in with another professional body, the British Association of Counselling and Psychotherapy (BACP) and its trade journal, *Therapy Today*. Stephanie went to a BACP conference to hear how they were talking about the issue, and why they couldn't see any risks in their affirmative approach. She thought the session about gender identity was naïve at best, harmful at worst, because it was just accepted that children and teenagers could be trans, with no exploration of why. There was no recognition of factors like the high correlation with autism and with same-sex attraction.

She wrote to *Therapy Today* pointing this out. After her letter was published, the editor met her and wrote a long, balanced piece on the issues, interviewing people on both sides of the debate, including Bob Withers and James Caspian. But before the piece was published, she was told that all her comments had been cut, as had those of Bob and James. The final piece, 'Putting Gender on the Agenda', was nothing like the draft Stephanie had seen. All criticism of the gender-affirming approach had been cut from the article. It was all about affirmation.

Furious, Stephanie wrote to *Therapy Today* to complain. This second letter was also published, but this time there was no constructive meeting with the editor. The magazine got a deluge of complaints. Stephanie and Transgender Trend were accused of being transphobic. Somebody started a petition about them. Activists criticised Stephanie personally, going way beyond the healthcare issues. They posted comments on her sculpture website saying she exploited parents, was a talentless failure, and so on. Really personal stuff. Then the editor of *Therapy Today* published an apology saying Stephanie's letter should not have been published. Total capitulation. This was because the BACP's commitment to the MoU meant no one was allowed even to keep an open mind.

This was Stephanie's lowest point. Transgender Trend had been smeared by activist groups and individuals as an 'anti-trans hate group', but this was the largest counselling body in the UK effectively accusing her of supporting conversion therapy. She thought it was the end for Transgender Trend. She also realised that the hidden purpose of the MoU was to silence debate, to prevent anyone from questioning the gender-affirmative approach. BACP not only ignored her request for a retraction or right of reply, they deleted her original letter from the online version of *Therapy Today* and in the next issue they published in full the petition that defamed Transgender Trend as an "anti transgender rights lobby group." She engaged a solicitor and sent a letter before action to BACP for defamation, but as Transgender Trend was not a legal entity at that time she was advised that it was too risky personally to take it further. Transgender Trend became a limited company in July 2019.

Stephanie felt awful about all of this for about a week and then got over it. Like other dark times, she says, it became part of the past.

Hot Topics: Transgender and Gender Diverse Children

In early 2017, Stephanie went to a conference in London hosted by the Royal College of Paediatrics and Child Health called 'Hot Topics in Child Health: Transgender and Gender Diverse Children'. She was struck by the event title. Here was the Royal College of Paediatrics, the leaders in child medicine in the UK, talking about 'transgender children' as if it were a simple fact. That was a big move on from the Cambridge event the year before which was about 'treatment dilemmas' in 'gender non-conforming children'. Suddenly there were no treatment dilemmas, and gender non-conforming children had been replaced by transgender ones. When the term 'transgender child' was used, it was as if people forgot they were talking about children. All they heard was 'transgender'.

The event was set up by the NHS's gender identity clinic for children, GIDS, in partnership with two pro-transition charities, Mermaids and GIRES. These two charities promoted the idea that being transgender was innate and immutable. To them, some children just were trans, and their bodies needed to be changed to match their inner identities. Susie Green of Mermaids was sitting a few rows in front of Stephanie. The co-founder of GIRES, Terry Reed, was a speaker, along with the top GIDS people.

The Hot Topics conference was a big moment. Stephanie had met Dr Bernadette Wren in 2016 at the Cambridge seminar, but this time Dr Polly Carmichael and Dr Sarah Davidson were there too, the other two leaders of GIDS. They were all welcoming and friendly, saying things like, "Oh, you're Stephanie, Transgender Trend. What you're doing is so important. You must keep writing." No one said what exactly was so important, but it was already clear that GIDS were under pressure from Mermaids to be gender-affirming and to provide puberty blockers to younger children, almost without question. At lunchtime, Dr Carmichael came over and sat with Stephanie and her sister Helen. They had a good chat, the first of a few at various events over the next year or so.

Back in the conference, Stephanie stood up and asked a question. Many people would find that daunting. Now imagine you're at a medical conference and you're not a clinician. Add to that the certain knowledge that the audience will resent your question. Some may even be thinking you are a bigot or a hateful person who doesn't care about distressed children. Stephanie knew what she was facing. But, she says, "My logic was that, in a way, it didn't matter if my question was answered or not. The point was to get it out there so the whole audience heard it." She felt the prevailing narrative could not go unchallenged, especially when she saw the medical people from GIDS working so closely with the campaign groups that were pushing for puberty blockers and an affirmation-only approach.

Stephanie asked her awkward question about the huge rise in teenage girls presenting to the clinic as trans. This introduced a somewhat discordant note to proceedings. Up to that point, everybody had been saying, these poor marginalised, misunderstood kids, it's terrible the discrimination they face, we must affirm them. And then Stephanie got up and asked Dr Carmichael, who was on the panel, "Why so many girls?" She said it couldn't be because of trans visibility in the media, because most of those are the opposite of these girls. They are men transitioning to a version of womanhood that these girls reject completely, a sexualised or glamorous version of womanhood that these girls feel uncomfortable with. Anyway, greater acceptance might change the numbers but why would it change the ratio, when historically it was mostly boys? She went further, asking why it wasn't seen within the framework of adolescent female mental health, rather than that, as soon as it's seen as trans, those girls are no longer girls and we can't talk about them as girls any more.

There was a sort of frisson in the hall. Stephanie believes that Polly Carmichael felt it too, that she was aware of the courage it took to stand up and say something different. The answer was that they didn't know why there were more girls. Dr Wren ventured that being female was lower-status than being male, so social factors worked on teenage girls to make them not want to become women. Stephanie was encouraged by that but frustrated that they could say this and then carry on affirming trans identities and doling out puberty blockers and cross-sex hormones.

Also presenting at the Hot Topics conference was a Dutch academic called Thomas Steensma. It seemed to Stephanie that the GIDS leadership team – Polly, Sarah and Bernadette – were in awe of him and a bit smitten. She says he was like the Justin Timberlake of the gender professionals world. He worked in the Dutch clinic that pioneered the 'Dutch protocol' for the use of puberty blockers for 'transgender' children. Stephanie talked to him. He didn't know who she was, but she knew that he was one of the most influential people in the push to give puberty blockers to children. He was presenting a research paper about that work, but like all their research it took as fact that some children simply were transgender, rather than

Stephanie Davies-Arai and her twin sister Helen Saxby in Brighton, 2019
Photo courtesy of Lily Maynard

exploring what this meant or why it happened – or even how you could diagnose it. He talked about the study they were doing but was vague about the results. Coming away from these events, Stephanie did not know whether she had achieved anything. But it had to be better than not questioning and not scrutinising the evidence.

Meanwhile, Helen had gone to hear about a different Hot Topic in the afternoon session, a seminar about school toolkits. She too stood up and asked a question. She was at the back of the room so she had to watch the whole room turn round to stare at her with hatred. When she asked a follow-up question because they didn't answer the first one adequately, the two men presenting the session told her to be quiet now, saying, "I think we *all* know exactly what *you* think." This sounds excruciating, but Helen was already battle-hardened. She remembers an earlier event, a meeting of human rights lawyers hosted by Garden Court Chambers, that was even more daunting. She and Julia Long were there, and it felt like they were in enemy territory. It was obvious from the way things were being discussed that their caution around transitioning children would not be a popular view. When it came to question time, she thought about standing up from her seat but found her legs were shaking so much she couldn't do it.

The first time Nicola Williams went with Stephanie to one of these meetings, Stephanie suggested Nic might stand up and ask a question, but she didn't feel ready. All the same, Nic says this was an important part of her early training in activism. When she later branched out on her own, as spokeswoman for Fair Play For Women (see Chapter 2), she followed the same tactic. She found it almost as scary as Helen had, but at least by then she'd had some practice under Stephanie's tutelage. Nic's first question in a public meeting on gender issues was when they went together to an NHS public consultation on specialised gender identity services early in 2018. Nic asked about the rise in teenage girls identifying as boys. Stephanie asked about detransitioners; she was told that regret was not necessarily a "failure."

At that time, almost no one was speaking out. Stephanie went to as many medical and educational conferences and Westminster Policy Forum events as she could, specifically to ask questions publicly:

> Even though I could always feel the hostility from the room and the panel, I felt there must be more people there who had the same doubts as I did. I wanted to show them that you're allowed to ask questions just as in any other subject.

Schools Guidance

Teachers were contacting Stephanie, cautiously, saying it was difficult to know what to do for the best when a trans-identifying child wanted to change their name and pronouns, and access the areas of the other sex. Everyone wanted to accommodate the child – especially if this was what might alleviate their distress. But this affected the other pupils who would have to go along with it, changing their words, too. The Department for Education had no guidance on this and Stephanie could see that many local authorities were using guidance provided by transactivist groups. Guidance from a Brighton-based group called AllSorts was being widely circulated in schools all over the country. It was all about affirming the needs and rights of 'transgender' children, with no regard for the impact on the others.

In 2017, she read in a newspaper that the Equality and Human Rights Commission (EHRC) was going to fill this void by issuing schools guidance. The EHRC is the UK government body responsible for monitoring how equality law is being complied with, ensuring rights are protected and that the right balance is struck when there are conflicting rights. Their involvement should have been good news. But the report said that they had already held a round table meeting with all the stakeholders, meaning trans lobby groups – Stonewall, Mermaids, GIRES, AllSorts. Stephanie contacted the EHRC and requested a stakeholder meeting of her own. She brought along a therapist and a couple of parents. Nicola Williams went too as she was in London for her appearance on *Good Morning Britain* talking about men in women's prisons. The civil servants listened but there were no minutes of the meeting and no official record of the concerns being raised. Afterwards, Stephanie sent them a document outlining her three areas of concern about the trans guidance that was circulating in schools.

The EHRC had declared its intention to publish in March 2018. Stephanie realised she wouldn't be able to stop publication or even influence it to be balanced. She decided Transgender Trend would produce its own schools guidance and get it out ahead of the EHRC's. This was a big deal. It took months of work, with input from a teacher and from a safeguarding expert. It was published as a free downloadable pdf on the website in February, a month before the EHRC guidance was due. Trans lobby groups, and some teachers, "went ballistic" in Stephanie's words. Stonewall put out a statement saying the Transgender Trend guide was deeply damaging and wrote to local authorities saying they should avoid it. Articles in a teachers' magazine, *Schools Week,* denounced it as an "anti-trans guide." So did a headteachers' newsletter. The head of Stonewall Scotland said it was dangerous and posted a picture on his social media showing it in the bin. Others said it was a modern version of *Mein Kampf.* Pro-women campaigner Lily Maynard wrote an entertaining account of the reaction called 'Ban it! Bin it! Shred it!' on her blog.[5] The reaction generated massive awareness of the new publication. It was a brilliant example of the Streisand effect.[6] Downloads quickly reached 15,000.

The published abuse was deeply unpleasant, some of it defamatory, but it was clear that many parents and teachers welcomed the guidance. Stephanie felt vindicated. She decided to get it printed so parents could give copies to schools. Maybe it's because she's a sculptor that Stephanie likes real, tangible objects. Transgender Trend launched an appeal to fund the print run. Even that was tough. Activists demanded that Crowdfunder UK, which hosts crowdfunders for all sorts of causes, close down the Transgender Trend appeal. They did so, to the sound of much crowing on Twitter by trans groups. A headline in *The Independent,* a national newspaper, said, 'Crowdfunding platform suspends campaign to distribute "deceitful" school resources on transgender young people'.

When Stephanie contacted Crowdfunder UK, she was told there had been reports that she was raising money for something hateful and that they had to investigate. That was another moment where she thought maybe Transgender Trend had hit the wall. If a supposedly independent company like Crowdfunder UK were to determine that Transgender Trend was too hateful to be allowed to raise money, that would be the end. But after six days it confirmed they had found no

5 <https://lilymaynard.com/ban-it-bin-it-shred-it-transgender-trends-new-guidelines-for-schools-the-activists-that-hate-it/>.

6 The Streisand effect is when an attempt to hide, remove, or censor information instead increases public awareness of the information. In 2003, Barbra Streisand tried to block a photograph taken to show coastal erosion in California because it also showed her home. The result was much greater awareness of where she lived.

evidence of hate and no legal reason to stop her either – as if it had tried. The crowdfunder was reinstated and around £40,000 raised in just a few weeks. This included a couple of large anonymous donations. There was speculation that JK Rowling was behind these but no one knew for sure. This was more than a year before JKR got involved openly on social media on this issue.

The Transgender Trend schools guidance was requested by lots of parents. The EHRC gave up, announcing in 2020 that nothing would be published after all. Schools guidance remains a hot topic. The Department for Education took up the baton dropped by the EHRC but they found it equally tricky. Eventually a draft was published for public consultation in 2024. It was a sign of how far Stephanie and others had shifted the narrative that this new document referred not to transgender children but to 'gender-questioning children'. Perhaps it will be finalised in 2025.

My Body Is Me!

The other pressing issue for Stephanie was the growing number of trans picture books being published and stocked in school libraries. She wanted to publish an alternative children's book that challenged sex stereotypes but did not deny the reality of biological sex.

In August 2018, she met with local illustrator Jessica Ahlberg to discuss ideas. Jessica discussed the project with her friend Rachel Rooney, an award-winning children's poet, and Rachel came up with the inspired idea of a joyful poem about being yourself, in rhyming couplets.

After over a year of intensive work, the book *My Body is Me!* was launched ready for Christmas 2019. The book is adorable – Rachel's entrancing words[7] surrounded by Jessica's playful drawings. They didn't anticipate the ugly reaction from transactivists. Rachel suffered a barrage of vicious criticism, some of it led by other children's

7 <https://www.transgendertrend.com/rachel-rooney-reads-my-body-is-me-2/>.

authors and librarians. The sustained attack on her livelihood included contacting the company that booked school visits for her. She eventually stopped writing children's poetry altogether.

No Outsiders

Just as the schools guidance crowdfunder was closing, having exceeded its target, Stephanie and her sister Helen went to the Woman's Place UK event in Hastings. "It was the one with the bomb threat," she says casually. Woman's Place UK was set up in 2017 by Labour Party and trade union women to host public meetings at which the impact of transgender demands on women's rights could be discussed. They had been refused meeting space by several venues and the one they finally got was kept secret until the day. That didn't stop activists from threatening them but the event went ahead peacefully, with private security and police in attendance. At the pub afterwards, an ex-BBC journalist called Shelley Charlesworth and her sister Stacey came over. They knew each other on Twitter and they were thrilled to meet in real life. Shelley said if Stephanie ever wanted her to write for Transgender Trend, she'd be happy to help.

A few months later, Stephanie got in touch asking her to find out about the row that was going on in Birmingham over the teaching of a programme called 'No Outsiders'. A primary school with a 98% Muslim pupil intake was facing daily protests from parents demanding that their children not be taught about LGBT issues. The creator of 'No Outsiders', the school's assistant head teacher, Andrew Moffat, had been awarded an MBE for services to equality and diversity in education. Politicians and media commentators had waded in, mostly against the parents, calling them bigots and homophobes. Stephanie wanted a deeper look at what was in the 'No Outsiders' programme and why parents objected to it.

Shelley found that Andrew Moffat was teaching primary-school children that some children can change sex and that this is a good thing, to be celebrated. Parents were concerned that this was confusing for such young children. The resulting article on the Transgender Trend website was called 'No Outsiders: Queering the Primary Classroom'. It was the start of an increasingly close collaboration between Stephanie and Shelley, researching and writing about activist groups and their materials, books targeted at children, and the like. Their skills were complementary, Shelley analysing the materials these groups were putting out, Stephanie providing the link to child development and their impact on children. In time, Shelley took on more work, like managing and responding to emails. This freed Stephanie up to do much more. It was also brilliant to have someone else on the end of the phone who was equally committed to the work. They became a close-knit team.

Stephanie already had a support group she called the Transgender Trend gang, a hand-picked group of academics and parents of trans-identifying children whom she had met online and in real life. She knew the value of that kind of working group from her 'No More Page 3' gang. "I felt I was out there doing the media work alone. I needed trusted people to talk to," she says. With this WhatsApp group, she had her gang again, this time without self-censorship. They shared her concern and they could step in with professional skills like website support and document production.

She also got plenty of encouragement from a lesbian group she'd first met back in 2014 in a pub after a FiLiA conference. They shared her doubts about puberty blockers, seeing them as a threat to young lesbians, and they'd encouraged her to set up Transgender Trend. She met up with them from time to time and found their support very valuable at a time when so few people, even feminists, were prepared to put their heads above the parapet. They later formed the lesbian campaign group Get the L Out. There was also a private Facebook group with campaigners who were working on other aspects of women's rights which was useful for chatting about issues.

All these networks were important, but it was Shelley's arrival that really made the difference to Stephanie. Here was a trusted, kindred spirit to share the workload and day-to-day decision-making, and take on some of the research and writing that Stephanie alone could not cover. Shelley's background as a BBC and ITN journalist was invaluable. Stephanie describes her as the perfect partner. "She brought a new level of investigative research to Transgender Trend and as a mother and grandmother has a grounded understanding of safeguarding."

For a while after setting up Transgender Trend, Stephanie carried on doing Communicating with Kids work, writing blogs and running workshops. But it seemed that the people who'd published her before, Mumsnet, *Huffington Post* and others, didn't want her stuff now. Paid work dried up, and she worried about what would happen in her workshops with teachers or parents if the trans issue came up. Money got tight. When her savings were gone, she had to claim housing benefit and tax credits to pay her rent. At one point she was approached by a Christian organisation offering to support her, but even though she needed the money she felt it would have been a compromise. Transgender Trend had to be free of any affiliation or dependency that could call its independence and integrity into question. She would work with other groups who had a shared interest but would not take money from them. In 2019, Transgender Trend ran a second crowdfunder, this time to raise money to pay Stephanie a modest salary so she could keep going. The organisation has survived since then on that fund, plus donations from concerned individuals, typically monthly payments of £10 to £20, a couple at £2 and £3 a month, and very occasionally a much larger sum from a supportive individual donor. Critics of Transgender Trend like to declare on social media that there is sinister American alt-right or Christian fundamentalist money flowing in, but so far Stephanie has seen no sign of it.

For transactivist groups it's a different story. They get grants from the UK, Scottish and Welsh governments. There are fees for training and consulting, paid by corporates as well as universities, local authorities and government departments. Stonewall's membership schemes have generated millions of pounds annually. Mermaids,

Stonewall, Gendered Intelligence and GIRES were so well-in with the UK medical establishment that they were invited to speak at medical conferences, and medical people would speak at their events, while Stephanie had to pay to attend.

Mermaids had blocked Stephanie from its conference back in 2016, but she looked for opportunities to hear from the other side and take her challenge to them. She spotted a Stonewall Education conference in 2019. Into the lion's den, you might think. She booked and paid for a conference ticket a month in advance. On the day before the event, she got an email from Stonewall saying she could not come and they would refund her money. This was because she had

> booked under the name of a group with well-publicised anti-trans views and that has produced materials and documents that promote the idea that trans people don't exist and that LGBT inclusive education presents a threat to children.

By this stage Stephanie was neither surprised nor upset, just annoyed.

No More Friendly Chats with the Gender Identity Development Service

In early 2019, relations with the Tavistock GIDS team soured. At first the senior staff there had been friendly and encouraging when they met at events. Stephanie heard through a GIDS clinician that Dr Wren used the Transgender Trend website resources in training sessions with junior GIDS staff. She also knew Dr Carmichael had recommended the site to a parent at a conference. They seemed to welcome Stephanie's questioning approach, perhaps as an antidote to the push for affirmation and earlier medical intervention from Mermaids. Dr Wren and Dr Carmichael both spoke of their approach being much more cautious than that of gender clinics in the USA.

So what changed? In March that year, Transgender Trend published a report by a sociologist at Oxford University called

Dr Michael Biggs. He had invited Stephanie and Nic Williams to speak at Oxford. His first attempt was cancelled by the university after activists got wind of it and complained. Michael was told if he wanted a university venue, he would have to co-sponsor with the Queer Studies Network. Some months later, he helped Woman's Place UK run an event on a non-university site. Even that was not easy. Attendees had to run the gauntlet of 50 protesters outside the door, screaming at the top of their voices. One Oxford student came disguised with hat, scarf, and sunglasses in case she was recognised by the protesters. A mother who came with her baby in a pushchair was called a paedophile and was photographed, despite pleading with the protesters not to take photographs of her daughter; she was in tears. But the event went ahead. This was the start of a collaboration between Stephanie and Michael.

His report described the puberty blockers trial at GIDS, finding and publishing outcomes from the study for the first time. Back in 2010, the GIDS team had wanted to run a trial of earlier use of puberty blockers on gender-confused children, similar to the Dutch clinic work. The Dutch team published academic papers and frequently presented talks on their work, but although this UK 'Early Intervention' trial had run, no results had been published. Michael Biggs had pieced together a picture of how the study was going. He requested data from the Tavistock under the Freedom of Information law to see what the clinic knew about its young patients and their outcomes. He dug through published articles and talks by GIDS staff and Tavistock annual reports. Stephanie and her network sent him what they had.

He found that the puberty blockers trial didn't show an improvement in mental health outcomes after one year, and that puberty blockers had been rolled out to a much wider patient group before their long-term effects could be known. His most striking finding was that after a year on puberty blockers, children were more likely, not less, to want to hurt themselves or to have suicidal ideation. The result was embarrassing for the GIDS team, whose entire position was based on the claim that puberty blockers improved mental wellbeing and saved unhappy children from self-harm.

Michael subsequently wrote a series of articles, called 'The Tavistock's Experimentation with Puberty Blockers', published on the Transgender Trend website, and was interviewed for a *Newsnight* episode on the subject. He is perhaps one of the unsung heroes in this story. His work was pivotal in exposing the lack of evidence and bringing the subject to public attention, and he pursued it despite the risk to his academic career. Stephanie is very proud that his early groundbreaking work was first published by Transgender Trend.

Stephanie wondered how this treatment had got ethical approval. Any medical experiment or novel treatment has to be approved by an independent panel of suitably-qualified experts which decides if it is safe to run and if the risks to patients can be justified. Usually, this includes monitoring everyone in the trial, collecting and publishing data. But there was no evidence of a properly-controlled trial. Instead, GIDS talked about puberty blockers as if this were a long-proven and safe treatment.

A parent found, after weeks of digging online, that ethical approval for the study had been refused, before the team got approval from a different ethical review panel. This is not how things are normally done. If you don't get the answer you want at first, the usual thing is to adjust your planned trial to address the raised concerns and go back to the panel. Going and asking a different group looks decidedly ... let's just say, unusual. Discovering this felt like a breakthrough, and the parent got in touch with a reporter from *BBC Newsnight* to tell her what they had found. Stephanie had been about to publish this shocking discovery on the website, but the *Newsnight* journalist contacted her and said, please don't publish it yet. We want to report it. So that is what happened. It was a little painful not to get the credit, but at the same time Stephanie knew it was better to get it out there, on a credible and high-profile news programme. More unwelcome scrutiny for the GIDS team.

The change in the weather was signalled by Dr Carmichael approaching Stephanie at an event in Bristol saying something along the lines of: I have a bone to pick with you. Her beef was that Michael's article on the Transgender Trend website published trial results which were not yet public. Stephanie didn't feel defensive. She said her aim was to get reliable information and evidence out there, and that any time she reported on GIDS, say from hearing them speak at an event, she was always balanced, giving the good with the bad. Dr Carmichael didn't see it that way. She seemed upset that Michael's analysis of GIDS' use of puberty blockers was out there and she blamed Transgender Trend for hosting it. This was surprising since one source of information was Dr Carmichael, herself quoted in *The Daily Mail* in 2014. She'd said that the Early Intervention trial seemed to be going well so they'd decided to extend it to more patients.

In truth, tension had been building for a while. In 2018, two academics who were part of Stephanie's network, Heather Brunskell-Evans and Michele Moore, had published a book called *Transgender Children and Young People: Born In Your Own Body*. It was a set of essays providing a range of perspectives – a philosopher, an endocrinologist, the parent of a trans-identifying child, detransitioners, and campaigners. Stephanie's chapter had the punchy title of 'The Transgender Experiment on Children'. The book was published by Cambridge Scholars and it did well enough to go into paperback.

Heather and Michele were contacted by several clinicians at the Tavistock clinic wanting to tell their stories. They were worried about the affirmative approach there, and about other things, like the inability of the organisation to explain what being trans meant, and the lack of a therapeutic model to address it. But they were terrified of going public. Some had already left the clinic and gone to work in other fields. This spurred Heather and Michele to plan another book, published the following year, called *Inventing Transgender Children and Young People*. Notice the addition of the word 'inventing' to the title. While the medical establishment had moved from 'gender non-conforming' to 'transgender' children as their starting point, this book called them out on it. Heather's chapter was called 'The Tavistock: Inventing "The Transgender Child".' Michael Biggs expanded on what he'd written for Transgender Trend in a chapter called 'Britain's Experiment with Puberty Blockers'.

The Tavistock got wind of it and its legal team contacted the publishers demanding to see the book before it was published. When Cambridge Scholars failed to comply with this bizarre request, it received a legal letter from the Tavistock and Portman NHS Trust suggesting that they would be sued if they published. After several months of miserable uncertainty for Heather and Michele, the publishers went ahead with the book. The GIDS team must have had to buy it to find out if it libelled them, but there was no lawsuit. A Tavistock insider later reported that both books by Heather and Michele had been in the Tavistock library but that they'd been removed. Suppressing books is an unusual approach in any area of medicine. These books weren't promoting some radical treatment. They were questioning the diagnostic basis for medical interventions on physically healthy children that would make them sterile. Imagine thinking it necessary and reasonable to remove books so that clinical staff could not read dissenting views.

The combination of the books, both with a chapter written by Stephanie, and Michael's article on the Transgender Trend website was too much for the GIDS leadership team. After that, there were no more friendly chats. This led to some awkward encounters. Soon after the *Newsnight* coverage, Stephanie and Polly Carmichael were invited onto *Woman's Hour*. They arrived at the BBC building at the same time and had to go up in the lift together. There was no small talk.

But none of this – not the *Newsnight* stories, not the revelations about the paucity of evidence, not the feeble answers to questions given by Tavistock staff or activists from Mermaids – seemed to slow down the transgender train. The Gender Identity Development Service seemed unstoppable.

Heather Brunskell-Evans and Shelley Charlesworth campaigning in 2021
Photo courtesy of Lily Maynard

By this time, trans campaign groups were open about wanting to keep Stephanie quiet. Here's an example: in 2018, an Irish psychotherapist called Stella O'Malley fronted a programme for Channel Four called *Transgender Kids: It's Time to Talk*. As a child, Stella had felt certain she was really a boy. Puberty put her right. She believed that the affirmative approach now being taken would have led to her transitioning medically if it had been applied to her as a child. She wanted to explore whether so-called 'transgender children' were getting the right treatment. She set out to interview a range of people covering the spectrum of opinion. Olly Lambert, the director, was no stranger to difficult issues. He thought the trans issue would be straightforward by comparison with some of his work – he'd just made a programme called *One Day in Gaza* featuring Palestinian and Israeli voices.

At first, he had agreement from senior people at the GIDS clinic to participate and he was expecting to get Susie Green of Mermaids as well, and Dr Helen Webberley, a doctor based in Wales who ran a clinic called Gender GP which prescribed puberty blockers to children privately. After seeming interested, Susie Green refused to take part for a whole litany of reasons including that she didn't like some of the people Stella followed on Twitter. Susie Green told Olly Lambert that Mermaids would be discouraging people from taking part.

Helen Webberley said she would be in the programme only if they would assure her that certain people would not be. Who might these people be? Dr Webberley named two people. One was a Welsh Conservative MP, David TC Davies, who had questioned the wisdom of transitioning children. The other was Stephanie Davies-Arai. Olly Lambert had never come across this sort of condition, not even between the Israelis and Palestinians, and he had no intention of agreeing to it. As it happened, he and Stella had already spoken to Stephanie. Her position was similar to Stella's, a voice of caution and concern, focused on treating children as children, recognising their immaturity and concerned with keeping them safe. So similar, in fact, that they had decided they probably wouldn't include Stephanie. But he wasn't going to agree to Dr Webberley's conditions, so she did not participate in the film.

It was tough being cast as the unwelcome naysayer, a person with malevolent intent towards an already-marginalised group, but there were occasional positive signs. A supporter nominated Stephanie for the John Maddox Prize. This is an annual award made by the charity Sense About Science and the science journal *Nature*, which "recognises the work of individuals who promote sound science and evidence on a matter of public interest, facing difficulty or hostility in doing so." Out of almost 140 nominations, Stephanie was one of a handful shortlisted and invited to the 2019 awards dinner. In the face of so much hostility, and with nasty and defamatory things being said by pro-trans campaign groups and charities, it was encouraging to have an independent, respectable outfit recognise that she was acting in good faith and doing worthwhile work.

Making Connections

Two years into Transgender Trend, in 2017, Stephanie made her first appearance at the Palace of Westminster. She knew that for years trans lobby groups like Press for Change, Stonewall and Mermaids had been influential in British politics. They'd been invited to give evidence at the Women and Equalities Select Committee (WESC) hearing on trans equality in 2015, where the push for self-ID started. Two trans groups, Gendered Intelligence and GIRES, had helped many sports bodies in the UK to write policies for transgender inclusion, while women's groups had not usually been involved at all. Stonewall was widely consulted as the expert in how to accommodate trans people in the workplace. Gendered Intelligence had worked with the Government Equalities Office to produce a government document called Guide to Public Services, saying that in toilets and changing rooms in normal high street situations, trans people should have access to the facilities that matched their identity, not their birth sex.

Most people had no idea about all this, but Stephanie knew that these groups were shaping policies affecting millions of people. They were presented as the decent thing to do for the tiny minority of trans people, irrelevant to everyone else. But in practice, women were losing privacy in public toilets, shop and workplace changing rooms and toilets, hospital wards, and the rest.

Women's groups were coming late to the party, uninvited. Back in 2015, Stephanie had responded to the WESC trans inquiry. When no women were invited to give oral evidence to the committee, Stephanie and Julia Long took matters into their own hands. They requested a meeting with the Equality and Human Rights Commission (EHRC) to talk about the WESC report's recommendation to change the *Gender Recognition Act* to self-ID. The EHRC people advised them to wait for the public consultation on the proposals and to make sure they were stakeholders when that time came.

After several months, concerned by the silence, they asked to meet again. There were different people at this meeting, and it felt different. It wasn't openly hostile – that came later – but the civil servants seemed uninterested and disengaged. Stephanie asked one of them about the suggestion of adopting gender identity as a protected characteristic in UK law. This was another recommendation in the WESC trans inquiry report. He said no, there was no plan to do that. But the way he said it, so definite and confident, made Stephanie think he already had a clear plan in mind to do what the Women and Equalities Committee wanted, just without the need to make that change. She did not find it reassuring. As before, the advice was to wait for the public consultation and respond to that.

After the consultation had opened, Stephanie heard that a round table had been held with women's groups but she had not been invited. She demanded and got a meeting of her own and went along with her sister Helen. This one felt hostile from the start. They met the civil servant who was going to be in charge of the consultation on the *Gender Recognition Act*. Stephanie found the atmosphere made it difficult to speak plainly. "If I said 'male' or 'a man who identifies as a woman' the civil servants glared, the barriers went up." It was clear that if her side wanted to be listened to they had to be careful about the language they used. They couldn't speak freely.

Stephanie also felt that the people from the EHRC and the Government Equalities Office were confident they could make the planned changes and nothing would stop them. They talked as if they already had things all sorted. She says the hostility was "absolutely palpable." They saw it as a trans issue, nothing to do with women. Some seemed already committed to self-ID. She thinks that others, less committed, just thought that if there was a dispute between the trans lobby and feminists, well, neither side mattered too much so they didn't care who won.

Her own first Westminster appearance was at the invitation of the Welsh Conservative MP, David TC Davies, the one to whom Helen Webberley had taken exception. Stephanie had seen him make a comment in an article about the encroachment on women's rights by trans demands, and she'd written to thank him. She made a habit of contacting and thanking people who said anything public as a way to introduce herself and her organisation. He invited her to meet him. In late 2017, he set up a briefing meeting for law-makers called 'Transgender Law Concerns'. It was about the impact of self-declared gender legislation on women and children, with Stephanie as a speaker. Dr Nicola Williams also spoke. These briefing meetings are a quiet influencing tool used by lobby groups with political connections. All you need is one sponsor, an MP or a member of the House of Lords, to book a committee room and circulate the invitations to all members of both houses. They're unofficial, but political insiders know this is one way to reach MPs and influence them. People of any party may come along or may send one of their staff to see what it's all about. It was the first time that this side of the debate had been presented in Parliament. Not many MPs attended, but it felt like a breakthrough.

The host, David TC Davies MP, was accused of transphobia by his party's LGBT group, just for having allowed the topic to be aired. He was undeterred. At another meeting he hosted, Stephanie approached a government junior minister, Victoria Atkins MP, and gave Transgender Trend leaflets to her. The minister listened to Stephanie and asked a couple of questions. But a civil servant from the Government Equalities Office, which was in charge of the GRA consultation, tried to pull Stephanie away from the minister.

A few other parliamentarians were becoming concerned and getting involved. In 2019, a Labour peer called Lewis Moonie, a psychiatrist, chaired a meeting organised by Kellie-Jay Keen and Venice Allan called 'First Do No Harm: The Ethics of Transgender Healthcare' where Stephanie spoke about the potential harms being done to children. Kellie-Jay had been the first person to conduct a full interview with Stephanie about her work, for her YouTube channel. Lord Moonie was also investigated by his party for transphobia, in his case before the meeting even happened. He resigned from the Labour Party and went ahead with the meeting. He tweeted, "I feel free to carry on campaigning for women."

Kellie-Jay Keen and Stephanie Davies-Arai in London, 2023
Photo courtesy of Nicola Williams

It still didn't feel as if anyone with the power to change things was listening. Only two other parliamentarians attended the 'First Do No Harm' meeting – old faithful David TC Davies MP and Baroness Tanni Grey-Thompson. BBC journalist Hannah Barnes was there, who later reported on GIDS for *Newsnight*. But this event was pivotal, not so much for what was said in the House of Lords committee room but because of discussions in the pub afterwards. This is where the plan for a high court judicial review against the use of puberty blockers on gender-confused children was born, when Stephanie met a couple called Marcus and Susan Evans.

Susan was a psychiatric nurse who had worked at the GIDS clinic. In 2004, she had raised the alarm about what she saw as poor care of the children. A management report was written, but Susan did not see her concerns properly addressed, and she had left GIDS in 2007.

At the House of Lords meeting, a representative of the Tavistock and Portman NHS Trust, which ran GIDS, stood up and explained how the GIDS approach was careful and thorough. Listening, Susan says, her blood started to boil. She herself stood up in the audience and said, "I'm going to have to contradict you. I witnessed children being sent for hormones after four sessions." Until that moment no one other than her husband Marcus knew that she'd been a whistleblower, the first on GIDS.

Marcus had spent 25 years in adult services at the Tavistock and Portman NHS Trust. When he left for private practice as a psychoanalyst in 2018, he joined the Trust's board as a volunteer governor. But he had just resigned from the board after less than a year. Like Susan years before, it was because he felt that a report documenting clinicians' concerns about GIDS was being ignored.

This second report was by a psychiatrist in the Trust's adult service called David Bell, who also spoke at the House of Lords meeting. As the staff representative on the Trust board, he knew GIDS staff were worried about its approach. Several had come to him individually with concerns, and he'd written a report for the board. But his term as staff-governor was ending and he was not confident his report would be acted on when he left.

Marcus tried to get the Trust board to address the issues about GIDS in Dr Bell's report. Frustrated, he resigned and went public. This was perhaps the most critical step in getting the concerns into the public domain.

A solicitor called Paul Conrathe was at the meeting too. As a parent, he was worried about what was going on. He'd previously visited Stephanie at her home to hear about her work. It was Paul who'd introduced her to the Christian organisation who'd offered financial support, which she declined. Like Stephanie, Paul felt that vulnerable children needed to be protected from making life-changing decisions. How could informed consent to puberty blockers be given by children if no one could tell them what they were consenting to? The medics themselves admitted they didn't know the long-term effects. Added to that, children don't know about sexual function so they can't understand what they are giving up. Nor can they, at the age of 11 or 12, make an informed decision that they don't mind losing their fertility.

The Court Case That Made Them Stop

In the pub after the event, they talked about whether there was a legal mechanism to slow things down at GIDS. Paul's idea was to bring a judicial review. That is a legal process in which a judge is asked to determine whether something is lawful. A claimant brings the challenge against one or more respondents but it's not a criminal case. The claimant must have 'standing', that is, they must be personally affected by the matter so they have the right to ask for it to be reviewed. They file the case outlining why they believe it is unlawful. If the claimant has standing and the case is assessed to have merit then it is listed for a high court hearing. This is the 'judicial review'.

After years of lobbying, asking questions at conferences and responding to consultations, maybe legal action could shine a light on the troubling absence of evidence for radical medical interventions on children, and perhaps even make them stop. Susan Evans agreed to be the claimant, along with an anonymous parent of a GIDS patient. After the announcement of the planned judicial review – meaning that Susan was challenging the Tavistock and Portman Trust and NHS England in the high court – Marcus and Susan had months of anxiety about whether they'd made themselves unemployable by taking this public stand. No other clinician, and no one on the GIDS staff, not even those who'd spoken to David Bell, was speaking up. Marcus and Susan also risked financial ruin taking on the government in court.

Then Susan came across an article written by Joani Walsh in the *Daily Telegraph* called 'Meet the Detransitioners'.[8] It featured a former GIDS patient called Keira Bell. Susan contacted her to get a witness statement for the case. Keira was a 22-year-old woman who had been through five years of medical treatment in her attempt to become a man, before realising it was all an illusion. But she'd had irreversible treatment, including having both breasts removed. Years of testosterone treatment had given her a deep voice and a beard that will never go away. Her claim was that the gender clinic had been negligent in affirming her desire to become a man – something that was never possible anyway – and that they had taken direction from an immature young woman instead of treating her like the mentally ill patient she was.

She felt the GIDS clinic had let her down and if a court case would stop it from harming other young people she was willing to be part of it. As Keira later wrote:

> I had so many issues that it was comforting to think I really had only one that needed solving: I was a male in a female body. But it was the job of the professionals to consider all my co-morbidities, not just to affirm my naïve hope that everything could be solved with hormones and surgery.

Keira's personal history gives clues as to why she might have been unhappy as a young woman. Her home life was miserable, with an alcoholic mother and an emotionally distant father. She'd been a tomboy, happiest out playing with the boys. But when puberty hit she didn't fit anywhere. Then she started to feel attracted to girls. She interpreted this as having something wrong with her. By the age of 14, she was depressed and confused. She dropped out of school and stayed in her room.

Prompted by her mother, she fixated on the belief that she was meant to be a boy. She was sent to a psychiatrist, and at 15 to the

8 <https://www.telegraph.co.uk/women/life/meet-detransitioners-women-became-men-now-want-go-back/> 19 November 2019.

gender clinic at the Tavistock. Despite her history, they endorsed her belief that becoming a boy would make her feel better. She was put on puberty blockers at 16, then testosterone at 17. She had a double mastectomy at the age of 20. About a year later, she began to understand that she was not and would never be a man, and that she was a lesbian. She stopped taking testosterone and went back to her birth name.

Susan was moved to tears when she read Keira's witness statement. She proposed that Keira should replace her as the claimant. Keira was not seeking compensation or anything for herself. She wanted to stop the GIDS clinic from putting children on puberty blockers, on the basis that children could not agree to such radical treatment because they were children – and the effects are unknown. As Stephanie says, when they talk about 'transgender children' it's as if they forget they are children and only hear the transgender bit. There was also an anonymous claimant, the mother of a trans-identifying teenager being treated at GIDS.

Transgender Trend is Finally Heard in Court

In a judicial review, each side submits evidence from experts, but they don't appear in court. Their evidence goes in as written witness statements. The barristers on each side do all the talking. Dr David Bell and other medical experts were to be witnesses for the claimants, those challenging the use of puberty blockers.

An expert with something to contribute who's not been called by either side can ask the court's permission to intervene. For example, the EHRC sometimes intervenes in cases about human rights issues to say what their understanding of the law is and how it affects the case. For the case of Bell vs Tavistock, solicitor Paul Conrathe convened a working group to consider intervening. They had heard that Stonewall and Mermaids were planning to intervene, supporting the continuing use of puberty blockers. The best person to intervene opposing this would be Stephanie. Her years of following developments in the field meant she knew more than anyone about the evidence, such as it was, in the UK and around the world. She also had a good feel for what was going on at the GIDS clinic, reported to her by concerned staff and ex-staff.

Usually, an intervenor submits an outline of their proposed evidence, the judge decides whether they have anything useful to contribute, and then, if granted permission to intervene, they write up the whole thing. This time the judge asked to see the entire submission before deciding. This meant that anyone asking to intervene had to do all the work not knowing whether it would be accepted.

The court set a deadline, and it was two weeks away. So in the baking heat of the summer of 2020, Stephanie spent two solid weeks working round the clock, gathering evidence, talking to detransitioners and writing a 6000 word submission with detailed references to back it all up. She focused on the cultural environment of celebration and 'affirmation' of trans identities that was encouraging children to think they were 'trans', supported by evidence from detransitioners. She loves to swim in the sea so it was a sacrifice, after months of lockdown, to sit at her desk during a heatwave rather than going to the beach. But you don't argue with a judge. A court deadline is a deadline, or so she thought.

Imagine how the team felt when they found out that the other proposed intervenors, both Stonewall and Mermaids, had missed the deadline and been granted an extension. Mermaids' reason was that its chief executive Susie Green was on 'annual leave'. Stephanie was furious that she'd foregone the best swimming of the season and these campaign groups with their full-time salaried teams couldn't hit a deadline. Mermaids also missed the extended deadline, but the court accepted its submission anyway.

Then the judge had to decide whose evidence to allow. An intervenor has to bring something new and relevant. Stephanie's intervention was accepted but those of Stonewall and Mermaids were both rejected. The written response from the court said that they had raised issues that were not about the case – they did their usual stuff about the human rights of 'trans kids' but this case was about informed consent, and they had nothing to say about that, or nothing relevant. Stephanie felt this was a turning point. "For the first time, no debate won't wash, mate. Not here. You're in front of a judge now, you have to produce your evidence, and they didn't have any." After how she had been defamed, over and over, it felt like a huge victory. A high court judge had declared that her input had value; theirs didn't.

At the hearing in October, not many people were allowed into the courtroom because of the Covid pandemic. Keira was allowed in, as the claimant, and Stephanie was, as an intervenor, but Susan wasn't, because she was no longer part of the case. Everybody else was in another room, watching on monitors.

Stephanie was sorry Susan couldn't be in the room but she was glad to be there so Keira wasn't on her own. They sat side by side, and at times during the hearing they found themselves holding hands tightly. The two of them were sitting behind Dr Carmichael from the GIDS clinic and Gary Butler, the chief endocrinologist at University College London Hospital (UCLH). Psychologists in the UK cannot prescribe medication, so the GIDS psychologists would send children to UCLH's endocrine unit for puberty blockers. So these two were representing the defendants, as it were. They were not on trial, but in a sense their professional judgment and decisions were. Dr Carmichael and Dr Butler were the only two in court from the entire gender treatment team. Insiders later reported that the GIDS team had been so confident they'd win their case that they hadn't even considered the possibility of losing.

Maybe that changed as they sat in court for two days listening to the barristers. Even though she had heard a lot already from detransitioners and from GIDS clinicians, Stephanie was shocked by the revelations in court. Time and again it seemed like the medical team at GIDS had no evidence and no answers. More than once the judges expressed "surprise" at the lack of data, the failure of the clinic to follow up the children it treated, and hence the complete absence of reliable data on the effects, positive and negative, of puberty blockers. When a high court judge expresses "surprise", they're really saying WTF. There was an audible gasp from those in court when, in response to a statement about a 12-year-old expressing disgust at the idea of sex, the barrister for the Tavistock said some adults were asexual.

The decision wasn't announced until December. But there had already been two major developments. First, in September, shortly before the case was heard, NHS England announced an independent review of treatment practices at the GIDS clinic. This was victory for Transgender Trend and its supporters. All they'd ever wanted was a proper evidence-based approach to the treatment of distressed children who were confused or unhappy about their sex. The court case was to try to force the NHS to take an evidence-based approach, and this independent review would do that. An eminent retired paediatrician called Hilary Cass was appointed to lead the review.

The very next month, the Care Quality Commission inspected the GIDS clinic. The Care Quality Commission (CQC) is the government regulator for health and social care. It inspects hospitals, care homes and the like to make sure they are safe for patients. The inspection was done because various people including healthcare professionals and the Children's Commissioner for England had reported concerns about GIDS to the CQC.

In early December 2020, the key players on both sides of the judicial review gathered in the high court to hear the decision. Stephanie drove to London and met up with Keira, Susan, Paul, and a few others. Together they trooped into the court room to hear the judges say that they did not see how children could give informed consent to an experimental treatment which had lifelong consequences that children could not understand. The court wasn't making a judgment about the efficacy of puberty blockers. That was not for them to decide. But they did express surprise at the inability of the clinicians to answer those questions. They also disagreed with the GIDS' view that puberty blockers were a pause. The evidence was that almost all those put on blockers went on to cross-sex hormones, which meant that any talk of blockers being reversible was irrelevant. Blockers led to cross-sex hormones and loss of sexual function, and were effectively one single medical treatment, extended over several years. Pre-pubescent children couldn't sign up to that, so the clinic would have to stop putting confused, unhappy children on puberty blockers unless they got approval from the family court.

It was the win they'd had been hoping for. Keira made a statement to the waiting media saying it wasn't about her and she was not seeking damages – a judicial review can't do that. But she hoped this would protect other young people from what had happened to her.

Stephanie Davies-Arai, Heather Brunskell-Evans and Keira Bell after the judgment, December 2020, London

Photo courtesy of Heather Brunskell-Evans

Stephanie was feeling tired and decided that she wouldn't stay over in London that night as planned. She started to feel unwell, to the point where Susan and Marcus Evans asked her if she was okay. As she drove home, she found her left hand slipping off the steering wheel. She was finding it difficult to use that hand. This was the first sign that she had a serious illness. She was diagnosed with cancer soon afterwards. With hindsight, she felt that it was almost as if she had to get through the court case before she could be ill. The date is seared into her mind, as a sort of turning point:

> It's like all the tension, all the stress of doing this work over all those years. And then a result like that, which was, oh, my, we've done it. Oh my God, we've done it. It's like when you're working really hard, you have a holiday and that's when you get the flu. And it felt like that to me, all of those held-in tensions and stresses over the years could finally be released.

From that point on, the GIDS clinic was under public scrutiny, the kind of scrutiny that for years Stephanie had been pushing for. The case made headlines worldwide. The use of puberty blockers started to come under scrutiny in other countries, too.

The day after the court's decision, the Tavistock finally published the results of the Early Intervention trial. The results were inconclusive, except for the fact that only one child from the trial group did not proceed to cross-sex hormones. This backed up the court's conclusion that, far from being a pause button, puberty blockers were in effect part one of a two-stage treatment that included cross-sex hormones.

The CQC report was published in January 2021, after the court case, and it found the GIDS clinic to be "inadequate." That's the lowest possible rating. By then, the Cass Review was underway and puberty blockers had been more or less suspended after the judicial review. After the court judgment, the statement about puberty blockers on the NHS website was quietly changed. For years the NHS had said puberty blockers were entirely reversible. Now it says their long-term effects are not known. Too late for thousands of children and their parents.

In parallel with the court case, NHS England had commissioned independent reviews of the evidence for the use of puberty blockers and cross-sex hormones. These were done by a UK public body called the National Institute for Health and Care Excellence (NICE) whose role is to assess medical treatments and drugs and advise the NHS whether they work and are worth paying for. The reviews were published in April 2021. They concluded that there was no good evidence to support the belief that puberty blockers or cross-sex hormones were an effective treatment for children with gender dysphoria. This alone should have been a killer blow for the affirmative approach being practised by the GIDS clinic at the Tavistock (and the Sandyford, its equivalent in Scotland). Campaigners like Stephanie hailed this as a return to an evidence-based approach within the health service. Like the court case, the NICE reports got international attention. An expert, independent review of the evidence has value everywhere, so the NICE reports were something clinicians in other countries could rely on.

The Tavistock NHS Trust appealed the ruling in Bell vs Tavistock. Much later, the appeal court ruled that it was not for the court to decide on medical treatments, and that parents could consent on behalf of their children even if the children themselves could not give informed consent. It didn't matter. Stephanie's feeling was "we've won this case anyway because we've got the NHS independent review out of it." They'd got worldwide attention on the issue, too. The court case had triggered a cascade of scrutiny. The Cass Review, then the inadequate rating of the GIDS clinic by the CQC, the devastating lack of evidence and data from the puberty blockers experiment at the GIDS clinic, as revealed in court, and finally the reports by the National Institute for Health and Care Excellence, meant there was no going back to the old model.

In March 2022, Dr Cass published her interim review. It said clearly what Transgender Trend had been saying for six years.

Children presenting with gender distress were not getting the same standard of care as in any other area of paediatric medicine. Instead, all other co-morbidities were ignored in favour of a single-minded focus on their claimed trans identity, which was largely affirmed rather than explored. This was not a medical but an ideological response. The interim Cass report was proof that Stephanie's work had achieved its goal – the safeguarding of unhappy, confused children. The lost court case did not matter, because healthcare experts were now back in charge.

The Cass interim report went further. It said that the GIDS clinic should be closed and replaced. New referrals to the clinic were stopped right away and the clinic finally closed in 2024. The report also said that social transition was an active intervention that could affect the psychological development of the child. This was a very powerful statement, because it pushed back on Mermaids' demands for affirmation without question, in schools and by parents as well as at the gender clinic.

The final report from the Cass Review was published in April 2024. In almost 400 carefully-worded pages, it spelled the end of so-called gender-affirming care for gender-questioning children on the NHS. An immediate temporary ban on puberty blockers was announced. That decision survived a change of government in the UK in July 2024, with the new Labour government endorsing the Cass Review's findings and continuing the work of the previous Conservative administration. A legal challenge by transactivists against the NHS failed. An attempt to provide puberty blockers through a private clinic set up by Susie Green, who by then had left Mermaids, and others, was blocked. In December 2024, the UK government announced an indefinite ban on puberty blocker prescription for minors, whether via the NHS or private clinics. In parliament, the Secretary of State for Health, Wes Streeting MP, said, "It is a scandal that medicine was given to vulnerable young children without proof that it was safe or effective."

First Meeting with an Old Friend

In April 2022, there was a lunch with JK Rowling in London. It was reportedly organised by journalist Julie Bindel, who has a long history of feminist activism especially in male violence against women and girls, an area in which JK Rowling has long been involved and made substantial charitable donations. Those invited to the lunch were sworn to secrecy beforehand. There were about 15 present, mostly women well known for their activism on the front line between trans demands and women's rights, including Maya Forstater who won a legal action (see Chapter 4) and the founders of LGB Alliance, Kate Harris and Bev Jackson. A couple of them posted photos of the event on Twitter afterwards. This was JKR's first public engagement with women's rights campaigners on this issue.

Transactivists were livid. They scoffed at the wine and 'expensive' mobile phones on the table – as if this somehow lessened the women's relevance as campaigners. Twitter users responded with a series of jokes about women needing men's permission to meet for lunch, or to be the owner of a mobile phone. Other women posted photos of their own lunches, arranged without said permission. Someone created a spoof permission form which 'ladies who lunch' were supposed to complete if they wanted to get together. There was a huge amount of publicity. JKR making a personal appearance was a big deal. Women's rights campaigners, and those worried about children, were delighted. It was great to see women we knew getting recognition, and exciting to see JK Rowling with them as part of the movement.

A few of us talked among ourselves about who had been there. There are many worthy campaigners, and it was a personal choice for the organiser, so we had no complaints – except one. Stephanie was one of the first to put herself out there, to do the hard work when no one else was. Her future was uncertain because of her illness so it seemed a shame she had missed out on this wonderful event. She herself would never have suggested she was entitled to anything and nothing was said to her, as far as I know. I talked to Marion Calder of For Women Scotland about it. Marion said, "Leave it with me." Marion is someone who gets things done, so I left it with her.

Three months later, in June, Stephanie trekked up from her home on the English south coast to Scotland to speak at a long-planned event at Edinburgh University. She'd thought she should head home straight after, but Marion persuaded her to stay overnight, and not to rush off in the morning either. Next morning, Lisa Mackenzie from the policy group Murray Blackburn Mackenzie picked her up from her hotel, promising to take her to the best place in Edinburgh for coffee and cake. Chattering away in the car, Stephanie barely noticed when they pulled up in front of a pair of close-boarded gates. Susan from For Women Scotland was waiting there. She hopped into Lisa's car, the gates opened and they drove in.

At the top of the drive, Stephanie suddenly realised it was a private house, not a hotel, and Jo Rowling was standing outside the front door to greet her. They spent the best part of two hours over coffee in Jo's house. Stephanie says it was like meeting an old friend. They just chatted away. Jo mentioned the large anonymous donation Transgender Trend had received when crowdfunding to print its schools guidance. There had been speculation at the time but there was no way for Stephanie to know. She hadn't even felt she could thank JKR's agent, because what if it wasn't her! Finally she was able to say thank you, directly to Jo.

Stephanie tweeted wryly, "I'm in the best café in Edinburgh", with a photo of herself and JKR.

Stephanie meets JK Rowling at her home in Edinburgh in 2022

Photo courtesy of Susan Smith

Transing the Gay Away

There was a short window in which Stephanie felt that her work was done. After the Keira Bell ruling, GIDS had been stopped from putting children on puberty blockers and its affirmation model discredited by Cass, an independent adjudicator with impeccable credentials. It didn't last, though.

The transgender activist lobby wanted a law banning 'conversion therapy' – the practice of trying to change someone's sexual orientation. In some countries there is corrective rape of lesbians and physical torture of gay men but there is no evidence of such practices in the UK. LGBT rights activists in the UK suddenly started talking about it around 2017 and a previous prime minister, Theresa May, had pledged to bring in a ban. The problem, as Stephanie saw it, was that the proposals included banning conversion practices for gender identity too. That would mean that it would be unlawful to challenge anyone who said they were transgender. The MoU on conversion therapy already makes this difficult, but it's not a crime. This ban would make it illegal for therapists to explore in talking therapy why a child thought he or she was in the wrong body, or why a teenage girl did not want to grow into a woman.

The old model for gender-confused children was called 'watchful waiting', and it meant wait and see, support and accept the child, but don't assume any outcome one way or the other. It is not conversion therapy because it doesn't tell them they're not trans. The most likely outcome is that they will grow out of those feelings through puberty and it's quite likely they will be gay or lesbian. Not all little boys who like dolls and ballet will grow up gay, and not all gay men liked 'girly' things in their childhood. Nor are all lesbians tomboys as children. But being a so-called effeminate boy in early childhood is a predictor of being gay in adulthood. Susie Green has talked about this, how she thought she had a sensitive little boy who might grow up to be gay but that her husband wasn't okay with that.

If a young person thinks it is not okay to be as they are, perhaps because of homophobia around them, being trans might seem like a better option. There are also cases of butch girls being told they are really boys, because they don't conform to sex stereotypes, and especially if they are lesbians. It was reported on *BBC Newsnight* that clinicians at the GIDS clinic had a dark joke about this: that there would be no gay people left. A ban on conversion therapy would only make this worse, because it would mean these young people had to be affirmed as trans. A law meant to protect gay people from forced conversion could actually stop young gay and lesbian people from growing up unharmed. If they transitioned instead, they'd have no sexual function.

For years there was ample evidence that the vast majority of young people referred to the GIDS clinic were same-sex attracted. The patient profile at the GIDS clinic also included a massive over-representation of children with autistic traits – at least a third of them and maybe up to half compared with one or two per cent in the general population. Autism is associated with late emotional development and with rigid thinking. It's not hard to see how same-sex attraction or not fitting the stereotypes associated with your sex could lead a young person with autism to think they are the other sex.

Other factors that crop up at significant levels in the GIDS patient group are a history of sexual abuse or being looked after by the state. At the Hot Topics in Child Health conference back in 2018, Dr Wren had referred to the high incidence of autistic traits, and to patients with sexual trauma in their past. The Cass Review reported that almost 97% of the patients referred to GIDS had one or more co-morbidities – other factors like anxiety or depression, a history of abuse or parental abandonment, autism, self-harm, and so on. Transactivists say these are the result of being trans. But these issues could just as easily be the direct cause of the young person's distress and confusion. It's easy to see why someone might want to stop being themselves, or to escape their sex – particularly the burden of being female.

A conversion therapy ban would mean no one is allowed to even ask that question. But it's quite a subtle point to try to get across. What kind of person would oppose a ban on conversion therapy? That must mean you support conversion therapy! For the average member of Parliament, it's much easier and safer to agree that all conversion therapy is bad and should be stopped. Maybe it's a bit like when the fight against self-ID started. Politicians thought it was an easy win to allow people to self-identify their sex and change their birth certificate, because (they thought) it would only be a few and it didn't really affect anyone else. It took years of patient campaigning, raising awareness, trying to get media coverage, trying to get to the politicians so they could see it wasn't that simple. This issue is similar. Of course no one wants gay people to face attempts to make them straight. But the profile among children who think they are transgender is so full of red flags that adults have a duty to protect them.

All the gains made by Stephanie's years of campaigning, publicised by the Bell case and cemented by the Cass Review, are at risk if therapists are banned from considering the possibility that a young patient is not 'trans', but that she or he is gay, or abused, or confused. Remember that the British Association of Counselling and Psychotherapy already has its commitment to the Memorandum of Understanding on Conversion Therapy. The next step post Bell and Cass should be unpicking that, not making it a legal requirement. So, the work continues.

Honours Even

In June 2022, Stephanie was awarded the British Empire Medal for services to children in the Queen's Jubilee Honours List. This prompted a frenzy of delighted whatsapping among campaigners when we heard the news. Stephanie herself said:

> After years of hostility it's vindication not just for my work but for all of us who've been campaigning and blowing the whistle. And it's for all the parents who have been afraid to speak out or have been called bigots for doing so.

Her award was reported in *The Daily Telegraph, The Times* and *The Daily Mail* – all with "transphobic" in the headline. They weren't saying she was transphobic but it seemed they couldn't report the story without leading with that claim from the transactivists.

Despite the label, Stephanie is now regarded as an authoritative voice on these issues in relation to children. She's the media's go-to person for quotes on the vexed question of what should happen in schools when one or more children say they are the other sex. She is consulted by media, lawyers and policy makers. Stephanie and Shelley have met with politicians and spoken in the Commons and the House of Lords several times over the years.

It is now clear that there is a conflict of rights between the 'transgender' pupil who wants their identity to be accepted and the

Stephanie with Marion Calder, Nicola Williams and Shelley Charlesworth at Westminster, 2022
Photo courtesy of Karen Varley

other children who will lose the privacy of single-sex changing rooms and toilets, and the fairness of girls' sport, if that happens. That's before you address the gaslighting of forcing everyone to pretend they're not seeing what they are seeing, and to change their language to suit that one person. This was the thing Stephanie had noticed and reacted to in the media reports about transitioning children at school, way back in 2013. Finally, the concerns she had then are getting mainstream attention. The solutions aren't there yet, but the concerns are talked about, and she is part of the conversation. There's mainstream media coverage now; there's political awareness and attention.

Stephanie Davies-Arai started Transgender Trend to give parents and others an alternative to the simple 'trans is good, affirm them, give them puberty blockers' narrative of pre-2015. Since then, there's been an explosion of grassroots groups aiming to help children with gender confusion and their parents: supportive networks of parents like Bayswater and Our Duty, schools-focused groups like

Safe Schools Alliance, clinical groups like Thoughtful Therapists, Genspect, CAN-SG and SEGM. She's being contacted by women in other countries asking for advice on how to set up their own groups. Stephanie did what was needed when only a few were speaking up, when parents had nowhere else to go. Now she feels massive relief that so many are sharing the burden. When parents contact her looking for advice, she can direct them to the most suitable group. That frees up Transgender Trend to focus more on providing evidence and analysis and on influencing policy. But Stephanie hopes that work too will end. "I can see a time when Transgender Trend won't be needed, and that will be success for us. When I feel the transgender trend is fully over, that's when I will stop."

2

Dr Nicola Williams

IN EARLY 2017, NICOLA WILLIAMS WAS OUT FOR A WALK with a friend who said to her, "Oh, God, there's all sorts going on on Mumsnet at the moment about terfs." Nic wasn't on Mumsnet and she had never heard of terfs. She asked her friend to explain. Her friend said women were posting on Mumsnet that there were trans women wanting to be considered women, that they were going into women's spaces. Nic's first thought was, well, I don't know much about transgender people. "I presumed they'd all had surgery and I didn't think there were many of them. And I thought, live and let live."

The topic came up in chats with this friend a few times. She wasn't an activist trying to recruit Nic or 'peak' her – as we might say now, when someone raises 'the trans issue' and tries to show you it's a problem for women. It was just an interesting conversation. One day, her friend told her that these transgender men were saying they were lesbians. Only she didn't call them transgender men, she called them 'trans women'. Trans women were lesbians. That got Nic's attention. She thought, that's odd. Live and let live meant largely turning a blind eye, playing along if you needed to. But pretending a man was a lesbian? That wasn't possible.

Nic wondered where people were hearing all this because she hadn't seen it anywhere. The friend said she was in a Facebook group. This was a private group that had migrated across from Mumsnet talk boards. There were feminism chats on Mumsnet where, for a few years, women had been talking about this emergent issue – the problems caused to women and girls when men wanted to live as women. Then it seemed to get all too sensitive and difficult to discuss. Mumsnet had complaints about the things women were saying about trans people. Terms like 'trans-identifying male' were deemed offensive. Mumsnet is a moderated forum and it tightened up on what language was allowed. Posts and even whole threads could be deleted if they broke the guidelines. Repeat offenders could be banned from Mumsnet completely. Someone suggested they set up a secret Facebook group where they could speak freely.

The group had a sort of parody Women's Institute name which it changed from time to time. You couldn't just apply, you had to be recommended. Security was tight because it was such a controversial topic that they needed to make sure they knew and could trust everyone there. Nic asked, "Can you get me in there?"

Nic's friend vouched for her, and in she went. There were a few hundred in the group, women who mostly knew each other only online. Nic didn't know it then but pretty much all the women who were talking about trans stuff back in 2017 were there: Julie Bindel, Stephanie Davies-Arai, Julia Long, Sheila Jeffreys, Kellie-Jay Keen, and later Venice Allan. There were other journalists, academics and campaigners too, and lots of Mumsnetters who had started thinking there was a problem for women's rights which the mainstream was unaware of, or maybe was ignoring. Other than Stephanie, most were not doing anything more than talking to each other in the group. Just like on Mumsnet, they posted about what they'd seen or heard ("Oh, my God, have you seen this?") or shared the occasional news item, and talked about what it meant and why it mattered.

As a newcomer to the issue, Nic learned all the basics there. She was barely aware of the *Gender Recognition Act* or the *Equality Act*. None of that was part of her life. She'd been a scientist, doing a PhD in biochemistry and then working in pharmaceutical research. She found herself joining in the discussions and wanting to know more.

It quickly went from 'this is interesting' to 'this is important'. If it was both interesting and important then she wanted to find out for herself. Maybe it was her scientific background, but she wanted to become an expert.

Nicola had left the pharmaceutical industry not long before and set up a small business as a handywoman, doing painting and decorating, plumbing, odd jobs. It was a conscious downshift away from the stress of the corporate world. She looked after other people's dogs too, which, as a dog lover, didn't feel like work. It was meant to be a relatively stress-free life.

She joined Twitter as @AskNic. Almost straightaway she found herself engaging in Twitter conversations with people on the trans issue. "I realised that there was a lot of nonsense talked about it. There were no real numbers, there were no proper facts. It was as if they were making stuff up. But they were preposterous claims." What sort of claims? Airy statements like: brain scans show that trans women's brains are more like women's brains than men's. Nic's view was that, before anyone could even make a claim like that, it had to be established that women's brains were somehow similar to each other and different from men's. She had two biology degrees but she didn't know if this was true. She started digging around in scientific journals online. She found no evidence for the brain scans claim, and only weak, contested evidence as to whether female and male brains were different in ways that pointed to different personalities or behaviour. (Of course, male ones are usually bigger – just as every other male organ is, on average, compared to a female one.)

When she saw claims like this, she would look into them and form her own conclusions. She was arguing on Twitter about them and she started to become quite knowledgeable, writing up little reports on what she found and posting them in the Facebook group. She was, in effect, taking activist talking points, looking for evidence for and against their claims, and then writing it up with her conclusion. She has a striking ability to discard received views and go right back to primary sources to find out what was really what. Some claims, like the brain scan one, could be debunked. Sometimes there was no information at all and people were making claims with no evidence.

Stephanie Davies-Arai, who was on her second year of Transgender Trend, asked Nic to help her with researching the claims about the awful suicide rate among trans youth. Nic found that these were, fortunately, not true and wrote a post for Transgender Trend on that.

Stephanie saw Nic's analysis of other topics and asked if she could take a look at the media coverage of trans issues, which seemed to be nothing other than acceptance and celebration of young people declaring a trans identity. At this point they had never met and only knew each other through the Facebook group. Nic organised volunteers from the Facebook group and shared out the task. That was her first project with other people. It was easy to get volunteers because everybody was interested. Each volunteer was allocated some part of the media to monitor, reporting the stories they saw and classing them as positive, negative or neutral. At the end, Nic did the analysis and made some nice charts to show the results and Stephanie wrote the report. It was clear that media coverage of trans issues was overwhelmingly positive. The report is still there on the Transgender Trend website, a little snapshot of Nic's analytical mind.

Men in Women's Prisons

Then Nic's attention was caught by talk of men with transgender identities being put in women's prisons. Women in the Facebook group were sure it was happening, but no one knew how many there were. "I thought, how can we not know basics like that?" She submitted Freedom of Information requests to the Ministry of Justice and the Prison Service in the UK. Every year they publish detailed data about the prison population by types of offence, sex, age and so on. But the Freedom of Information requests came back with nothing. They didn't seem to have a record of transgender prisoners, male or female, what they were in for, or where they were housed. They didn't even know how many there were.

She called for volunteers in the group again, to piece together the information. Knowing nothing about prisons, they searched online. Prisons have their own websites, and the Inspectorate of Prisons publishes reports on prison visits which sometimes mentioned transgender prisoners. They patched together the best picture they could, knowing it was incomplete. Then Nic wrote it up like a proper research study, with the method, the results, the conclusion, the flaws in the study, trying to do it as scientifically as possible.

She found that there were at least 128 male prisoners who claimed to be transgender in prisons in England and Wales. Most of these were not in women's prisons, as far as she could tell. But she didn't know for sure, and the Ministry of Justice (MoJ) couldn't or wouldn't say. Her Freedom of Information requests confirmed that the policy was, more or less, that they would take a convict at his (or if he insisted, 'her') word, and transfer them to the women's estate if risk assessment permitted. That might seem bad enough. But her real discovery was that half of all the trans-identifying males in prison in England and Wales had been convicted of violent or sexual offences. It was an incendiary conclusion.

It felt important but it didn't belong on the Transgender Trend website, which was only about children and young people. A woman in the Facebook group had a blogging site called Fair Play For Women where she collected women's stories about unfairness in sport and in life. She and Nic agreed that her prisons research report could go there. That is where Andrew Gilligan, then a *Sunday Times* journalist, found it. He contacted Nic through the website and wrote a story headlined, 'Up to half of trans inmates may be sex offenders'.[9] He had some startling examples from Scottish prisons, which seem to have led the way in the UK on this. He wrote:

9 <https://www.thetimes.com/life-style/beauty/article/up-to-half-of-trans-inmates-may-be-sex-offenders-26rz2crhs>.

> The effect can already be seen in Scotland where this policy is broadly in place and most trans prisoners are allowed to transfer to women's units without a gender recognition certificate. Scotland has 18 transgender prisoners, including 13 male-to-female, far more than England and Wales for its prison population size. Most are in female accommodation. One of the 13, Paris Green, was convicted of murder as a man and has twice been allowed to transfer to women's units before being moved out again after having sex with female inmates.
>
> Another trans inmate, Tiffany Scott, convicted as Andrew Burns for stalking a 13-year-old girl, assault and other offences, punched a prison officer and threw a chair at the prison nurse. The offences, which took place when Scott was asking to be known as Mighty Almighty, led to a court hearing at which Scott screamed that the presiding sheriff was a "f****** transphobe bastard" for referring to her by the wrong pronoun.

It came out in *The Sunday Times* on 19 November 2017. That evening, Nic got a call from a popular breakfast TV show called *Good Morning Britain*. Could she come down to London? They'd put her in a hotel and she'd be on at 7 a.m. the next day. This was exciting and terrifying, live TV being well outside Nic's experience, and not something she'd looked for or expected. It was a mad rush. They sent a car for her, she stuffed a few clothes into a bag and was on her way to London within the hour. She was put in a hotel with a very early morning pick-up to go to the studio. But when she got to the hotel and opened her bag, she hit a snag. She'd brought a tunic-style dress meant to be worn with leggings ... but no leggings. She headed out into the London night looking for somewhere to buy a pair of thick tights. Trawling round convenience stores at 3 a.m. wasn't great preparation for her first ever TV interview.

After only a few hours' sleep, she was on set with Piers Morgan and India Willoughby. India was a trans-identifying male best known at this point for an ugly scene in *Celebrity Big Brother*, in which he'd got furious at being referred to as 'he', and had bellowed at an 82-year-old lesbian, "I am a *real* woman!" Nic was mortified in her improvised outfit, which felt to her like she was wearing the shortest of mini-dresses. Fortunately, only her top half showed on camera.

Piers Morgan conducted the interview. India Willoughby was a regular in the *Good Morning Britain* team at that time but, luckily for Nic, on the big screen from another studio, not in London in person. There was a slight but audible quaver in Nic's voice at the start, but that soon disappeared, especially when India Willoughby interrupted. It's startling to look back at this interview, because Nic brought up all the key issues – the risks of the proposed change in the law to self-identification for changing legal sex in the *Gender Recognition Act,* and the issues around affirming gender-questioning children as the other sex. India Willoughby said, "We should remember that transgender women are women, they're not men, it comes down to that genuine aspect." He talked about "genuine transgender prisoners" and cited the contested statistic that "one in two transgender people contemplate suicide."

Piers Morgan asked whether transition should be barred until after puberty, on the basis that children change their minds. India Willoughby said no, because "transgender people know who they are from an early age." Nic challenged his claims that puberty blockers are harmless, "like a pause button on the old video recorder machines" Predictably, he interrupted her to say you can't have non-trans people talking about trans issues. Nic said you don't have to be transgender to have views on the risks to children and that over 80 per cent of children who have questions about their gender change their mind if they go through puberty. India Willoughby resorted to "the actual suicide rate among transgender people has been terrible." It was a robust exchange, back in the days when such conversations were allowed to happen.

"The media stuff was terrifying," says Nic:

> I had never done anything like that. I'm naturally an introvert, I don't enjoy attention. I am a scientist so I hate to say anything without data and references to back it up – in a way I'm an interviewer's nightmare. I never make generalisations or lurid claims so

> I'm not great for soundbites. But the prisons story didn't need to be inflated. It was shocking.

The BBC picked up the story, but not as you might expect. Its Reality Check Team claimed Nic's findings were not reliable. It confirmed the numbers she had collated, but said they excluded transgender prisoners on shorter sentences and also "transgender people who haven't identified themselves to the prison service." The logic was, if there are many more transwomen in prison who aren't known to be trans or who are there for other offences, then the proportion of trans-identifying prisoners who are sex offenders might just be the same as for the general male population. I'm not sure how this helps.

For there to be transgender prisoners not known to the authorities, either they need to be men in men's prisons who have said nothing about their inner woman, or men who have been put in a women's prison with no one realising they were born male. At this point, only around 3000 gender recognition certificates had ever been issued to people born male in the UK. Maybe some of them were in women's prisons, with a reissued birth certificate marked female, passing unnoticed and therefore missing from the transgender prisoner stats. It seems implausible that among the few thousand women in Britain's prisons there could be hundreds of trans-identifying men undetected and registered as female – particularly when you know that getting a gender recognition certificate doesn't require any medical transition. Nic's later research showed that most would not have had surgery. Even if true, there couldn't be enough of those 3000 in jail to make a difference, not if you believed the BBC's hypothesis that they were no worse than other men.

Alternatively, there could be prisoners in the men's estate presenting as men whilst privately feeling they were women. If there were enough of these undetected transgender prisoners convicted of other offences, then the proportion convicted of violent or sexual offences would be less than the 41% Nic had calculated. The BBC report did not dispute the headline number of sexual and violent offenders who were claiming to be trans, and it had nothing to say about how being in prison with such a person might affect women. Its issue seemed to be that the story was making trans prisoners look bad. *The Independent* ran a similar story. It was an early sign of how tough it would be to get any consideration of the impact of transgender demands on women. As Nic comments:

> You might imagine that an issue so crucial to the safety of the female prison population would have been the subject of a nationwide, evidence-based, government study. But you'd be wrong. When I asked the Ministry of Justice (MoJ) for the relevant facts, they wouldn't produce them. Even my MP was stonewalled when he raised a parliamentary question on the matter. The MoJ couldn't answer even the most basic questions: how many trans prisoners are already held in the female estate? What crimes have they committed? How dangerous are they? And how many transgender males could be eligible for transfer to a women's prison?

After the *Good Morning Britain* interview, Nic met Stephanie for lunch. Stephanie had lined up a meeting at the Equality and Human Rights Commission about its proposed schools guidance and Nic went with her. Suddenly she was out there as a campaigner. Her name was public, and she rapidly became a go-to person for the media. There was really only Stephanie, Nic and Kellie-Jay Keen doing media interviews then. Stephanie was measured and concerned for children. Nic was evidence-based and careful. Kellie-Jay's approach was different. She was outspoken and challenging on Twitter and Facebook, and on mainstream media when she got the chance. Julia Long had done a few interviews too, also pretty uncompromising, but she wasn't leading a campaign as they were.

By now Nic was knowledgeable across a whole range of related issues because of her research. She had realised that a form of self-ID was already operating in many aspects of life. Not just in prisons but in sport, changing rooms, rape crisis and domestic violence services, bail hostels, almost everywhere, it seemed. She could see straight away that the proposal from the Women and Equalities Committee to amend the *Gender Recognition Act* (GRA) to be based on self-ID would only make things worse. If someone like Paris Green or Andrew Burns could simply declare themselves female and get a birth certificate to say so, they would be in women's prisons as of right. Even if the prison service had a way of dealing with that, it could only make it harder to keep women safe in prison.

The abject failure of the prison service so far, and its willingness to accept these violent men's declarations of womanhood, gave her no confidence. The proposed GRA change would make it virtually impossible to push back on any of it. Suddenly, it became more urgent. She and Stephanie were among those who saw the threat of self-ID early, even before the public consultation on changing the GRA in 2018.

Stephanie Davies-Arai with Nicola Williams in London, 2019

Photo courtesy of Lily Maynard

Hands Off My Rights!

Not many people follow parliamentary committees but you'd probably assume they are considered and reasonable. When the Women and Equalities Committee had inquired into 'transgender equality' in 2015, as described in Chapter 1, the topic was treated entirely as an issue for 'trans people', whom the MPs talked about in a matter-of-fact way as if they were a clearly defined group. They don't seem to have considered women much, although they were warned by prison psychologists in written evidence that male convicts could and would take advantage of self-ID.[10] This could be for any number of reasons, including getting into a softer regime or getting access to women. Ignoring that, and any other inconvenient input, the Women and Equalities Committee published a report recommending the adoption of self-ID as an evolution of the *Gender Recognition Act*. In 2017, the recommendation was adopted by the UK government, with a plan to issue proposals for a public consultation. They called it 'reforming' the GRA, and isn't reform a good thing?

There were people who were aware much earlier of the issues around accommodating the wishes of trans-identifying people. Julie Bindel and Germaine Greer had both been deplatformed for it years earlier. But the general public was clueless. The established women's groups like the Fawcett Society seemed to have nothing to say about it. Women who tried to host public meetings, as Venice Allan did, faced harassment, cancellation and even violence (see Chapter 3).

A new women's rights group, Woman's Place UK, was set up by Labour Party and trade union women to hold meetings and raise awareness. Nic and Stephanie both spoke at Woman's Place UK meetings. They too had trouble with venues, even though they were mostly middle-aged women and there was barely any noise, and no violence or trouble of any kind. In a way, this more official form of cancellation is more worrying. You can dismiss a few young activists

10 <https://committees.parliament.uk/writtenevidence/57375/html/>.

as outliers, but when church groups won't let you book their meeting room, it suggests you are beyond the pale, or at the very least that you hold views that other people want to distance themselves from. How did women's rights become so unacceptable?

The trouble with booking venues for meetings showed how difficult it would be to challenge anything to do with transgender demands. Women who tried to do so faced resistance at every turn. While politicians insisted there was no conflict of rights or needs, that self-ID was a private, administrative matter for a few transgender people, anyone who tried to suggest otherwise was ignored or silenced. Nic went to a meeting at Westminster hosted by a Conservative MP, David TC Davies. It was to brief MPs about what this GRA reform meant for women and why they should not nod it through. But the event was poorly attended. A journalist, Jo Bartosch, later discovered that MPs from all the main parties had been strongly advised by their party whips not to attend. This was during a public consultation on a proposed change to the law. You'd think that MPs would want to be well-informed. Instead they were being pressured not to listen to women.

Seeing the lack of political engagement, Nic decided that raising awareness of the public consultation would be her mission. But how? After the early success on *Good Morning Britain*, media coverage was hard to come by. The media felt generally hostile. As novice campaigners, she and Stephanie had few media contacts and little know-how. They knew a couple of journalists who took an interest – Sanchez Manning at *The Mail on Sunday*, Andrew Gilligan at *The Sunday Times* and Janice Turner at *The Times*. Nic did get onto the *Victoria Derbyshire* show, a daytime show broadcast live on the BBC. There was a panel discussion about GRA reform with four guests, two women and two trans-identifying men. Nic wasn't in the original line-up, but some brave women who worked at the BBC objected to the inclusion of an academic called Sally Hines, because she was so pro-trans that this would make the panel three to one in favour of self-ID. So she was dropped and Nic added.

Before they went on air, Nic and the other woman, Sarah Ditum, were summoned to the show's control centre. The editor asked them whether they thought trans women are women. It felt like a purity test. Nic was walking a tightrope, needing to be safe enough for the BBC to give her a platform but clear enough on air to make the point. Nic felt the best they could get away with was saying that trans women are trans women and that trans women have different issues from those facing women. It was a tactical decision, pushing it as far as she could, knowing that if she said that trans women are men, she wouldn't have been allowed to appear on the show. Imagine how that affects your live TV performance, which is hard enough, without the added pressure of knowing you have to be so careful not to say the 'wrong' thing.

Nic also tried to get onto *Woman's Hour* on BBC Radio 4, but they wouldn't touch the issue. In fact, *Woman's Hour* didn't cover GRA Reform until the week *after* the public consultation closed, in late 2018. They had Nic on the show then, as one of a range of voices from both sides of the issue. The timing meant it was too late to respond to the consultation.

Nic and the other women knew the topic was considered controversial:

> So the question was, if there's a consultation, how do we get the word out? Because we realised that the general public had no idea what it was. Whereas if you did speak to somebody about it… Straight away, as soon as you say, did you know the government is going to change the law to allow any man to get a new birth certificate saying he was born a woman? The reaction of the ordinary man on the street was, that's crazy.

The Facebook group was the answer. Nic called for volunteers across the country who would be willing to go out onto the streets and speak to people. She didn't know anything about campaigning but she knew that when people understood what was being proposed, they tended to see there was a problem. Her idea was to connect volunteers who lived in the same area, to create little hubs across the country. It became a logistical project with Nic at the centre, trying to organise and manage as many local hubs as possible to be able to go out and do their own little bit of street campaigning. Once each local group was connected, they could organise themselves.

Around 100 women in the Facebook group signed up. Nic set up about 20 secret Facebook groups for regional groups and connected women who were in the same area. Then each local hub, some with just two or three women at first, could recruit others they knew in real life to join them. There were close to 200 women across the country prepared to do street campaigning. In fact there may have been more, because Nic only had contact with the core group who'd come from Facebook.

There was a bit of luck as well. A filmmaker got in touch offering to make some short films illustrating the issues. She helped with messaging, and she knew a designer, so they got a logo and a style for the campaign, all done for free. They coined the campaign slogan: Hands Off My Rights. Campaigning on the street would require leaflets or flyers to hand out. The idea was to show ordinary women, of all ages and backgrounds, and to show why they were concerned about the self-ID proposal. Through the Facebook group and the network it created, they were able to sign up individual women who were willing to be featured as faces of the campaign.

Some of these women have become high-profile since: academics Kathleen Stock and Raquel Rosario Sanchez; barrister and former fire fighter Lucy Masoud. But at the time they were not well-known. Another volunteer, a professional photographer, took their pictures. They would feature on a series of postcards, each with a message about one of the problems of self-ID. Nic set high standards for all the materials, both in how they looked and what they said. She's always been precise and careful about detail and accuracy.

One of the Facebook volunteers, Rebecca, who knew about fundraising, suggested a crowd funder to pay for printing postcards and flyers. They called it the 'Campaign for female rights'. Ten years earlier, this would have been a lot more difficult but now anyone can create a crowdfunder online. If it's any good, people give you money. It felt like a kind of miracle to Nic. Rebecca knew how to structure the case for funding and managed the whole process. They shot through their £10,000 target and then the stretch target too, raising £22,950 in a month. More than 600 people donated. This was an encouraging sign.

Bolstered by the support, Nic and Rebecca ordered striking red T-shirts with the 'Hands Off My Rights' logo in black, with the help of a friend of Rebecca's whose business was producing branded clothing. These were for the campaigners to wear on the streets so the message was unmissable. There were tote bags too, for all their campaign materials. As the campaign progressed across the summer of 2018, they'd reorder booklets and postcards. Nic's house looked like a small warehouse, because everything was delivered to her. "Huge boxes and boxes. The whole place was full of boxes." She had to select items from each box and package up mixed parcels for each hub, to make sure they didn't run out. She even asked people their T-shirt size. None of your 'everyone gets a large'.

That summer she spent a lot of time making parcels and going to the post office:

> It was more than full time. I was living it. I was waking up, starting and then going to bed and then waking up and starting again. I mean, it was 18-hour days for the campaign. It went on like that for a couple of months. I didn't have a summer that year.

Normal life was suspended. Nic's normally tidy house was chaotic, but for those few months she did nothing else. She was writing content for the website as well, because once the street campaigners got somebody interested with a postcard, there needed to be somewhere to go to read more about it.

She was also trying to generate profile for the campaign on social media. The street campaigners would send in photos of themselves out and about in their red T-shirts all over the country, and she added them to a gallery of images on the website, Facebook and Twitter. That in turn helped with recruitment, which meant more requests for more T-shirts and postcards. People were getting in touch asking to buy the T-shirts, so they set up an online shop offering T-shirts, bags and kitchen aprons to make a bit of money. The website looked slick but it was so fast-moving that behind the scenes it was all done by the seat of their pants. Nic and Rebecca pushed each other on, Nic determined to maintain a professional front at all times, and Rebecca saying, "Why not? We can do this. What is Stonewall after all, it's not so different, just a website and a bit of money." She had no doubt they would win, because she was sure they were right.

It was scary for these women to go out on the street. Most of them had never done anything like this. So there was a lot of nervous excitement. But after the first weekend, when they'd found that people didn't know about this issue and when they did find out they were on side, it felt a lot better. One of the street campaigners recalls:

> The buzz was huge because people were coming back, going, my God, we've done it. And actually we weren't chased out of town. People were really interested in it, people wanted to know more. And that fuelled it even more.

During July and August 2018, these local groups organised themselves to get out into town centres, every weekend if they could, to hand out postcards and leaflets.

The goal was to get people to go online to the government website and respond. Street awareness was one thing, but they needed to get people to register their feelings. Nic and Rebecca set up another crowdfunder, this time called Hands Off My Rights, and raised another £10,000 in two weeks. Compared to the sums raised later for legal cases this seems modest but Nic says that in those early days "it felt like massive amounts of money." In this second crowdfunder they were able to report how much they had already done. They'd already distributed 150,000 pieces of printed information, including flyers, postcards and guide booklets, and more than 300 T-shirts –

all hand-picked, repackaged and despatched by Nic from her front room. By the end of the campaign they'd distributed half a million printed items.[11] No wonder it was all-consuming.

They spent the money on more materials and a tool on the website to make it easy for people to respond to the consultation. With one click they could fill in responses automatically. Then, as the campaign was building to a crescendo, trying to get as many responses as possible, the website went down. Nic thinks it was sabotaged. There was frantic work behind the scenes in the last week to keep the site up. Fortunately, Nic had a volunteer who knew about building and managing websites, and he took care of it, eventually cloning the whole site and setting it up afresh when the original site was corrupted.

During the campaign, Nic started meeting with policymakers. After that first meeting with the Equality and Human Rights Commission together with Stephanie, and because of the campaign, Fair Play For Women was becoming known. By persistently emailing the EHRC and the Government Equalities Office – the civil servants driving the consultation and the proposed changes to the GRA – she got herself invited to meetings as a representative of Fair Play For Women. Sometimes these were meetings with multiple groups represented, but sometimes she was on her own. She remembers the hostility.

There was one meeting at the Government Equalities Office where it must have been Pride week or something, because the GEO offices were plastered with Stonewall posters. Nic remarked on it to them and said, "Will you put up a Fair Play For Women poster?" Of course they didn't take that seriously, so Nic said, "Well, why are you doing all this?" Their position could not have been clearer. They sat down and Nic laid out her concerns about self-ID, how it would

11 The Fair Play For Women campaign films are at <https://fairplayforwomen.com/social-media-videos/> and an archive of the campaign materials can be found at <https://fairplayforwomen.com/gra/>.

affect prisons, and so on. But she felt as if the civil servants didn't take any of it seriously and that they were just going through the motions by meeting with her.

Can Boys be Girls?

That spring, one of the women in the Facebook group, Helen Watts, had been kicked out of Girlguiding along with another group leader, Katie Alcock. It was a girls-only organisation, but Girlguiding declared that this included 'trans girls' – that is, boys who identified as girls. It had published a new policy on 'transgender' children, what to do (let the trans kids do whatever they want) and who to tell (no one). The worst part in Helen's and Katie's view was that no one was to be told if a 'trans girl' was on an overnight trip, where they could be sharing accommodation with other Guides. In other words, teenage boys and girls would be sharing a bedroom, while the parents were told it is a girls-only trip. This is against safeguarding rules, which are a big deal in any organisation where children are involved.

Nic got the story into *The Times*. She organised an open letter to Girlguiding with almost 800 signatures and got that into *The Times*, too. Among those who signed, along with lots of women involved with Girlguiding, were Stephanie of Transgender Trend, Judith and Ruth of Woman's Place UK, academic authors Heather Brunskell-Evans and Michele Moore, Kellie-Jay Keen, and of course Nic herself. There are other names that became known later, such as Kate Coleman who went on to set up Keep Prisons Single Sex. It's a good list to scroll through.[12]

The story was back in the media in late 2018, after Helen and Katie had appealed in vain against their expulsion from Girlguiding. Helen had featured in *The Times* story but she didn't want to go on TV so when Victoria Derbyshire's show called, Nic did it. This was right in the middle of the campaign to get people to respond to the GRA

12 <https://fairplayforwomen.com/guiding/>.

consultation. The producer didn't look pleased when Nic turned up in her 'Hands off My Rights' red T-shirt. They asked her to change and she said she had nothing else with her. The interviewer didn't look pleased either when she walked on set moments before the interview started and saw Nic. And that set the vibe for the interview.

Nic could see there was no other guest to debate her in the studio. It was just her one-on-one with the interviewer. She didn't know until they 'rolled the VT' that there was a recorded interview with a mother and a trans-identifying child. Here was this cute little 'trans girl' called Lily who wanted to be in the Brownies, with her mum talking about how lovely she was, and how important it was to her. Shown only from behind, it was not obvious that ten-year-old Lily was a boy. "And then it was me, the nasty transphobe, talking about why I thought that lovely little girl shouldn't be in Girlguiding, Brownies," remembers Nic.

Nic doesn't mind being the one saying the unpopular thing, but it's a tough situation, going into battle. She's not keen on being the centre of attention, so live TV isn't her natural place. She did it because she felt someone had to. The Girlguiding story felt like a success because it got a lot of attention, although Nic also got harsh criticism from other activists for not being hard-hitting enough. Nic knew most people hadn't thought about this issue but that they'd be sympathetic to the little 'girl'. She did not want to alienate people by being too strident. She also didn't want to risk being deemed too hateful or transphobic to be allowed on in future. Getting on national television had huge value, and she'd seen already how difficult it was. A few women said on social media that she was a sell-out. But she was the one on TV, and she felt her way was effective.

The week after the consultation closed in mid-October 2018, BBC *Woman's Hour* did a feature on it, with guests on each day arguing the two sides of the issues. They had ignored approaches by Nic and others while the consultation was open. Nic was invited on to talk about sport, against a trans-identifying male who worked for Stonewall at the time, called Bex Stinson. But Bex would not talk to

Nic, because there was 'no debate' – Stonewall's policy of not talking to anyone with opposing views. Instead, the presenter Jane Garvey recorded an interview with Bex Stinson first and then cut back and forth between it and her conversation with Nic in the studio. As a fan of *Woman's Hour*, this was exciting for Nic but also tense, feeling the pressure to get the points across clearly in a short time.

Maybe it was because of the GRA consultation, but talking about trans issues had become even more sensitive. "It was somehow known that you didn't really speak about it. You had to speak in whispers. You have to be careful who you told." In the private Facebook group, women would say to Nic, "I've just been in such-and-such feminist group, and I posted your *Times* article about the prisons, and I've been booted out of the group and everyone's piled on me." So they all knew you couldn't say anything in the usual liberal feminist circles. Nic knew, too, that Stephanie had found herself having to leave her close-knit group, the 'HQ' for the 'No More Page 3' campaign group.

Nic made a conscious decision to be careful and measured while saying difficult things, because she knew how easily people would be frightened off if she said something that jarred with them. "That was our modus operandi. That was just the way we did it. People did different things. We got criticised for it sometimes, but we were very effective." The priority was to be someone policy-makers, politicians and the media would be willing to listen to. She wanted Fair Play For Women to appear moderate and acceptable, while not compromising on policy demands. She wanted to make clear these were men, not women, but it had to be in terms that mainstream media would tolerate at the time or she would have no voice at all. She got her foot in the media door by using terms like male-bodied so that she could win people over, and gradually it became easier to speak plainly.

Waiting

Once the GRA consultation was done and dusted, there was a feeling that they had done all they could do. Nothing would happen for months, maybe a year, while the government digested the feedback and developed its response. After the huge summer of GRA activity, that project was over and the street campaign ended. Nic remembers:

> I thought, I'll carry on a bit longer and keep doing a bit more, because we'd made a lot of progress over that year and we'd come out with huge numbers in the consultation for us. It felt like it had been a very successful campaign. But also, I could see there was loads more still to do, in other areas.

Nic turned her attention back to prisons and found that the media attention a year before hadn't changed anything. She also got more proactive on sport, and she shared her experience of resisting sex self-ID with women in Scotland campaigning against their government's plans to bring in their own self-ID law.

She decided she could continue as the front person:

> I didn't really have anything to lose. I didn't have any reputation to damage. I was working for myself. I wasn't working for a company that could have felt I brought them into disrepute. I didn't have children that I was going to embarrass.

It did mean working for nothing, because her other work had all had to stop for the campaign. There wasn't a plan as to how long this would be, but she felt she could continue to work full-time on Fair Play For Women for a while longer. She set up a new Facebook group for all the women who'd been in the Hands Off My Rights campaign hubs. That became a lively chat group and a place where Nic could ask for volunteers for ad hoc pieces of work.

From working full-time coordinating the GRA campaign, moving T-shirts and leaflets around and involving lots of people, Nic found herself in a new kind of full-time unpaid role. Right back from her first media appearances, women were contacting her through the website asking for advice on their own situations, like being made to share toilets at work with a newly-transitioning male, or wanting to know what they could do about the female changing rooms at their gym being open to 'transwomen'. There was nowhere else for them to go. It was a heavy burden. For a few months she was on her own, which was hard. She didn't consider it a job because it wasn't paid, it was just something she did all the time – probably more than most people do in a paid job. This was when I came along, at the end of 2018. I emailed Fair Play For Women, asking how I could get more involved. Nic and I met in London and started working together.

Nicola Williams with Marion Calder in Edinburgh, 2020

Photo courtesy of Bryndis Blackadder

The Prisons Court Case

Near the close of the GRA consultation, Nic heard a whisper from a journalist that a 'transwoman' had assaulted a woman in prison. It was almost impossible to get information out of the prison service but this journalist had heard something and he wanted comment from Nic because of her track record of uncovering and campaigning on the issue. This time, the *Today* programme on BBC Radio 4 wanted her on. Being on the UK's flagship national morning news programme, the one politicians listen to, is a big deal. It was another early morning in the studio, where she was interviewed by Justin Webb.

When she came down from the studio to the BBC lobby, she saw the Minister of State for Prisons, a Conservative MP called Rory Stewart, on his way up. So she loitered in the foyer and when he came back down she introduced herself. He was a bit taken aback, but she says she spoke to him "in a very business-like way, hoping not to come across as a crazy woman." It worked, because he stayed and talked to her for a few minutes, standing there in the BBC foyer. "There was a lot of grabbing the moment and just being brave and diving in, trying to maximise every little scrap of opportunity that came along," she says.

The prison assault story featured on *Victoria Derbyshire* in September 2018, with Nic as a guest in the studio, in her campaign T-shirt again, and a trans ex-prisoner, Tara Hudson, on the screen. He agreed with Nic that the policy was wrong, because, he said, the prison service was letting people declare as trans while in prison and letting people change "willy nilly," and this made it harder for "real transgender people like me." Nic agreed that "people like Tara" should be kept safe in prison, but so should women. With 13,000 male sex offenders in British jails, transferring men who claimed a transgender identity into women's prisons put women at risk. But Tara Hudson wouldn't stop talking when Victoria Derbyshire tried to end the interview. They had to cut his mike because the show was live. As Victoria Derbyshire turned away, Tara Hudson could be seen on the big screen behind her flipping the bird.[13]

There were a few radio interviews too. And *The Mail on Sunday* planned a photoshoot with Nic outside a women's prison. A guard came over and said no photos were allowed and wanted to confiscate the camera. The photographer refused and jumped in his car and drove off, leaving Nic on her own. Two police officers turned up in a squad car. She was summoned to the prison reception area and given a lecture by the prison governor about how you are not allowed to take photos of prisons. Nic explained why she was there. She was told not to hang around outside prisons in future and allowed to leave.

Once again Nic thought that this media exposure would trigger change. But the Justice Minister dismissed the Karen White affair as a "procedural error" and not a policy failure. Trans campaigners went on the offensive, accusing Nic of suggesting all transwomen were sex offenders. This person is not really trans, they said. Because look what he's done. They said that people like Nic who tried to use this unfortunate case against transwomen were scaremongering, smearing an already oppressed group. Nic stood her ground. "All I was saying was, don't let criminal males who tell you they're women into women's prisons." But it seemed people couldn't hear it.

Nic was in touch with other prisoners' advocacy groups too, like Richard Garside of the Centre for Crime and Justice Studies, who also spoke up. They met with the Ministry of Justice and Her Majesty's Prison and Probation Service to discuss their policy in late 2018. But the Ministry of Justice insisted that the Karen White case was a one-off. The policy would not change. He was eventually given a life sentence which he is serving in Wakefield, a high-security men's prison.[14]

After a flurry of media interest about Karen White, it all went quiet. Despite the GRA consultation, the media backed right off

---

13 <https://www.youtube.com/watch?v=eaDibfKnKbc>.

14 <https://www.bbc.co.uk/news/uk-england-leeds-45825838>.

trans issues. The problem of men in women's prisons wasn't getting coverage any more. Nic tried another route. She launched a petition from Fair Play For Women asking the government to review their transgender prisoner policy and not to put male sex offenders in prison with women. It was shared on Facebook and Twitter and gathered more than 10,000 signatures, enough to trigger a written response from the government. Finally, there was a statement from a minister saying that the policy would be reviewed, and that the implications for all prisoners would be considered. Nic was relieved but still worried. After all, none of this could be a surprise to the prison authorities. Prison psychologists and psychiatrists had warned the Transgender Inquiry held by the Women and Equalities Committee in 2015 that male prisoners would exploit the opportunity to get into a 'softer' prison and perhaps to get access to women.

A new version of the transgender prisoner management policy was published in 2019 with the tiniest of adjustments. It distinguished between male-born prisoners with a gender recognition certificate – a small number – and the much larger number who self-identified but remained legally male, like Karen White. Those without a GRC would be risk-assessed as males before a transfer could be authorised. Prisoners with a GRC would continue to be placed in the women's estate as a matter of course, risk-assessed as females, and only separated from the general female population in a prison if deemed too risky. For these prisoners, a new unit was created at Downview Prison in Surrey.

Downview is a closed prison which holds around 300 women and girls. It has a large main building and a couple of smaller separate buildings, one of which was due for renovation to become a unit for women getting ready for release. Instead, this unit, known as E wing, was now designated for transgender prisoners who had a gender recognition certificate and were therefore legally female. Information was hard to come by but Nic heard that there were three male sex offenders there. They were deemed not safe for free association in the general population but they were given access to the main prison building during the day under supervision. A source told Nic that female prisoners reported being observed by these male prisoners during exercise classes and in the gym. Each trans prisoner was escorted by two officers at all times, but it was deeply uncomfortable for the women.

Nic had been in regular contact with senior civil servants at the Ministry of Justice (MoJ) pushing for change. When a new policy was adopted in March 2019, she asked to see the Equality Impact Assessment. This is a process which public bodies are required to go through to check that a new policy does not adversely affect any group protected by the Equality Act. She was told there was none as "there are no novel elements to the accommodation at Downview so there was no Equality Impact Assessment."

She kept asking to meet to discuss this revised policy, and eventually the MoJ held a round table discussion with Fair Play For Women, Women in Prison, the Howard League and the Centre for Crime and Justice Studies. The campaign groups were shown the latest version of the policy to read in the meeting, but they were not allowed to take copies away. They relayed their concerns about how this policy did not consider the psychological, possibly traumatic, effect on women of being in prison with violent males. It was made clear to them that the policy was not open to review.

It was obvious that Karen White was unlikely to be the only case. But it was hard to get reliable information. So in the summer of 2019, Fair Play For Women placed a paid advertisement in the prisoners' magazine, *Inside Time*, asking women to get in touch in confidence if they had anything to say or any experience of transgender prisoners. Nic started hearing terrible stories. It wasn't just sexual assault and physical abuse, though there was that too. It was also the widespread fear among women. Bear in mind that two-thirds of female prisoners have themselves been victims of male abuse. Most have low self-esteem and low confidence. These men seemed to take pleasure in terrorising the women, knowing they could not complain. A prisoner who dared suggest such a person was not a woman could be sanctioned. Again Nic sounded the alarm, writing up the stories but getting no media take-up. Still the prison service would not review its policy.

Finally, in late 2019, one brave prisoner approached the Centre for Women's Justice, the campaign group founded by solicitor Harriet Wistrich, partner of journalist Julie Bindel. With their help she filed a request for a Judicial Review of the Care and Management of Transgender Prisoners policy. Fair Play For Women was asked to provide evidence as an expert witness. The anonymous claimant, known as FDJ, said she'd been sexually assaulted by a trans-identifying male, not Karen White but another one, in an English prison. Her claim was that the MoJ's policy was unlawful. FDJ was also challenging the operation of E wing, the special unit for high-risk transgender prisoners at Downview women's prison. FDJ wanted the court to consider that the disproportionate allocation of resources to the transgender prisoners – both the dedicated building and the staff escorts – meant that female prisoners were losing out and the policy was discriminatory. The case was filed in late 2019 and was expected to come to court about a year later.

Meanwhile, Nic organised a group of volunteers to look at how the police were dealing with this thorny issue. Through Freedom of Information requests, they discovered that many UK police forces were recording suspects' sex according to self-declared 'gender'. Typically-male crimes such as sexual assault, child sexual abuse (both 98 per cent committed by males) and of course rape (which in English law requires a penis) were being recorded and reported as committed by women. Their findings were reported but after momentary outrage there was nothing. The story reappeared years later, when a couple of members of the House of Lords took an interest and raised it there. To our bemusement, it was duly reported in the papers as if for the first time. But we were grateful to see it out there.

The focus of campaigning was on trans-identifying prisoners because convicted men in women's prisons created terrible problems

Nicola Williams, Stephanie Davies-Arai and Karen Varley (Conservatives for Women) at House of Lords cross-party briefing, 2022
Photo courtesy of Fiona McAnena

for female prisoners, who have no power and little voice. But it's also a problem for staff. A female prison officer (or police officer) does not want to search a man who says he feels like a woman. Consider the women officers in Bronzefield Prison who had to search Jessica Winfield or in New Hall Prison patting down Karen White, possibly with 'her' erect penis (as newspapers described it when reporting his assaults on female inmates). The practical consequences of the 2016 transgender prisoner management policy were now coming to light. The Prison Officers Association did not want its female members to have to search the likes of Karen White and Jessica Winfield. They asked for guidelines to be drawn up so that women staff would not be forced into that situation.

This time, the prison authorities included groups advocating for women in the consultation. Nic had her say at a meeting at the Ministry of Justice, along with other prison campaign groups. Then, silence.

There were trans-identifying staff, too. In the prison service, and in the many police forces across the UK, staff LGBT groups were demanding that their felt gender be recognised. They wanted to be permitted to dress, change and work as if they were the other sex, with the usual claim that it was their authentic self, and that it didn't affect anyone else. The fact that it affected female staff who found themselves sharing their changing rooms with male colleagues was disregarded. The harder problem to dismiss was this: imagine a woman is to be searched. She may be a suspect, undergoing an intimate search for weapons or drugs. Or she may be a remand or convicted prisoner inside, subject to regular searches. She could even be a visitor to a prison. Standard procedures in the police and prison services are that a person may expect, and may ask, to be searched by an officer of the same sex. But a trans-identifying officer wants to operate as if they are the other sex. That's a clear conflict of demands, but the requirement to believe that a woman is anyone who says they are a woman means open discussion is not allowed.

FDJ's judicial review of the transgender care and management policy finally got into court in late 2020. It was an in-person hearing at the high court on The Strand. Covid restrictions meant that there was no public gallery. Instead, a separate courtroom was opened, with individual desks set apart from one another and a couple of screens to show the live proceedings in another courtroom. Public attendance was limited to however many of these odd little workstations could be accommodated, about fifteen. Nic and I went along, giving the vague impression we were journalists so that we wouldn't be turned away.

The audio was poor and it was hard to follow what was going on. But the gist of it was that the defendants – the MoJ and the Secretary of State for Justice – had relevant information that the court and the claimant's team had not seen. The barrister for the MoJ said there was information "material to the case," which is to say it was relevant, but that they did not have the Secretary of State's permission to disclose it. There was a back-and-forth between the legal teams and the judges who sounded exasperated with the excuses being given for this failure of process. The Court adjourned for the judges to consider what to do.

The Times columnist Janice Turner was there too. She already knew Nic. I thanked her for her work in exposing women's concerns, saying that lots of women were grateful to her for doing what so few other journalists would.

We were recalled to our little desks, straining to hear what was going on in the other room. The defendants were given a date by which they had to sort it all out and get the information to the claimant so that a new date for a hearing could be set. With that, and without a word of evidence being heard, everyone was dismissed. The claimant's legal team, plus supporters, adjourned to a nearby restaurant where I was awed to be in the company of Julie Bindel and Harriet Wistrich, who acted for FDJ, as well as her barrister Karon Monaghan and several other legal feminist luminaries.

The case finally got a two-day hearing in February 2021. This time there was online access for the public. The arguing in judicial reviews is done by the barristers, so neither the claimant nor the Secretary of State for Justice were called upon. There was a good deal of argument about data and the lack of it. One of the judges asked how many transgender prisoners were in prison in England and Wales. The defence counsel couldn't say exactly. It became clear that prisoners with a GRC were recorded only under their legal sex. So there was no record of how many transgender prisoners with a GRC were in the system. Worse, these were the ones most likely to be in the women's estate. But, said the barrister for the MoJ, "Anecdotally we believe it is around …" And she named a number. "We do not make policy by anecdote," was the judge's steely reply.

The legal issue was whether the policy itself was lawful, but it was already clear that the policy had been adopted without sufficient regard for its implications. It seemed that it was being operated in a somewhat cavalier fashion.

Quite how this situation had arisen was not discussed in court. But once the case had been heard, Nic's evidence about how the policy had been developed could be published on the Fair Play For Women website. She'd used Freedom of Information requests to get hold of the MoJ documents showing what had been discussed. Although she'd been told in March 2019 that there was no Equality Impact Assessment for the transgender unit at Downview, the separate building known as E wing, it transpired that there *was* such a document, and it duly appeared through the FOI requests.

E wing was the solution to the problem of where to accommodate high-risk male prisoners who have acquired a GRC and so were treated as legally female. Some of these prisoners were dangerous sex offenders who under normal circumstances would be considered too high-risk to mix with women. But the MoJ decided that their GRC meant they had to be treated differently from the trans prisoners without a GRC.

This is significant when you think about the proposal to change the Gender Recognition Act to allow people to get a GRC on request. Transgender pressure groups claim that a GRC is "just admin" and that having one wouldn't have any impact on women's single-sex spaces. Here's proof that it would indeed grant violent men access to vulnerable women, and in the most shocking circumstances.

It turned out that the MoJ had considered two main options. That a separate wing was required for these high-risk trans prisoners wasn't in doubt. The question was where to locate it: on the female prison estate or the male estate. The documents obtained through the FOI request showed how the MoJ weighed up the pros and cons:

> **Option 1:** A bespoke and separate unit in the women's estate enables these high-risk transgender women to be located within the women's estate with access to the women's regime including risk-assessed association with other women. Placement in a bespoke unit would allow greater control over the management of these prisoners to ensure the safeguarding of the other female prisoners whilst also enabling the individual's access to a greater regime than would be provided on a unit in the male estate or in segregation.

> **Option 2:** A bespoke and separate unit in the male estate would ensure that the rights of female prisoners were protected. However, whilst female services could be delivered to the unit, it would be very limited compared to what could be offered within a women's prison. In addition, any level of association would be difficult in the male estate. Therefore, it was decided that a unit in the female estate would be the most appropriate way forward.

Once you're over your shock at the use of "other female" in Option 1, as if Karen White and his ilk were female, look at that "however" in Option 2, and what comes before it. The desire of male sex offenders to mix with women, go to the hairdresser and lurk at the back of their exercise classes won out over protecting women. The possible impact on the female prisoners was not considered, beyond the most basic protection from physical assault. Giving the transgender prisoners "association with women" and access to "female services" were the main drivers of the decision to locate this unit at a women's prison rather than a men's one.

Having these prisoners mix with women was not an unfortunate side-effect of the fact they had GRCs. It was considered a necessary and important part of the regime provided to the high-risk trans cohort that can include dangerous male sex offenders. Put another way, exposing female prisoners to these sex offenders was a deliberate choice for the benefit of the male transgender prisoners. It's scarcely believable that they wrote all that down.

It's fascinating, in a troubling way, to see the mental gymnastics required to figure out how to manage male sex offenders in prison with women, while trying to treat these men just like the 'other' women. At first, the idea was that the E wing would be for high-risk women in general ('trans or not trans'). This was so that high-risk trans prisoners didn't feel singled out. Ensuring they were treated no differently from high-risk women would, it was claimed in the MoJ document, "foster good relations." But they soon realised that could not work in practice, because, as they carefully put it:

> ... transgender women can pose specific risks to other women which do derive from their transgender status. These may be from their offending history (e.g. sexual offences, or violent offences), or may be as a result of their anatomy/physiology (e.g. their size/strength/genitalia). Other women do not, at least in the prison service's experience, tend to pose a similar level of risk.

Indeed.

Where were trans-identifying women in all this? The use of testosterone can make women more violent than typical females. Occasionally a 'transgender man', a woman who identifies as a man, has requested a transfer to the male estate. But such requests are given short shrift. Why? Because they, the trans-identifying women, would not be safe. As the MoJ documented:

> If the operational requirement arose for transgender men in the male estate, the operational need for transgender men may be for a unit which is to safeguard them from potential harm in the male estate. The Transgender Complex Case Board will however have to consider this carefully when making decisions around transgender men moving into the male prison estate.

There was one other awkward issue to be considered. What if a 'transgender woman' got another woman pregnant? This was touched on briefly in the Equality Impact Assessment. It said that:

> ... a transgender woman in the women's estate who is attracted to other women may find her relationships come under extra scrutiny compared to relationships between non-trans women. There may be legitimate concerns regarding pregnancy etc. but also a potential risk of bias and unfavourable treatment if risks aren't assessed holistically.

Remember, here they are talking about sex between a female prisoner and a male prisoner who is too dangerous to be allowed to mix with women unsupervised. No real consideration is given to the risks posed to the woman in that dynamic or the possibility that the sex is non-consensual, whether through coercion or rape. Yet again the main concern is possible unfairness against the transgender prisoner.

This was the policy against which FDJ took legal action. In June 2021, the ruling was handed down. Her case had failed. The judge ruled that the policy was capable of being operated lawfully. We wondered, as we often did, what sort of person the judge had in mind when making this decision. A delicate, perhaps effeminate, perhaps gay young man who would be one of the girls, and who would not be safe in a men's prison? Men's prisons are dangerous places for everyone, but especially for vulnerable prisoners such as those who are young, old, or physically disabled, or who have learning difficulties, or who get into debt to other prisoners, as many do, usually for drugs. That's before you consider the convicts whose offences make them 'fair game' for other prisoners: child killers, paedophiles, former police officers. None of these gets a transfer into the women's estate.

FDJ's experience was of a brutish heterosexual man with a history of violence and deceit. 'Karen White', formerly Stephen Wood, was the same. Decision-makers seemed to be way behind in their understanding of how trans identification was being used and how different some of these people were from the population for which the GRA had been conceived. But accusations of transphobia and bigotry were always there for any campaigners who dared to point this out.

There were positives to be taken from the case and the judgment. The court was clear that its remit was to rule on the "lawfulness, not the desirability" of the policies. The stern telling-off about the paucity of data was echoed in the written judgment. This did lead to a change. The prison service had been revealed to have no idea how many prisoners with a GRC were in the system, and where they were. After the case, they began to keep records, which started to be included in published prisons data later that year.

How the Papers Told the Story

There was one more chapter to the FDJ story. In July 2021, after the ruling had been given, *The Daily Mail* published an article based on an exclusive interview with FDJ, the anonymous claimant in the prisons judicial review. It was headlined 'I was sexually assaulted in a women's prison ... by a fellow inmate with male genitalia'.[15] Referring to FDJ as Amy, the piece recounted her experiences of assault in prison by a male inmate, quoting her story:

> Just before she assaulted me, she was seen with the shower curtain open, her genitals in full view of the other women [...] She leered at me before lunging forward and grabbing my breasts hard. She squeezed them and I cried out in pain. I was terrified she would rape me.

The complainant was quoted as saying that the incident "brought back feelings of trauma about all the previous times when I've been attacked by men," adding that other prisoners were also scared of the individual "because she would rub up against them in the dinner queue with an erect penis." The complainant was also quoted recounting how she, and other women, had heard that the attacker had been sent to the segregation unit as punishment for not taking the medication that prevented her penis from getting erect, "which begs the question: 'Why was she still allowed around us?'"

But when FDJ had told this story to the reporter, she had referred to the attacker as he, not she. Seeing the published story, she was upset that her words had been changed. This made it seem as if she believed in gender identity ideology when she did not. It was also potentially misleading, as readers might think Amy had been assaulted by someone she perceived to be female. She was never in any doubt that the attacker was male. FDJ was a survivor of male sexual assault, describing in the article how the attack she experienced

15 <https://www.dailymail.co.uk/news/article-9819631/I-sexually-assaulted-womens-prison-fellow-inmate-male-genitalia.html> 24 July 2021.

in prison brought back traumatic feelings about "all the other times when I have been attacked by men." She felt she should be free to talk about her experiences without being misrepresented. So did we.

She wanted to remain anonymous so Nic agreed to complain to *The Daily Mail* and then to the media regulator, the Independent Press Standards Organisation (IPSO) on FDJ's behalf about their inaccuracy in quoting her. After a bit of a tussle over whether IPSO would accept a complaint via Fair Play For Women, demanding proof Amy really had given Nic permission to act for her, the complaint was reviewed and rejected. The reason was that although the newspaper had indeed changed her words, Amy had been told before publication that they would have to use female pronouns, otherwise they could not publish the story. The newspaper said that this was necessary in order to avoid an inaccurate and discriminatory reference to the 'transgender woman', who had a gender recognition certificate. IPSO did not consider whether Amy had been under pressure to agree to the proposed changes and did not accept that she was a vulnerable interviewee who didn't really have a choice other than to agree. Yet again, the needs of the transgender person came first.

Nic was really bothered by this sort of bad media reporting, which gave the impression that women were guilty of crimes that are in reality overwhelmingly committed by men. The general understanding that males are responsible for almost all sexual and violent offences, and that they represent a risk to females, is being eroded. It can seem as if women are just as bad as men these days. With that goes the general understanding of why single-sex provision is important. Prisons were the most acute manifestation of the erosion of hard-won rights to ensure the safety and privacy of women and girls. Media coverage was glossing over the whole problem. This is why Nic also campaigned hard to get the media guidelines changed, lobbying the media regulator, IPSO, over and over.

The media regulator's guidance on how to report trans issues had been shaped by one event several years earlier, the suicide of Lucy Meadows. Lucy was a primary school teacher, born Nathan Upton, who had married, fathered a child, separated from his wife, and begun a transition. The school's Christmas 2012 newsletter announced the news. "Mr Upton has made a significant change in his life and will be transitioning to live as a woman after the Christmas break. She will return to work as Miss Meadows."

The story was reported in local and then national press. Under the headline, 'He's not only in the wrong body ... he's in the wrong job', *Daily Mail* columnist Richard Littlejohn suggested this was all very well for Meadows but inappropriate for young children. He quoted a parent who said the news had left his ten-year-old son worried and confused:

> For the past three years he has been taught by Mr Upton but has now been told that he will be punished if he continues to call 'Miss Meadows' 'Mr Upton' after the Christmas holidays. My middle boy thinks that he might wake up with a girl's brain because he was told that Mr Upton, as he got older, got a girl's brains [sic].

The teacher complained to the Press Complaints Commission (IPSO's predecessor) about media harassment. Three months later, Lucy Meadows committed suicide. Trans campaign group Trans Media Watch had helped Lucy Meadows complain to the Press Complaints Commission about Richard Littlejohn's article, and a petition circulated calling for him to be sacked. He wasn't. In May 2013, an inquest into the suicide heard that Lucy Meadows had written notes which did not blame press intrusion but stated the teacher had "simply had enough of living." But, while concluding the press was not to blame for the death, the coroner criticised the media for the intrusion into Lucy Meadows' life and recommended that guidelines around press reporting of private lives needed to be tightened.

This made editors wary of publishing negative stories about trans people, or even mentioning their trans status. In 2015, specific guidelines were developed for reporting on trans issues by IPSO, the new voluntary body which replaced the Press Complaints

Commission. IPSO worked with trans groups like Trans Media Watch to draw up the new guidelines, based on the principle that no one should be 'outed' in the media as trans. The media response was to report using preferred pronouns at all times so as to avoid revealing a person's trans identity. This is how we got to Karen White and 'her' erect penis.

The problem with this approach is that the media report crimes by trans-identifying males as 'women'. That led to novel stories like women exposing themselves in public places, using pornography in a hospital bed, or raping women. Great clickbait, but of course also confusing the public. Most people would see these headlines and read these stories thinking they were about women. Sometimes a photograph of the accused would counter the pronouns, but overall a false narrative was being created. The general public was being misled into thinking that women commit these crimes too. Our worry was that if people thought women were a risk to other women just as much as men were, then it was no longer right to think that single-sex spaces were important for women's safety and peace of mind.

Over the years, Fair Play For Women made multiple complaints to newspapers and to IPSO pointing out that these stories were inaccurate, because the offences were being committed by males not females. Our beef was not that the public should know these people were transgender, but that they were male. Their gender identity was their business and perhaps should be private, but it was being reported as if it was their sex. No one reads 'she' and 'woman' and thinks it refers to 'gender identity', still a novel concept which many readers would not know. Those words imply female. But Nic's attempts to get the media to report the *sex* of these people accurately were rebuffed time after time.

IPSO rejected every complaint Fair Play For Women made about this. Often they simply said that it was not inaccurate to report what was said in court. In other cases, where the court reporting referred to their transgender status, thus revealing their true sex, IPSO had a different defence against reporting reality. Only the person affected by the claimed inaccuracy could complain. None of the rest of us could know someone's true sex, and they, IPSO, certainly couldn't make a determination of it, they said. So they would only consider a complaint about accuracy if it was made by the subject of the story. In other words, only if one of these sex offenders objected to being called a woman. Otherwise, no dice. In vain Nic argued that women, and indeed the general public, were affected by this misleading reporting, since it distorts public understanding about who commits crime and who represents a risk. Can you believe what you're reading in the news? A woman sexually assaulted someone ... was it really a woman? A girl stabbed another pupil ... was it really a girl? There is no way of knowing.

Through sheer doggedness Nic got a face-to-face meeting with the chair of IPSO, Lord Faulks. He was one of those 'my trans friend' people, referring to a well-known trans person from years back who passed very well. He seemed incredulous that Nic wouldn't call his friend a woman. There was a brilliant moment when his face fell as she pulled out of her pocket a page she'd printed out showing the faces of all the men that newspapers had called a woman in headlines. She showed him this rough-looking bunch of men and started reciting the shocking headlines – 'Woman caught with thousands of child porn images', 'Woman exposes herself in car park'. In time, IPSO issued improved, albeit not perfect, guidance. Maybe the reality check Nic gave Lord Faulks helped to push that along.

Lowlights and Highlights

Going into difficult meetings was par for the course. As long as she knew she was being reasonable and evidence-based, Nic would head into battle. Facing pure hostility was something else. Those were the times that left emotional scars. Perhaps the worst episode was in an international sport meeting hosted by World Athletics in Switzerland, although being on a television programme about 'womanhood' was almost as bad.

We heard about the World Athletics meeting at an event at a London law firm that worked with the International Olympics Committee (IOC) and many international sports federations. We were there because it was a chance to get to decision-makers in sport, whose trans-inclusive policies were so unfair to women and girls. After the formal part of the event, which was a panel discussion about the case of Caster Semenya vs World Athletics, Nic introduced herself to the senior lawyer who had acted for World Athletics. He told her his client was hosting a workshop on the issue of transgender inclusion in female athletics. She asked if he could get her invited. The next day, he emailed the organiser at World Athletics and she was invited to go.

The meeting was on a Saturday in Lausanne, finishing with dinner and an overnight stay. It was hostile from the start. There were about fifteen people, mostly from a range of international sports federations. Advocating for transgender people was the trans-identifying male who'd advised the IOC to adopt testosterone suppression in 2015 – Joanna Harper, who had transitioned to a female identity in mid-life. Nic soon found she was the only one strongly advocating for female sport to be limited to those born female. When, early on, Nic said something about male-bodied athletes, someone jumped in and said that language should not be used. Nic pointed out that she needed those words to discuss the issue, which was the role of birth sex in sporting performance. Reluctantly, it was agreed she could do so.

As the day wore on, it didn't get any easier. The atmosphere was markedly chilly each time Nic spoke. The microphone was taken away from her. At lunchtime, she approached another delegate saying she'd like the chance to talk to her. The woman replied, "I have nothing to say to you," and walked away. When they broke up before dinner, Nic texted me from her hotel room. Knowing where she was, I called her. She sounded quite shaken. Later she told me she had been in tears just before. She felt so unwelcome. It was difficult to speak up knowing that others did not want to hear her. She did not want to be defeated by the hostility, but was worried that other participants would walk away if she tried to talk to them. "You don't need to talk about the issues any more," I told her. "You've done your work. Just show them you're a normal person now. Go down, have a drink, make friendly chit-chat about anything at all. Then if you can't stand it any longer, go back upstairs and get room service."

First Nic had to steady herself to do a pre-booked phone interview on Australian radio, then she went down to dinner. She got through it. The conclusion of the workshop was that further work was needed and that those present would be involved; this was confirmed by email. Then Covid hit and it all went quiet. Two years later, there was a follow-up meeting at World Athletics' headquarters in Monaco, with much the same line-up as before. Joanna Harper was present, putting the transgender case, but Nic had not been invited. She didn't even know about the meeting until afterwards.

The other horror show was the same year, when she was invited to be part of a BBC documentary called *Womanhood,* in which "six female celebrities spanning different age ranges, backgrounds and experiences come together to tackle some of the most hotly contested issues facing women today." In an episode on 'trans rights' they interviewed a trans-identifying man and, separately, Nic. His interview took place in a night club and was mostly sympathetic and fawning. Her interview was in a changing room at a swimming pool. She found herself backed into a corner against lockers being grilled by these celebrities. The celebs who took the lead, the younger ones, were aggressive and totally unsympathetic. It felt like a lynch mob. Immediately after that, Nic was required to change into her swimming costume and do laps in the pool for the camera. The stuff of nightmares.

Experiences like that would be hard for anyone. For someone naturally shy and introverted, it was brutal. But as time went on, things got easier, especially as more campaigners got going with other groups.

Access and influence remained a problem. That's why Nic was willing to put herself through those awful encounters. The trans rights agenda had got as far as it had not through open debate but through influencing politicians and policy makers under the radar. Established charities advocating for women's rights like the Fawcett Society were now trans-inclusive. They would not speak up against self-ID or in favour of female-only spaces, services and sport. The new women's activists had to get political access too.

An email from a stranger in mid-2019 brought a political breakthrough. It was from a woman who said she had been involved in politics and that she was interested in supporting Fair Play For Women. Nic and I met her at a café in London. She had been a government advisor but was out of a job at that point, part of the natural ebb and flow of politics. A new Conservative Party leader was about to be elected and she was hopeful of a return to politics. I counselled her to be careful of revealing her 'terfy' views before she landed secure employment. Little did I know she was all-in with the terfs and with the new leader. A week later, Boris Johnson was elected as the new Conservative Party leader and UK Prime Minister, and she confirmed that she had a job as a Special Advisor in Boris Johnson's new team.

This led to two highlights of Nic's time as an activist. This contact invited her to meet at UK HQ, 10 Downing Street. Going up to that famous black door, and then going in, was a huge thrill. There, she bumped into Andrew Gilligan, the former *Times* journalist who had become a Johnson advisor himself. Andrew welcomed Nic with a hug. From the earliest cloak and dagger days of trying to get the story out, here they both were at the heart of government. She stroked Larry the cat, too.

It was almost two years later when the Special Advisor told Nic there was someone influential called Baroness Anne Jenkin who now understood the issue and wanted to get involved. They connected over WhatsApp and agreed to meet on a sunny June afternoon in 2021 outside the Houses of Parliament, in front of the statue of Millicent Fawcett, the pioneering campaigner for women's rights in the UK. Nic and I stood nervously waiting to meet this peer of the

Nicola Williams at 10 Downing Street, London, 2021
Photo courtesy of Fiona McAnena

realm, who came towards us in her bright pink suit, wheeling her bicycle, and started chatting as if we were old friends.

Anne had taken a while to see the difficulties of letting men decide they were women and therefore could access all areas on that basis. Like so many, she'd thought it was a tiny issue affecting a very few men. Once she understood how many women and girls were affected, and the impact on children, she was mortified that she hadn't cottoned on sooner. She became very involved and did a lot to make up for what she felt was her lateness to the fight, saying in the House of Lords, "It's not shameful to defend women's rights."

Winning on GRA

Almost a year after the public consultation on the GRA changes closed, a decision was announced by the then-Minister for Women and Equalities, Liz Truss, on 22 September 2020. Couched in careful language acknowledging the need for dignity, acceptance and so on, the proposals for self-identification of sex were dropped. As a sweetener, the fee for applying for a gender recognition certificate was cut from £120 to £5. The government report on the consultation said that almost 103,000 people had responded. Thirty-nine per cent had come through an online form hosted by Stonewall, 18 per cent through Fair Play for Women. When you think that Stonewall was an established charity with millions of pounds of annual income and Fair Play For Women started in the year of the consultation, that is an astonishing achievement.

By then, the women campaigning to protect sex-based policies and laws had realised that the fight to stop self-ID was only the start. Fair Play For Women, Woman's Place UK and other grassroots groups had sprung up to respond to what they saw as an emergency, but it was clear that even without a change to the *Gender Recognition Act*, sex self-ID was already the norm in practice. Thanks to effective lobbying over many years by campaign groups like Stonewall and Gendered Intelligence, men who identified as women were presumed to be entitled to have access to women-only facilities. GRCs and birth certificates just didn't come in it.

Many people seemed to think it was rude, and perhaps illegal, to state a person's sex honestly if that person claimed to be the other sex. In sport, in changing rooms, public and workplace toilets, in hospital wards, even in rape counselling services and domestic violence refuges, 'trans inclusion' had become the norm. That meant women who wanted male-free spaces, services or sport could no longer have them. Even lesbian bars were expected to include men who said they were lesbians. Lesbian dating apps booted off women who dared express a preference for biological females. Winning on GRA reform boosted us and gave us the confidence to believe that we could undo some of this vast knotweed of misinformation and bad policy. We pressed on.

Over the next four years, Nic focused on accurate recording of sex in data and language, as well as continuing the work on sport, which I led. Prisons were less of a focus, partly because after FDJ's judicial review, even though she had lost, the prison service began to operate a more cautious approach, and also because there was a new dedicated campaign group called Keep Prisons Single Sex.

A highlight was in March 2020 when Fair Play For Women took the UK government to court over the census. Nic and others had been talking to the Office for National Statistics (ONS) about their plan to allow some men to answer "female" to the question, "What is your sex?" The ONS was planning to say that they could do this if they had changed their passport, for example, even though this is easily done in the UK and does not require a gender recognition certificate. The ONS would not back down so we applied for a judicial review and we won. That forced the ONS to change the guidance they were giving in the census on how to answer the sex question. The ruling applied to England and Wales, and Northern Ireland followed suit, but Scotland had deferred the census by a year because of the pandemic. Their approach was even more wild: you could answer whatever sex you felt like, regardless of documentation.

Despite lobbying by Scottish groups as well as from Fair Play For Women, the Scottish government refused to drop self-ID in the census, and so we went to court in Scotland. That painful story is told in a chapter of the book about Scottish resistance to the erosion of women's sex-based rights, *The Women Who Wouldn't Wheesht,* edited by Susan Dalgety and Lucy Hunter Blackburn (2024). It also tells a more important story, about how the UK government was stirred into action to block self-ID in Scotland in January 2023. That was a team effort involving women in Scotland and those of us with access to the UK government in Westminster.

By 2024, Nic was ready to step back and let other people and groups lead the resistance. In 2018, she led a grassroots effort that opposed the intentions of the government and stopped the law from being changed. The campaign against self-ID brought hundreds of women onto the streets and thousands more online to defend their sex-based rights. It was the catalyst for greater awareness, resistance and campaigning for the rights of women and children in the face of the demands of transgender ideology. Nic's ongoing work is now less visible but the legacy of her Hands Off My Rights campaign is everywhere on Terf Island.

Nicola Williams and Kellie-Jay Keen at a private party in London in 2023

Photo courtesy of Nicola Williams

3

Kellie-Jay Keen

KELLIE-JAY KEEN, ALSO KNOWN AS POSIE PARKER, HAS A gift for branding. She has an eye-catching Marilyn Monroe vibe. She's given us multiple slogans and visuals with powerful cut-through, like the simple dictionary definition of woman: Adult Human Female. She uses accessible, clear language to defy the claim that this is all very complex. Unlike the other women in this story, she does her own thing without much collaboration or consultation. Where others lobby politicians and policy-makers, write articles and draft policies, Kellie-Jay talks and provides opportunities for other women to talk, and she films everything. There's not much on her website beyond those filmed events, though she sells merchandise which amplifies her message. Her straightforward language attracts a huge audience. She had the brilliant idea of being the billboard, and every woman can be that. Her reach is worldwide.

She appears to be utterly fearless and uncompromising. She's been visited by police multiple times. She's been assaulted at events, where she stands out in her jewel-coloured jumpsuits. Perhaps her mainstream appeal is also in part because of the contrast between her activism and her conventional lifestyle. She's married to a man and has four children. She says she is not a feminist. She's often critical of other women involved in activism in the UK, usually accusing them of being insufficiently hardline. This is a big draw if you're frustrated and feel that no one else is getting anything done.

Kellie-Jay is determined to be authentic and she's suspicious of anyone who seems calculated in any way. That includes campaign groups that share her position, but are more circumspect in their language. She despises that as compromise. Despite, or maybe because of, her natural talent for branding and marketing, she's wary of anything more professional. She rejects all the unsolicited advice she gets on what else she could be doing or how to do it better. She refuses to answer to anyone. That's why she doesn't sign joint letters. She's not a collaborator even in the most positive sense of that word. Instead, she empowers women to speak and to act.

Her activism goes back to 2015. As a Labour voter in the UK, she was shocked when the Conservatives won an overall majority in the 2015 general election. She joined a political activity group on Facebook called Amazing Lefty Women which quickly grew from around 400 members to 20,000. That's where she first came across men who called themselves women and who were in this women-only group. She noticed that women in the group would compliment the trans-identifying men, who would post soft-focus photos of themselves and be told how fab they looked, and how great their make-up was, and how the women wished they looked as good. The women didn't post photos of themselves. Only the trans-identifying men did that.

When one of these trans-identifying men made what Kellie-Jay felt was an old-fashioned sexist joke, she commented, "Are you sure you identify as a woman?" In response, she says, "He went nuts. But worse than that, all the other women went absolutely nuts, too." She saw how other women in the group rallied round this trans person and realised she couldn't speak about it. But, she remembers, "That's all I wanted to speak about. When somebody said, 'You can't talk about that', I'm like, 'Why can't we talk about that? I want to talk about that.'"

She was in a few left-wing political groups, mostly related to the Labour Party. She started asking the question, "Does my 11-year-old daughter have the right to use a female-only space and not see an adult penis?" She thought it was a clever gotcha question with such an obvious answer. She was astonished by the responses. "I was told, 'No, she's a pervert for staring at people's genitals'. 'You're raising a transphobe'. 'Why are you allowing your daughter to stare at people? No one looks'. 'You're upset at genitals'. 'You're obsessed'." Then she was kicked out of the groups for having the audacity to ask this question. It was also asked some time later on Twitter (now X) by Helen Staniland and became known as the Staniland Question. Kellie-Jay is sure she asked it first.

By late 2016, she was in the same secret Facebook group as Stephanie Davies-Arai and Julia Long. Like Nic Williams, who joined it later, Kellie-Jay was brought into it by a friend, in her case a Mumsnetter who recognised her on Facebook and sent her a message: there's this group, you should join us. The name Posie Parker, by which she is now also known, was her Mumsnet pseudonym – everyone uses a pseudonym on Mumsnet. Where did the name come from? That most conventional thing, the list of baby names she made when she was expecting her first child. Posie and Parker were two names she didn't use for her daughter, and after her fourth child she decided she wasn't going to need any more baby names.

Kellie-Jay was very active on Mumsnet because she loves an argument. But she hadn't seen anything on there about the trans debate or the threat to women's rights that it posed. She was aware of men who wanted to be women, or men who called themselves transwomen, but not that they were actually claiming to be women and demanding access to women's spaces. It was not until she joined the Amazing Lefty Women's group that she saw it.

This Facebook group is where she first heard about children being given puberty blockers. There was talk about the 2016 Olympics as well, because the International Olympic Committee (IOC) had recently changed its rules so that it would be much easier for a man to compete in women's events. Instead of needing to have surgery to remove their testes, they just had to take medication to reduce their testosterone levels, and only for the 12 months prior to competition.

The requirement for an extreme, irreversible and rare procedure had been replaced by a simple, reversible and relatively benign one. Kellie-Jay wasn't much interested in sport but she could see how it had the ability to peak people, and to reach men.

Kellie-Jay has a distinctive look, with platinum blonde hair and strikingly colourful outfits. But this wasn't a calculated move. She had her natural brown hair when she first started her activism, and she changed it to blonde for a fancy dress party. When Kellie-Jay was young, people used to tell her she looked like Marilyn Monroe in her brown-haired phase. Dressing up as Marilyn for her 40th birthday party, she was going to wear a blonde wig and then thought, why not just go blonde instead? The jumpsuits came about after an event in Bristol, early on, where there was trouble from trans activists. This was the event that was filmed for the Channel Four documentary, *Trans Kids: It's Time to Talk*. Kellie-Jay had recently lost a bit of weight and was enjoying being able to wear a jumpsuit that her husband had bought her. The trans activists followed her through the streets, and she realised afterwards that this block colour jumpsuit meant that anywhere in a photo she could be seen. So she decided she'd stick with bright all-in-one outfits as a sort of uniform.

No one will be surprised to learn that Kellie-Jay says she was born confident. She says she was always competitive and always confident, confounding stereotypes by hanging out with boys and beating them at maths. But she has a very shy daughter, and she sees the trans debate through her eyes. She knows her daughter would not challenge a man intruding in her space. She started to get more worried and more aggrieved that she couldn't talk about it openly. "The pressure to stay silent was getting greater and greater and greater. And I realised that more and more people knew about it but weren't allowed to speak about it."

Kellie-Jay started talking across social media about how trans demands were a threat to women. She interviewed other activists like Stephanie Davies-Arai for her YouTube channel, which she called

Kellie-Jay at the centre of a Let Women Speak event in Bristol, 2022
Photo courtesy of Karen Varley

'Posie on the Parapet'. There wasn't a strategy or a long-term plan. She just felt a burning need to call out what was happening.

In late 2017, she phoned into a radio show hosted by James O'Brien, who is best-known for making his callers look foolish over political issues. They had a long conversation in which he trotted out all the now-familiar tropes: about trans adults knowing from an early age they were really the other sex inside, and how trans children become suicidal. How changing rooms in shops don't matter because women are more likely to be raped at work. And he made it personal. "What are you worried I might do, Kellie?" She was calm and determined, insisting that her comfort and privacy mattered. "So you want some sort of Islamist segregation in place, because men can't be trusted?" he jeered, as if that was a ridiculous idea. Of course, the presenter always gets the last word so when she said sarcastically, "Yes, because I'm a right-wing fascist religious nut," he retorted, "That was the conclusion I was arriving at. I'm glad we agree," and ended the call. Some people would ruminate over that. It might make them think twice about doing it again. Not Kellie-Jay. In fact, when she called in to James O'Brien's show, she was already in trouble with the police.

Trouble with Tweets

The previous month, October 2017, Kellie-Jay got a text message from West Yorkshire police. She thought it was a joke, probably from a transactivist, because she was beginning to be known as Posie Parker, with her Facebook and Twitter activity, and she knew that transactivists had got hold of her mobile number. But the texts kept coming and then someone called and left a message. She rang back and found herself talking to a friendly police officer.

He explained the problem. She had posted a tweet about Susie Green, who was then the chief executive of a children's charity called Mermaids. She'd written that Susie Green had taken her son to Thailand to be castrated. Susie Green apparently complained to the police that this description could amount to a criminal offence. Kellie-Jay said Susie Green was a public figure who herself had written and spoken about this very thing, albeit not in such graphic language, so she was fair game. The police officer seemed understanding, saying he'd had conversations with his kids at dinner and how difficult it can be to find the right thing to say. But he wanted to interview her under caution about half a dozen tweets relating to Susie Green and another transactivist known as Janet Mock, who Kellie-Jay had called Mr Mock.

Kellie-Jay thought this was quite dramatic and exciting. In a way, it was what she wanted: a chance for the world to hear what was going on, what affirming 'trans children' actually meant. She was sure she'd done nothing wrong. She'd never had any dealings with the police and she had no reason to think they would see a statement of fact as criminal behaviour. The only difference between Susie Green's account of what she had arranged for her son and Kellie-Jay's was her use of the word castration. But that was the whole point. She says:

> I didn't really worry. And also there's a little bit of me that says, all right, let's go into a court of law then. Let's go and say it so everyone can hear it. Because I'm just thinking, once everybody's heard it, it's game over.

Through the Facebook group, she found a solicitor, Bill Bache, who was willing to represent her pro bono. He was famous for having overturned a high-profile miscarriage of justice, the conviction of a mother called Angela Cannings who was jailed for killing her two babies. Bill Bache had succeeded in showing how wrong the medical expert witness had been. Angela Cannings was freed and the medical expert was struck off the medical register.

Kellie-Jay remembers Bill as a lovely man, very tall and well-spoken with a commanding presence that gave him instant authority: "If he paused mid-sentence, I think people would have waited five minutes." His interest was free speech. He was interested not in the specifics of what she had said but in her right to say it. Having him on her side, and for free, was reassuring, but the police didn't like it at all. As soon as he phoned to say he was acting for her, the friendliness they had shown towards her disappeared. (Bill Bache died from Covid in 2021.)

Four months later, in February 2018, two officers from the West Yorkshire police force travelled to Wiltshire to interview her. For them, this was a two-day trip with an overnight stay. She had to meet them at her local police station. Her husband was worried, and she took the precaution of hiding all her devices – her computer, laptop, phones and everything – in a friend's garage, in case the police wanted to seize them. That would have given them access to the groups she was in, so could have caused problems for other women. One of the charges the police floated was conspiracy, though they never said what she was allegedly conspiring to do beyond having an opinion. The list of possible crimes she had committed also featured public order offences, nuisance and malicious communications. Hate speech, too, even though that wasn't actually a crime.

One of the officers was a dedicated 'hate crime' officer, and and the two of them did a bit of good cop/bad cop. On Bill Bache's advice, she had a prepared statement, and then said, "No comment" all the way through the interview. By the end it was starting to sound weird, in that way words do when you say them over and over. She stuck to the script. She looked at the officers with a steely gaze while she said her two words every time, while inwardly she was thinking, 'Fuck you for having me in here'.

At the end of the interview, they asked her solicitor what they should do next, which she thought was very odd. They didn't take his advice though, because they sent the file off to the Crown Prosecution Service to see if they could make any of the charges stick. After months of hearing nothing, it came back with a no. She hadn't been worried but it was good to know the threat was over.

Trouble with Her Own Side

This marked the start of her breakthrough year in the UK. She got media contacts through the secret Facebook group and talked about the Susie Green police report to Andrew Gilligan at *The Times,* who had covered Nic Williams' report about trans-identifying men in women's prisons a few months before. That was one of the first stories about the police taking an interest in people because of what they said about transgender issues. As a free speech issue, it got attention in the USA as well.

This was also when the controversy about alleged racism first arose, an issue that flares up from time to time. Kellie-Jay had been invited to speak at an event arranged by Woman's Place UK. One of them was also in the secret Facebook group. She was a bit surprised to be asked, because she wasn't close to them and wasn't involved in their campaigning. They were explicitly party political, whereas she had been booted out of unofficial Labour Facebook groups. Although

Labour losing the general election had been the start of her activism, she didn't feel aligned with the Labour Party any more. The event was to be in Truro, Cornwall, in May 2018. Cornwall is a long way from London but Kellie-Jay lives half way between the two.

It was a real shock when one of the Woman's Place UK founders contacted her late one night to tell her they were going to rescind her invitation because of comments she had made on social media. That hit her harder than when the police had called. She worried about how it would look – how could they uninvite her without showing a fracture in the movement? At first, she says, she was more concerned about that. "Not how people would view me, but how the enemy, which was vast, funded and cohesive, we thought, how they would view it and how they would capitalise on it."

The next morning, before she could talk to them about what to say, WPUK put a statement out. It began, "Posie Parker will no longer be speaking at our Cornwall meeting as we object to her stated views on race and religion." That was all that was said about her. The rest of the statement was about their principles and aims. The problem from Kellie-Jay's point of view was that they didn't say what she had supposedly said. She felt the statement had, in effect, labelled her racist. Of course there was chatter online about what had happened. She'd commented on news stories at the time about 'Muslim grooming gangs'. One tweet said, "Are we allowed to notice where these men are from and question the culture in which they've grown? I mean, we seem to be able to blame rape culture but not Pakistani/Muslim rape culture." Someone had dug out a few similar comments from 2017 as well.

"And then the antagonism and the nastiness against me, because I was seen as a lone wolf at that time, just exploded." She was bombarded with abusive messages from transactivists. She's a tough cookie but this really shook her. She says it was the first time she'd cried about something, other than something deeply personal, for a very long time. It was horrendous. Being called a racist is a powerful silencing tactic. And then she bounced back. "I thought – and it's a familiar thought for me – 'Well, fuck you' … I still wanted to do work, but I've been so badly damaged by those accusations I wanted to do it anonymously." That was when she started using Standing For Women as the campaigning name for her work. She'd already registered the name and a Facebook page when she thought she might do something political, so it was there, ready to use.

Adult Human Female

In 2018, when the UK government was running its public consultation about simplifying the *Gender Recognition Act* so that anyone could change the sex on their birth certificate, women who were already active on the issue like Kellie-Jay knew there was a problem. It was becoming clear that the word 'woman' was under attack, that transactivists were taking it for their own purposes and trying to stop women using it for theirs:

> They were diluting the word woman to mean lots of other things, and also making it not mean the thing that it means. We, as women, can't use women. But other people can use woman and it means whatever they want.

But she worried that most people had no idea of what was unfolding. How could they raise awareness? She and a few other women – Venice Allan and Joani Walsh among them – kicked around ideas. What about a full-page advertisement in the newspaper, showing the dictionary definition of woman? This seemed like a brilliant way to draw attention to the issue. The transactivists would make a fuss about it, and everyone else would think, "Why is that a problem? Everyone knows what a woman is." Says Kellie-Jay:

> I thought, well, I'll do this and everyone will go, oh, my goodness, and it'll be over. It'll be such a stroke of genius. It will be, 'What, the dictionary definition of woman is up for grabs? Oh, my goodness. That's crazy!' And it would break the spell.

She found out a page in *The Times* would cost £20,000 or more. Way too much. Then she had the idea of buying an advertising billboard instead. She'd worked in media sales when she first left university, so she knew this might be possible. She found out that she could hire a single poster site for a few weeks for £840. It didn't need to be anything fancy, a simple paper poster would do, and it didn't need to be anywhere special. The point was to get the definition up so that the transactivists would get annoyed. Social media could do the rest.

The next question was where to get the money. The idea of asking for money for nothing in a crowdfunder didn't appeal. Selling T-shirts and stickers with the definition seemed like a better way to go, and they could be promoted through Facebook. She spent a bit of time getting the design right. It had to be obvious that it was a dictionary definition. Showing the phonetics for pronunciation would do that. She googled it and found a nice simple one to copy. She wanted a simple typeface, so simple it could be aimed at schoolchildren, because the point was that it was in fact very simple. She went for white writing on a black background for visual impact, picked a font size for the writing, and sent it off to the poster company. Meanwhile, distinctive black-and-white T-shirts bearing the statement Woman: Adult Human Female were starting to appear at women's events. Stickers with the same design were being posted in public toilets and on lamp posts. It was just a generic dictionary definition but for ages, it was Posie Parker's definition.

Lots of women were talking, and still do, about the importance of language. As Kellie-Jay says, "If we can't speak about ourselves and have words that easily communicate what we're talking about, then we don't have any rights. I don't think I'm a particular genius for understanding that." But she's the one who did it.

She says, "That's why I love arguing, because eventually, you just come down to that one point of difference. And the word woman is that point of difference, and everything stems from it. Everything."

By the time she had raised the money, it was autumn and the Labour Party conference was coming up. She requested a poster site in Liverpool where the conference would be held. The poster went up. The very next day it was taken down. The poster company didn't contact her to tell her. They just put a message on Twitter saying they should have been warned when they saw the copy. That they should have understood, when they saw it, that it was unacceptable. And that they'd taken it down because it never should have gone up. Kellie-Jay is not sure whether she got a refund.

"That Woman Who Was on Sky News"

This time, the media came to her, and not just the newspapers but the big television programmes as well. The first was a live interview on *Sky News* in evening prime time with a trainee GP called Adrian Harrop who was introduced as "an LGBTQ activist." He seemed proud of being the person who had reported the poster to the billboard company, saying it was hate speech and dangerous for transgender women. He was asked what was wrong with displaying the dictionary definition of woman, and he said there was nothing inherently wrong with it. The thinking behind it was the problem, that Kellie-Jay was behind a campaign against trans people and particularly against transwomen, demonising them and suggesting they were dangerous sexual predators.

Kellie-Jay said that the point of the campaign was simply to highlight the absurdity that in 2018, saying woman equals an adult human female is an offensive thing to say, and that Harrop had "delightfully proven that point by having a tantrum." She was, of course, wearing her definition T-shirt, as the *Sky News* presenter pointed out. Kellie-Jay pushed back, asking, "Why is it offensive?" Dr Harrop's answer was that it was because Kellie-Jay specifically excluded transwomen from the definition of women, and that was "not appropriate in a modern progressive society." She asked him for his definition, to which he said, "A woman is a person who identifies as a woman."

She didn't hold back. "What you and your misogynistic allies seek to do is erase what it means to be a woman in law and in life, and that's why this campaign has been absolutely essential." She pointed out that if other people were not replacing the word woman with terms like cervix-haver and menstruator, women would not need to assert the fact that the meaning of woman is 'adult human female'.

The presenter said, "What do you have against transwomen?" Kellie-Jay didn't hesitate. "I don't. I just don't think they're women." Dr Harrop said she'd led a transphobic campaign, to which she interrupted saying he'd led a misogynistic campaign. The two ended up talking over each other, which she says is the only bit of this interview she would do differently. The presenter pointed out that Kellie-Jay's Twitter accounts were suspended and that she had been questioned by the police over the Susie Green tweet. Kellie-Jay jumped in to say what the offending tweet had said – that she thought it was wrong to castrate a 16-year-old child. In using words like castration, was she being deliberately provocative, the presenter asked her. "No, I'm being deliberately truthful in an age where it doesn't seem feasible that people can just speak the truth."

Dr Harrop was challenged about the right to free speech. He claimed there was no problem with the definition of woman, but that she had "appropriated" it for her transphobic campaign.

She appeared confident but she says she was quite nervous "because he was a doctor and I thought he might be clever, and he might make me look wrong." No chance. At one point she said to him, "If you can't see the absurdity in what you are saying then I don't know if anybody can help you." And then when he said "appropriated," she laughed. She looked relaxed.

The interview gave her everything she'd hoped for from the poster. She played Dr Harrop's logic back to him on national TV: "A dictionary definition on a billboard makes men feel unsafe?" He missed his cue to point out that transwomen are women. He said it was the symbolism behind it and she said:

> The symbolism is black-and-white plain English truth ... we knew when we put the billboard up that chaps like yourself would think that they could control what we think and what we say ... It's absolutely time that women are allowed to talk about ourselves, our spaces, our rights and our legal rights without men like you telling us that we are not allowed to speak.

And this time she got the last word.

As she was leaving the studio with a friend, Hannah,[16] a man in the street said to her, "Oh, my God, you're that woman who was just on *Sky News*. My whole office stopped and watched you. You were amazing." So she felt pretty good.

If the media coverage of the police interview six months earlier had launched her media profile, this TV appearance boosted her to a wider audience. *Sky News* doesn't have huge ratings but the interview circulated on social media. Lots of other women told her they had seen it. It's still on *Sky*'s YouTube channel, with hundreds of thousands of views and several thousand supportive comments. Among the most popular comments are: "She destroyed him so hard, I even think he himself was secretly impressed by her flawless comebacks, this woman is incredible and inspiring!" and "I love how a man explains to two women how offensive the definition of a woman is." Who could blame her if it went to her head a little?

Two days later, she went to the ITV studio to do a live interview on *This Morning* with Ruth Langsford and Eamonn Holmes and with transgender guest India Willoughby, formerly a regional weather presenter called Jonathan. On the ITV YouTube channel it's captioned, 'Feminist Blogger Believes Trans-Women Aren't Real Women', even though Kellie-Jay says she's not a feminist. When Ruth Langsford pushed back on her claim that the word woman was being erased, saying women were being celebrated, Kellie-Jay talked about Philip Bunce, a man who had just won an award for women

---

16 Hannah was central to the Man Friday campaign, as described in Chapter 5 and here: <https://www.telegraph.co.uk/women/life/happened-spent-day-identifying-man/>.

in business despite being a man who "wears a dress one day a week." Ruth Langsford asked for her definition of woman but before she could answer, Eamonn Holmes chipped in with the observation that she was making the word female more exclusive than inclusive, that she was claiming it back. He then introduced India Willoughby who, he said, "transitioned from male to female three years ago" and said to Kellie-Jay, "Why does she threaten you?"

She replied, "When you decide that men can come into a women's space it's no longer a women's space." To which Eamonn Holmes said, "But she sees herself as a woman." And he asked India Willoughby how he reacted to what Kellie-Jay had said. Things took a bizarre turn at that point. India turned to Kellie-Jay and said:

> I just want to ask you, Kellie, what would make you happy? Would you want to shave my head? Would you make me want to wear boys' clothes? Take my driving licence away and change it back to a male driving licence?

Kellie-Jay just said, "Of course not," and that he was free to live as he wanted but that should not translate into legal recognition as a woman. India said, "What is it about trans people that makes you so angry? … You've said in tweets that trans people are out to annihilate women," which Kellie-Jay denied she had said.

The situation rapidly became hostile. The rest of the interview consisted mainly of the other three challenging Kellie-Jay to accept India's choices, identity, 'journey' and so on, while she held her ground and said, carefully pronoun-free, that she just didn't see India as a woman.

When she said that India's choices affect women, Ruth Langsford helpfully asked how. Kellie-Jay gave the example of a transgender police officer who is male being allowed to intimately search a woman. But no one took that on. Instead, the two presenters challenged her to accept India's belief, since India was, they said, living as a woman. Kellie-Jay challenged them to say what living as a woman meant but no one could answer.

"What if I were raped on a night out?" asked India. "Would I go to a women's refuge?"

"No because then it wouldn't be a women's refuge, would it?" replied Kellie-Jay.

Eamonn Holmes asked her, "Do you have any sympathy that you're looking at a woman who was trapped in a man's body?" and later, "You don't respect her journey in any way?" But none of them explored the flip side. No one asked India whether a woman might not want to be intimately searched by a man three years into "womanhood."

Later, Eamonn Holmes brought up the poster that had been taken down, and said to her, "Are you proud to be transphobic?" Somehow she kept her cool, but even before she could answer she was interrupted by India saying to her, "You've actually been investigated by the police for malicious communications" and, just as in the *Sky News* interview, Kellie-Jay seized the opportunity to say exactly what the offending tweet had said, not shying away from talking about castration. "But why is this your business?" asked India.

Eamonn Holmes came in with, "Are we agreed there is just terrible confusion and there's a long way to go with all of this?"

Kellie-Jay instantly shot back at him, "No, I think I am agreed that this is an absolute assault on women and womanhood."

Eamonn Holmes tried again with emotional pressure, saying he didn't understand why Kellie-Jay didn't respect India's journey. Surely Kellie-Jay should empathise or understand. She just said, "I don't see why that matters."

Eamonn Holmes' take on this is quite telling. He said, a couple of times, that "as a man, outside all this ..." The implication was that there were two kinds of women in front of him, Kellie-Jay and India, and he wanted to encourage them to find common ground. India had full hair and make-up so maybe Eamonn Holmes really did forget. But at no point did he seem to think that the debate was anything to do with him, even though his then-wife was sitting beside him and he has both a mother and a daughter.

The two presenters read out comments from viewers that were hostile to Kellie-Jay. Brutal stuff. It ended with Eamonn Holmes sounding like a disappointed parent whose children won't make up after a row. "I thought we might have been able to get some agreement but there is a complete mismatch here in the studio. Thank you both for your opinions."

These two interviews propelled Kellie-Jay into the public eye. There was newspaper coverage about the poster as well. She feels the breakthrough was that she dared to say, on *Sky News,* "No, I just don't think they're women." And when she said to India Willoughby, "Well, then it wouldn't be a woman's refuge, would it?" This is her trademark. She made no allowance for the trans person sitting next to her, which can't have been easy, especially with both presenters pushing her to do so. But she did not water down her message. She was the woman who had said those things, very pithily and without qualification or apology. "Those sorts of things have stood the test of time, I believe."

'Cognitive Dissonance, Gaslighting and Fuckwits'

Kellie-Jay was thinking about how to gain more attention, and the need to reclaim the definition of woman. She had tried paying for advertising posters and was denied, so she went for a bit of rule-breaking. She thought it would look fantastic to project 'adult human female' in lights onto public buildings at night. This is guerrilla marketing – advertising somewhere you haven't paid for and without permission. She knew someone who could do it, albeit at a cost of several thousand pounds. She hired a photographer as well. It was exciting, getting up close to BBC Broadcasting House to install the projection. They also projected the message at the Royal Opera House in London and a couple of buildings in Leeds, selected because it was the home of West Yorkshire Police, who'd interviewed her about her Susie Green social media posts. The projections looked great, and the fans loved it. But there was no media interest. The useful, if expensive, lesson was that it wasn't news because it was just the poster in another guise.

It was still a hobby for Kellie-Jay at this point, although she was selling some merchandise, and the TV interviews and the poster row helped with that. She called her campaign Standing For Women and started doing talks on Facebook Live. She got tens of thousands of views in just a few days. That showed there was demand for someone like her, who would not shy away from saying what needed to be said. Her first talk was called 'Cognitive Dissonance, Gaslighting and Fuckwits'. It was inspired by a feminist meeting she'd gone to in Glastonbury where everyone was asked their pronouns. When she'd raised issues about girls in school and private spaces, it caused an argument, where she felt completely out of step with these women who called themselves feminists but seemed happy to redefine women to include men. There was an exhibition about the history of feminism, highlighting campaigns over the years. One display among them was about so-called terfs and how they were a bad influence. Kellie-Jay was furious. It felt like attacking women who didn't accept men as women. Women like her.

Kellie-Jay is happy to argue, but she's also quite happy on her own, speaking live to the camera on her YouTube channel, unscripted. She discovered she was pretty good at it: "I can get very angry and still be quite articulate." She felt she was channelling what many women felt but could not say. She moved from the study to an office next to her house and started to make her Facebook Live broadcasts regularly.

Kellie-Jay is best-known around the world for her public meetings, called Let Women Speak. They are open to all, usually held outdoors, and live-streamed. Anyone can speak. All you have to do is step forward and catch her eye. They didn't start like this though so it's worth tracking back a few years to when public meetings on this issue started. We also need to consider two other women whose role was foundational: Julia Long and Venice Allan.

Julia Long and Venice Allan at the Millicent Fawcett statue in Parliament Square, London, 2019

Photo courtesy of Venice Allan

Thinking Differently — Julia Long

Julia is a feminist academic and a lesbian. She's always had an absolute conviction that women-only organising is crucial. For years she had felt it was being sidelined by younger women whose approach was, bring your boyfriend along, you'll change his attitude and he'll change his friends and that's how we'll change society. As a counter to that, back in 2012, Julia had staged a women-only conference in London. But she'd got a lot of pushback about excluding men.

There was also, even then, pressure from trans-identifying males to be included in women's events. Julia's agenda in 2012 was mostly about male violence against women and opposing the sex industry, but a trans-identifying male called Roz Kaveney complained to the venue, Conway Hall, that the event was women-only and there was an invited speaker who promoted hate speech. He spelled out in an article for *The Guardian* that he meant Sheila Jeffreys, a feminist academic. Seemingly befuddled by this, Conway Hall management cancelled the booking, saying it was sex discrimination to have a women-only meeting, and also something about Sheila being a problem. So as far back as 2012, a women's meeting had to find another venue, the police had to be alerted, and participants had to meet in a public place to walk together to the new venue rather than making its location public in advance.

Over the next few years, Julia was involved in ad hoc protests with a few others, giving out leaflets at Reclaim The Night and the Dyke March about violence by men who call themselves women, and generally getting a very hostile response. She organised the UK launch of Sheila Jeffreys' 2014 book *Gender Hurts: A Feminist Analysis of the Politics of Transgenderism.* Alerted to the issue, she saw the risk in the political initiatives in the UK around trans demands, culminating in the 2015 trans equality inquiry held by the Women and Equalities Select Committee. In 2016, Julia planned another meeting at Conway Hall, again with Sheila. This one was called Thinking Differently. The speakers included Stephanie Davies-Arai, Lierre Keith, Mary

Lou Singleton and Magdalen Berns. There was also Jackie, a 'trans widow'.

Perhaps the management had changed because this time Conway Hall didn't renege on the booking. Stephanie remembers this meeting as ground-breaking, even though she was extremely nervous, feeling that the others were accomplished speakers and she was a novice. Julia recalls inspiring speeches followed by a great night at the pub with songs from singer-songwriter Ali Bee.

We Need To Talk — Venice Allan

The following year, a mutual friend introduced Julia to a committed Labour Party member called Venice Allan who was planning a debate on the clash between trans and women's rights. Venice had been worried for a while. She'd watched all Magdalen Berns' videos, listened to the Canadian Meghan Murphy's podcast, read all of her blogging on *Feminist Current.* She had been horrified to hear that transactivists had gone into the Vancouver Women's Library and vandalised it. She was a big fan of the then-leader of the Labour Party, Jeremy Corbyn. When she heard him say that he supported the Conservative government's proposals to 'update' the *Gender Recognition Act* and introduce self-ID, she reasoned that somehow he must not have heard about why self-ID was a problem: "If only Jeremy heard our arguments. I thought he would listen to me."

Venice wanted to take the argument off social media and into the real world. She was a regular volunteer at her local public library so she booked a room there and planned a debate with speakers for and against self-ID. She was surprised when her local Labour Momentum group, of which she was a member, said they wouldn't take part and refused to promote it to members, but she went ahead without them. She contacted Stonewall and they put forward two speakers. A friend suggested she ask Julia Long and a trans-identifying man called Miranda Yardley to speak on the other side, against self-ID.

Her friend kept saying it was not going to happen. Venice thought, "Why not? It's all booked."

Six days before the meeting, the lead Stonewall speaker, a trans-identifying man called Bex Stinson, dropped out. This was a year before he refused to go on *Woman's Hour* live with Nic Williams (see Chapter 2). He'd got a last-minute opportunity to go on a hiking holiday. The other Stonewall speaker, a woman, said she couldn't do it if there wasn't a trans person speaking so she was out too. Venice and Julia decided to go ahead. And then, with two days to go, the library was inundated with complaints. Venice is pretty sure that her local Labour Momentum group was involved, and a Labour member of parliament and some LGBT campaign groups. The library board cancelled the event, saying they didn't have the "risk appetite" for it, which Venice says was "the first time I'd ever heard that rather sweet little expression."

Julia posted in the secret Facebook group about this cancelled meeting and added Venice to the group. This was how she got to know Kellie-Jay. Someone else in the group said she could book a room at the University Women's Club. It cost £200, which was a lot for Venice. The library had been free so she hadn't sold tickets, just set up a Facebook event page. In desperation, she charged it to her credit card. Rather than risk the new venue being targeted as the library had been, the plan was to give attendees a meeting point and then they'd be told the venue. Venice thought, "Speakers' Corner, that's symbolic. We'll meet there."

She was expecting opposition because two campaign groups, Sisters Uncut and No More Class War, had put up a Facebook page saying let's go and protest against the terfs. Sure enough, there were about 50 young people with signs saying, 'Trans misogyny is misogyny' and 'No Debate', which was ironic at Speakers' Corner. They were singing and chanting, but Venice and Julia didn't take it too seriously. "I was so naive," Venice says. "I had no idea about any of it because I thought the people who were protesting were sort of my people." She means left wingers and anarchists, like people she would run into at her local pub.

Afterwards, when footage of the confrontation was played and replayed because of what happened next and the subsequent court case (which we'll come to), friends told her it was hard to tell which side she was on, because she was dancing along to the transactivists' chants. She had said to them, "Don't be ridiculous, come to the meeting." Their response was that they weren't coming and the meeting mustn't happen. The audience for Venice's meeting had grown because of Julia talking about its cancellation in the Facebook group. As Venice points out, "If they had just let us have our stupid little meeting in New Cross, then a lot of what happened afterwards wouldn't have happened."

They gathered at Speakers' Corner. Her mum was there, and a few of her friends, but there were plenty of women Venice didn't know. Everyone had their phones out to film and take pictures. A small woman of about 60 called Maria MacLachlan was taking photos of the protestors with a proper camera. Three young men dressed as women approached her, grabbed her and wrestled her camera away. She resisted and in the scuffle the camera was knocked to the ground and Maria got punched in the face. Julia saw it happen. She had been singing and larking about, excited that the meeting was going ahead, laughing at the protestors, and then she saw these big guys assaulting Maria. She was utterly shocked. She and others called the police but by the time they arrived the assailants had run off. One, a young trans-identifying man called Tara Wolf, was later convicted of assault but got off with only a fine and court costs. He refused to name the other assailants. Maria was chastised by the judge in court for referring to Tara Wolf as 'he' when she gave her evidence and was denied compensation.

After all that the meeting went ahead. Venice hoped that by going in small groups of four or five, walking or in taxis, they could avoid the protestors. She handed out little bits of paper with the address on it. She says it wasn't hard to tell who was genuine and who was a pro-

Maria MacLachlan in London, 2025
Photo courtesy of Fiona McAnena

trans protestor. The police were of no help. When Venice explained to the police they were being followed, the police said that was allowed. There were protestors chanting outside while the meeting was going on, which made it difficult to hear the speakers. This was also something of a surprise to the University Women's Club.

In a state of mild shock after seeing Maria assaulted, Venice and Julia carried on with the meeting, and then everyone stayed inside until they felt sure it was safe to leave. Julia ran through some slides, "mainly pictures of men in dresses," naming them unequivocally as men, but what she remembers most was Sheila Jeffreys standing up in the audience and saying:

> We have to understand transgenderism as a men's sexual rights movement.
>
> The same way we understand pornography, prostitution, all of this is an attempt to extend men's domain of their sexual rights, and that's how we have to understand it.

"And she was absolutely spot on and brilliant," says Julia.

Janice Turner at *The Times*, whose columns on the issues arising from transgenderism have been so important in raising mainstream awareness in the UK, was one of those who went to Speakers' Corner to join the meeting. A couple of months earlier, she'd interviewed Maria Miller, the MP who'd led the Women and Equalities Committee's trans equality report. Headlined, 'How do you solve a problem like men in women's changing rooms, Maria?', the interview went straight to the heart of the issues, and Maria Miller seemingly had no answers. Janice showed her photos of 'transwomen' such as Danielle Muscato and Alex Drummond, whom she described as "a lush-bearded British psychotherapist who claims to be a woman, without any transition, who is 'expanding the bandwidth of gender.'" Quizzed about "the epidemic of girls wanting to transition," Maria Miller picked up her handbag and threatened to leave.

Aware of the proposal to amend the *Gender Recognition Act*, Janice had discussed with other journalists the idea of organising a public debate on self-ID. She'd seen on social media that there had been problems with venues cancelling, and she was intrigued. At that stage, she says, she had no agenda, just went along out of interest. And then, "it all kicked off." She was shocked by the aggression from the transactivists. She published her first piece on it soon afterwards, and she has continued to write important, well-informed columns on all aspects of this issue.

After that, Venice thought, we need to keep having more of these meetings. The problem was venues. The first difficulty was that, like New Cross library, they might cancel. This had happened to several different groups and continues to happen. But Venice had another worry, after what happened to Maria. "Every meeting after that that I organised, I would wake up in the middle of the night and think, 'Oh, my God, is someone going to get hurt?' Every single time." Back then, before there was any media interest, before there had been any legal cases, and before the public support of JK Rowling, Venice felt genuinely scared that something awful might happen.

In fact, Maria was not the only one who was assaulted at that meeting. Venice says that a trans-identifying man called Miranda Yardley who was involved in her events in defence of women's rights was also punched to the ground, "but he never wanted to report it or anything because he didn't want to take the spotlight off Maria." So she didn't see the assault on Maria as a one-off that was unlikely to happen again.

A few weeks later, there was trouble at the London Anarchist Bookfair. Two women leafletting about the GRA were mobbed by trans activists, including some who had been present when Maria was attacked. A woman called Helen Steel who'd seen the attack on Maria came to their aid. She helped the women get away but on her return to the main hall she herself was surrounded by the trans activists screaming abuse. No one actually hit her, though she fended off a male hand aimed at her face. Friends formed a protective cordon around her and a noisy stand-off went on for over an hour and ended only when the fire alarm went off and the whole building was evacuated. Despite the fact she'd not actually said anything herself, Helen was denounced by people she'd thought were friends and allies. This sort of experience leaves lasting emotional scars, though it didn't stop Helen from speaking up. Weeks later she was the first speaker at the first Woman's Place UK event.

Venice set up a group on Facebook called We Need to Talk. The group description was "Fighting against the war on women, children and truth." In the next year or so, Venice put on several events across the country, with help from Sheila, Julia, Heather Brunskell-Evans and others. Kellie-Jay was involved with a couple of them. One of the first events was in York that November, called 'We need to talk about the GRA', with Sheila and a lesbian politician called Linda Bellos. That event led to Linda and Venice being taken to court. Something Linda had said was represented as a threat of violence. Because Venice livestreamed that event, she was issued with a court summons as well. But that wasn't until the following July. They didn't know they were in trouble until then.

They Have Debates in the Houses of Parliament, Don't They?

The venue in York cancelled and another one had to be found. The same thing happened in Glasgow in January 2018. Next, Venice was planning a meeting in London for March 2018. She had booked a large room at Millwall Football Club. Millwall FC is notoriously rough. Its fans have a long track record as football hooligans. They chant, "No one likes us, we don't care." You'd think that would be a venue that Venice could rely on. She was liaising with a helpful woman in the office there and it was all going swimmingly. On a Friday morning a couple of weeks before the event, she announced the venue on Facebook and started selling tickets to cover the room hire charge. By the end of the day the venue had called it off. She got a call from the nice woman in the Millwall FC office apologising, saying she was trying to make it happen, but didn't think it would be able to go ahead. The club had been bombarded with phone calls complaining about them hosting this hate group. Later it was rumoured that among the complainants were a local MP and a well-known boxing promoter who had transitioned in his sixties from Frank to Kellie.

Venice had the idea of booking a meeting room in the Houses of Parliament: "I thought, well, this is the place where we have debates, isn't it, in parliament?" She phoned the parliament hospitality line. They said it was ten thousand pounds to hire a room. For Venice that was a non-starter. And then they said, if a member of Parliament sponsors the meeting, use of the room is free. She thought of a Conservative MP called David TC Davies who'd been in the news just a few days earlier about trans issues and women's rights. A socially conservative right-wing politician was an unlikely ally for a fan of Jeremy Corbyn, but he had dared to speak up when no one else had. So she found his number, picked up the phone, spoke to his assistant and told her what she wanted to do. He called her back five minutes later and said he would very much like to help.

There were some tricky issues to negotiate. She'd already sold tickets to over a hundred people, so they needed a big room. That's a lot of people to get through security. Charging for admission to these rooms is not allowed, so those who had already bought tickets would have to be refunded. It was decided to make the event women-only. Even with an MP as sponsor, it was not easy. Venice and David had to meet with the Serjeant at Arms, the official in charge of security at the Palace of Westminster. David TC Davies told Venice that he'd organised meetings in the past with actual terrorists, but nothing was as bad as organising this meeting of women talking about their rights.

The event was called 'Transgenderism and the War on Women'. The speakers were Sheila, Julia and Anne Ruzylo, an all-lesbian panel. It was only a week after Kellie-Jay had been interviewed by the police about the Susie Green tweets, so she was invited to speak from the floor about being reported to the police and the interview that followed.

Despite the gulf between them politically, David TC Davies and Venice worked well together and were both delighted with the event. The MP was particularly tickled about the lesbian panel because he'd been accused of being homophobic. He had mentioned in a media interview that he used to go boxing with a gay friend which led to him being accused of beating up gay men for a hobby. Here was his proof that he wasn't homophobic. Venice also was pleasantly surprised to get on so well with a social and political conservative.

Around this time, she was suspended and then expelled from the Labour Party. She was investigated because she had, as a joke, changed her Facebook profile to say her job was leader of the Labour Party. She was also posting stuff on Twitter as Dr RadFem that they didn't like. For example, a picture of Eddie Izzard saying, "Eddie Izzard on the all women shortlist? This is what misogyny looks like." A trans-identifying man reported her and she had a disciplinary interview to investigate her 'transphobia'. A barrister called Amanda Jones went with her for free.

The interview was, in Amanda's words, "completely surreal."[17] The investigator asked Venice things like whether feminism exists in the animal kingdom and whether her mother agreed with her. "It was proper Kafka," Venice says. "Slightly embarrassing as well, because I'm there going, oh, I'll treat them as honorary women if they're nice." She happily conceded that she was not, in fact, the leader of the Labour Party, but did not back down on her belief that people can't change sex. So she was out.

Private Prosecution and Litigation Stress

Then Venice ran into real trouble. In late summer she received "a weird handwritten court summons" sent to her at work. It looked so weird that she wondered if it was a spoof. She was lucky to have a barrister she could call – Amanda, who'd gone with her to the Labour Party disciplinary hearing – who told her it was real because it was listed to be heard at Westminster Magistrates' Court.

It was a private prosecution for malicious communications, based on something that Linda Bellos had said the year before. For Venice, this came completely out of the blue. She had livestreamed an event in York in November 2017 where Linda had spoken. The incident at Speakers' Corner when Maria MacLachlan was attacked was still fresh in people's minds, and Linda had said something like, "I'm 60-something years old and I play football and I box, and if one of those bastards comes anywhere near me I'll ..." You can't quite hear all the words on the livestream, but she says, "punch, hit, slap." A transactivist had reported Linda to the police at the time, and they had interviewed her, but nothing came of it. They hadn't contacted Venice at all. So this court summons was a terrible shock. "I had never even heard the term 'litigation stress' at that point in my life,

17 <https://mirandayardley.com/en/the-labour-party-is-no-longer-safe-place-for-women-venice-allan/>.

but I suddenly knew what it was. I'd never been taken to court before, you know, it's terrifying."

The next few months were utterly miserable for Venice. For several weeks, until the first court hearing, she couldn't sleep, she couldn't concentrate on anything else. "I was constantly distracted because I was constantly thinking about it, even though I felt like I hadn't done anything wrong and the police hadn't even interviewed me. That was the worst," she says, though she also jokes about discovering the benefits of being poor. Since she did not own a home, she wasn't in danger of losing it, and she qualified for legal aid. Amanda Jones and another barrister, Gudrun Young, did most of the work for free, telling the legal aid solicitor what to do. They got the case postponed from September to November, and in that time they got the Crown Prosecution Service (CPS) to step in. The night before the second hearing, the CPS intervened to throw the case out. There still had to be a court hearing of sorts for the proceedings to be closed down, so they had to troop down to the magistrates' court and face the activist who had started it all. A couple of dozen women gathered outside the courthouse in support – among them Kellie-Jay Keen and an unknown consultant called Maya Forstater who was taking her first activist steps on this issue. David TC Davies posted a video from outside the court on his Facebook page.[18]

Venice and Linda had to sit in the dock, although they didn't have to speak. The activist who'd reported them glared at them across the courtroom and complained that they were making faces at him. Linda was in a suit with a handkerchief in the suffragette colours of purple, white and green in her top pocket, and he complained about that, saying it was a political thing. Venice thinks that was one of the catalysts for women in the UK to start wearing the suffragette colours

18 <https://www.facebook.com/davidtcdavies/posts/recording-outside-westminster-court-with-campaigners-venice-allen-linda-bellos-w/1899603916789192/>.

again. The judge was having none of it. He basically said the case never should have come to court.

It did change Venice's behaviour, though:

> The process is the punishment. And it was a punishment. I couldn't sleep for two months, like, properly. I couldn't concentrate on my work, I couldn't concentrate on my kids. I think it was at that point my kids said, Mummy, Mummy, can you just stop it?

After the case was dismissed, she decided she would stop engaging on Twitter with these people, not even in the playful way she used to. She thinks the complainant came after her because she used to send him up, quote-tweet him and make jokes about him:

> So I walked out of that courtroom to all the lovely people outside who had come and protested, and I thought, I'm never going to say that bastard's name ever again. When these people come onto my Twitter now, I just grey rock, because there's no point.

That's when she started working with and for Kellie-Jay, happy to play a supporting role for someone who was willing to be the front person.

While Venice was struggling with her court case, Kellie-Jay planned an evening event in Manchester. It turned out to be the very day of the second court hearing for Venice and Linda's case, when it was thrown out. They caught the train from London to Manchester together straight after the hearing, in jubilant mood. For once Venice, the perennial behind-the-scenes person, spoke at the meeting. The UK government consultation on changing the *Gender Recognition Act* had just closed so it felt as if the fight, at least the political and legal fight in the UK, was over for a bit.

The First USA Trip

Kellie-Jay decided she wanted to go to the USA to protest her banning at the Twitter headquarters in San Francisco, and at Facebook as well. Lierre Keith and Kara Dansky of the US campaign group Women's Liberation Front, WoLF, advised her not to go to San Francisco, saying she would be killed, and anyway the protest wouldn't be visible. They said it would be better to go to Washington DC where the politicians are. They helped her plan a trip to DC and to New York in January 2019. She asked Venice and Julia to go with her. Later, there were accusations on social media that they'd taken money from American alt-right or conservative Christian sources but that was not true. Kellie-Jay was selling a lot of merchandise, which paid for flights for her and Venice. Julia paid for her own travel. Kellie-Jay and Kara Dansky paid for the accommodation in the US.

The trip was intense. Kara, Lierre and others helped set up lots of meetings and events. They met with politicians and their staffers in private meetings from eight in the morning until six in the evening, across a few days. They did manage to meet with representatives from both sides, even if the few meetings with Democrats were brief and rather chilly. It was a punishing schedule but, Julia says, Kellie-Jay was in her element. Charming, persuasive, energetic. They handed out cards with the definition of woman on one side and "This is hate speech in the UK" on the other. Julia went and met with a lesbian group one evening.

There was a meeting in a public library, with the Canadian campaigner Meghan Murphy as a speaker. Venice loved it, because it was, finally, the meeting in a library she'd first tried to arrange more than a year before, only in a grand public building in the USA instead of in the down-at-heel council-run library of New Cross in south east London. The library meeting was well-attended, with great speakers and no protestors, but people have forgotten that it even happened. Because then there was the meeting at the Heritage Foundation.

Kara Dansky and Kellie-Jay Keen in Washington DC, 2022

Photo courtesy of Kara Dansky

The push for this meeting came from a woman whose family had been devastated by her daughter's belief that she was male (and her daughter's decision to bind her breasts). The mother desperately wanted a public discussion of 'gender identity' ideology and the Heritage Foundation had agreed to host it when no one else would. It was called 'The Inequality of the Equality Act: Concerns from the Left'.

None of the British contingent had heard of the Heritage Foundation before they got to the US. They weren't familiar with the American Christian right and certainly weren't getting money from them. Venice remembers:

> Everybody thinks that we were paid to go there by the Heritage Foundation. I actually asked the Heritage Foundation could I do some photocopying and they said no. All I got out of the Heritage Foundation was a couple of really nice sandwiches.

All the same, when they heard people talk about this group they had some misgivings. Julia says she wasn't thrilled to be going there, even though she was only in the audience. But the speakers were women she respected: Kara Dansky, Julia Beck, Jennifer Chavez, all of WoLF, and a man named Hacie Horvath. She wasn't going to undermine the event by not going.

Kellie-Jay was a bit more blasé about the venue. Even now, after all the backlash and criticism they got, she says, "I've frequently said I'll stand with the devil himself if it stops another girl getting mutilated, so I don't really care." Venice was equally determined to hear these women speak. Her feeling was that it's the issues that matter. She knows that the Heritage Foundation get credibility from having lesbians and left wingers speaking, but her position is: "If you are confident in your arguments then why not make them everywhere you can? These people's values and beliefs don't rub off on us."

Even before the event at the Heritage Foundation, there was trouble. A fourth British woman had been due to go on the trip but changed her mind. Her main beef was that the trip would involve what she called "right wing links." In 2016, WoLF had accepted $15,000 from the conservative group Alliance Defending Freedom, ADF, to help fund a legal case to defend *Title IX*, a vital piece of American legislation that requires sex equality in federally-funded institutions. The ADF is anti-abortion, and the WoLF board had consulted its members before taking the money. Then there was the planned event at the Heritage Foundation. The woman objected and eventually decided she had to withdraw from the trip.

That was all behind closed doors, but on the day they were flying out, this other woman, who doesn't want to be named, published a blog post detailing various areas of disagreement with Kellie-Jay. She said she was going public because of a podcast released that day in which Kellie-Jay talked about the English campaigner Tommy Robinson. In the podcast, Kellie-Jay was talking about gangs of men who had sexually exploited girls in England, resulting in the conviction of dozens of men of mostly Pakistani origin. She said Tommy Robinson had called it out and that he'd filled a gap left open by feminist groups. He is known for being anti-immigration and many people accuse him of being racist. This other woman wrote that he used the grooming gangs to be "anti-Islamist" and not because he cared about the girls they preyed on, and that Kellie-Jay had been dismissive of the work of women who had tried to raise the alarm about the gangs.

This blog post was published while they were in the air, and when they landed in the US, there was already a whole lot of denunciation on Twitter. Being brave doesn't mean it doesn't hurt. Kellie-Jay was upset, feeling these were baseless smears and that she had no way to respond. She says she rage-cried that first evening in Washington DC. It didn't help that, as a nervous flyer, she'd had a few drinks on the plane. But then she pulled herself together and got on with it. Probably thinking her usual, "Well, fuck you."

The British women received a very warm welcome, especially from the parents of children and young people who had transitioned. They were so grateful that Kellie-Jay had come, and that she spoke up for them and for their children. She remembers that they said things like, "Oh, my God, Posie Parker, I can't believe you're here," and, "I wrote you on my ballot. I spoiled my ballot in the last election. I wrote your name." Very gratifying for the ego, although she says it was a measure of their desperation rather than of her brilliance. "They felt just so hopeless, so that I was this amazing thing."

At the private parents' meeting that followed the Heritage Foundation public event, they went around the table, one by one, telling their devastating stories. Kellie-Jay was moved to tears. There was a girl who was 18 and homeless. She'd had a radical hysterectomy. She had no breasts. She had a beard, and her mother didn't know how to help her. This girl clearly had mental health issues, which is why she was there in the first place. There was a lesbian Democrat couple whose daughter had gone away for camp and come back saying she was a boy. "It was just story after story. I felt like I didn't have any right to cry in that room because it wasn't happening to me. But it was devastating." That put all the drama about being at the Heritage Foundation into context. This was why they had come.

There was one more controversial event on the USA trip. While Venice was off stickering somewhere, Kellie-Jay and Julia were with women from WoLF, walking through the Congress buildings on a busy schedule of appointments. They saw a video being filmed in the corridor promoting the idea of 'trans children' and subsequently walked past a room where Kellie-Jay spotted a face she recognised, talking to camera. It was Democratic Congressman Joe Kennedy III, then-chairman of the Congressional Trans Equality Task Force. He was running a meeting where someone was talking about their four-year-old being trans. They carried on past but when they came back, a trans-identifying man called Sarah McBride, formerly Tim McBride, was there, looking at camera footage. At the time he was a senior person in the Human Rights Campaign, promoting trans rights at the Capitol.

Kellie-Jay knew who he was, and she asked the Americans they were with whether it would be illegal for her to go and ask this man some questions on camera. They said it wasn't so she asked Julia if she wanted to go and speak to him on camera. Julia didn't hesitate. Kellie-Jay set her camera on Live, and she and Julia went and asked him questions like why he hated lesbians. Julia asked about women in prison. It was completely spur-of-the-moment, a step into the unknown, but too good an opportunity to miss, and rather exciting. They wanted to make it quick and didn't want him to be able to say they were harassing him in case that got them into trouble. Sarah, formerly Tim, McBride didn't answer at all. It was a dramatic moment, streamed live and widely shared.

Kellie-Jay thought people would be delighted that she had tried to hold this person to account. She was shocked and upset when this event was added to the catalogue of her alleged offences against 'true feminism', as defined by other women back in the UK. A US Senator who had supported the Supreme Court nomination of Brett Kavanaugh, a judge who'd been accused of sexual misconduct, had been challenged in a lift by two women not long before, and everyone had celebrated that. But they reacted quite differently to this, some even saying she and Julia had bullied and intimidated Tim/Sarah McBride. That revealed to her for the first time that "those women really did not see him as a man; I just saw him as a man."

Venice says Kellie-Jay and Julia burned themselves out on that US trip, because they were both ill when they came back.

First Do No Harm

During the US trip, all fired up and full of ideas, Kellie-Jay had decided to do some targeted events back in the UK. In one week in May 2019, helped by Venice, she did three events in three different cities. One was an event in Brighton about the challenges in journalism, sponsored by Julie Burchill, a journalist involved in the trans debate from 2013, when an *Observer* column led to calls in parliament for her to be sacked. She paid for a room in the Odeon cinema and they showed one of the films made by a feisty lesbian activist, Magdalen Berns, who was known for her brilliant and often sweary videos in which she challenged transactivism. That was followed by a panel with journalists Jo Bartosch and Brendan O'Neill and the film maker Olly Lambert, who made the TV programme *Trans Kids: It's Time To Talk* with Stella O'Malley. This was when he talked about how it was harder to get both sides of the trans debate to agree to be in the same film than it had been to get sworn enemies in the Israel–Palestine conflict to cooperate with him.

The big event that week was at the House of Lords, where Lord Moonie, a Labour peer and retired psychiatrist, was their sponsor for an event about healthcare for children with gender confusion or 'transgender identities'. Stephanie Davies-Arai spoke about how she had been trying to raise the alarm for almost four years.The court case against the Tavistock was born over drinks in the pub afterwards (see Chapter 1). It took almost five more years before the National Health Service in the UK stopped giving such children medication that would block their puberty and lock in their transgender ideation.

Then there was an event called 'Lesbians on Chairs'. This might seem odd, but it was named after an incident in March when Julia Long, the journalist Joani Walsh, a radical feminist, Georgia Constantinou, and another woman who had to stay anonymous were thrown out of an event in a city firm's offices. The IT consulting giant Accenture was hosting an evening event for Transgender Day of Visibility. It was organised by Accenture's Pride network and Susie Green, then-CEO of Mermaids, was one of the speakers. It was billed as an inclusive event which was open to everyone so Julia and co registered online for tickets and went along.

While they were waiting for the event to start, enjoying the pizza slices and wine provided, they were approached by one of the organisers from Accenture. She said, "My panel does not feel comfortable with you here." She asked them to leave. She was accompanied by a police officer who said they were being disruptive.

Julia was intransigent, pointing out that the event was supposed to be inclusive and they had done nothing other than sit quietly in chairs and eat pizza. Eventually, objecting loudly, she was carried out by police officers and security, followed by the other three women, while Georgia filmed the whole thing. #LesbiansOnChairs trended on Twitter.

Always quick to spot a catchy slogan, Kellie-Jay set up a lunchtime event with an all-lesbian line-up including Julia and Sheila as speakers and Anne Ruzylo as, dare I say, the chair. The venue, the lower ground floor of a hotel in central London, was not released until the day of the event. Once everyone was settled into their seats, Anne announced the arrival of Martina. Cue flurry of excitement and disbelief – until a giant picture of lesbian icon and activist Martina Navratilova was carried down the stairs and installed in a chair of her own, at which point Anne declared, "Martina Navratilova is now a lesbian on a chair!"

In the Q&A session at the end of this event, Maya Forstater stood up and said that she had, rather cheekily because not a lesbian, asked Julia the week before whether she could promote her crowdfunder at the event. She was right at the start of her legal odyssey (see Chapter 4). But by the day of the event, her crowdfunding target had been met so there was no need.

Let Women Speak

After the frightening experience of seeing Maria MacLachlan attacked at Speakers' Corner in London in 2017, Venice and her old friend Katie, also known as DJ Lippy, had gone back there to mark the anniversary of the event a year later. That was also the day Magdalen Berns died. She was a mature student at Edinburgh University, and a boxer. She died from a brain tumour aged 36. She was forthright, fearless and funny, sparking lots of memes, like "Their minds are so open their brains have fallen out," and "I'd rather be rude than a fucking liar." After that, going to Speakers' Corner each

September and lighting candles became a ritual for them, both to mark the original incident and to remember Magdalen.

Venice and Katie thought, 'Why don't we actually do a speaking event at Speakers' Corner?' They chose International Women's Day, 2020. Kara Dansky and Marcia Matthews flew over from the USA to speak. Kellie-Jay was already quite well-known because of the police interviews, the Adult Human Female poster and the TV interviews she'd done, and she acted as host, and filmed the event. She thought it was brilliant and she said to the others that she was going to come back and do this every month.

Then the pandemic lockdown happened and they couldn't do any events for three months. In July 2020, at the height of Black Lives Matter protests, they were confronted by BLM activists, getting in their faces and shouting at them, calling them transphobes. Venice blurted out, "Oh, go worship your dicks!" But that was misquoted. People said, "She just went and told a black woman to go and wash her dick." Despite Venice's protestation that she'd said worship not wash, people starting calling both her and Katie racist. Venice feels this is because it's not a strong enough insult to label someone transphobic. She says:

> I'm not anti trans people, I'm anti transgenderism, anti trans ideology. But they can't just say that because it's not strong enough, because you can just go, yeah, you know what I mean? So they have to invent all these other bigotries – racist, homophobic, classist, whatever.

After a while they moved from Speakers' Corner to Reformer's Tree in Hyde Park because they couldn't hear themselves at Speakers' Corner. You're not allowed to use amplification there, so it's a cacophony of competing voices, mostly male, mostly shouting about God. As Venice says, "If you're talking about some trauma, and you're a regular woman without a voice, hardly anyone can hear you."

In July 2020, after JK Rowling wrote her essay explaining her position,[19] Kellie-Jay paid for a poster in the main train station in Edinburgh, where JK Rowling lives. It said "I heart JK Rowling," based on the famous 'I heart NYC' graphic. It lasted a couple of days before it was removed because of a single complaint.

Marion Calder with I HEART JKR poster at Edinburgh station, 2020

Photo courtesy of Nicole Jones

19 <https://www.jkrowling.com/opinions/j-k-rowling-writes-about-her-reasons-for-speaking-out-on-sex-and-gender-issues/>.

Kellie-Jay decided that she needed to host meetings outside London as well. She picked Nottingham because it was the first place outside London where there had been a Speakers' Corner. She planned an outdoor rally where any woman could come up and speak for a couple of minutes. That's a familiar format now but it was a big change from indoor meetings with a panel of experts and an audience. Some transactivists arrived and protested noisily, so no one could hear the speakers, even though there was a microphone and amplification. The women started shouting, "Let women speak!" And that's where the name came from. Kellie-Jay adopted it because it just seemed so perfect that "ordinary women who don't have a voice, who haven't got planned speeches, who are finding themselves silenced in their own life had come up with this." For her, it's about creating space to let women speak, demanding to let them speak. It's not asking for permission.

Social media companies had already decided that Kellie-Jay shouldn't be allowed to speak, at least not on their platforms. She had lost her Posie Parker Facebook account in late 2018. She was banned from Twitter before the Adult Human Female poster went up in September 2018. She was banned from Mumsnet, for some sort of language violation, after they got nervous about the use of terms like trans-identifying male instead of transwoman. She can't sell merchandise or raise money on Patreon or on various crowdfunding platforms. Two businesses that she was paying to provide Adult Human Female branded goods stopped dealing with her and she had to find different suppliers. She couldn't even sign a petition on Change.org. All for promoting the definition of woman.

Well, not only that. She has been very forthright in her views about how children fare when they get caught up in transgender ideology. She has said many times that transitioning children is abuse. She herself has not been intimidated or silenced by any of this, but she knows that many women are. No wonder she felt a compulsion to give women a platform to be heard. She can still operate on Facebook as Let Women Speak, and after Twitter became X she got her @ThePosieParker account back. But that was years later.

Let Women Speak Across the World

Since those first meetings at Speakers' Corner in London's Hyde Park in 2020, Kellie-Jay has organised dozens of outdoor rallies where anyone can turn up and speak about women's issues for a few minutes, across three continents.

An American filmmaker and Director of the Center for Bioethics and Culture, Jennifer Lahl, invited Kellie-Jay to speak at an event in New York in early 2022. Another American, Beth Stelzer, a former powerlifter who'd started a campaign called Save Women's Sports, said that she was going to go to the National College Athletics Association (NCAA) swimming championships, and asked Kellie-Jay if she would like to come with her. And obviously, the answer was yes. The NCAA organises national championships for students in American universities and colleges, across a range of sports. This is a very big deal: the American system of sports scholarships attracts top talent from all over the world. Competing in the NCAAs are current and future Olympians, not just from the USA but from other countries too.

Beth was talking about the NCAA swimming championships, held that year in Atlanta, Georgia. It was on her radar because of Lia Thomas, formerly Will Thomas, a student who'd switched from the men's swimming team to the women's team at the University of Pennsylvania and suddenly started winning. This was celebrated in the US media as 'Lia' being able to perform because of finding contentment as 'her' authentic self. Female students were told by their universities that they must accept Thomas in the women's changing rooms and that speaking to the media might get them expelled from college. As a result, there was almost no media coverage.

Beth organised a hotel and tickets for the swimming championship. There were other women activists there, too. When they found they were staying in the same hotel as Will Thomas, a couple of the other women wanted to confront him. Kellie-Jay said, absolutely not:

> We want this man to be really confident he's going to win the race. You don't want him to come last, and then to say he was persecuted in his hotel. You want him to have every opportunity to show the world exactly what's going on.

Off they went to the pool on day one of the four-day swim meet to watch the racing. As Thomas walked out, Kellie-Jay says, the silence was palpable. She felt that people were just afraid. As soon as she saw him, she shouted out, "You're a cheat!" although the NCAA rules at the time permitted Thomas to compete. She sees herself as the person who will say what needs saying, especially when no one else will.

Thomas duly won the race and was interviewed standing poolside. Kellie-Jay had decided she would make her presence felt, and she called out, over and over, "He's a man." She felt it was important for the other people there, the young women who'd raced, and the parents watching their daughters, knowing that their daughters had to get changed in changing rooms with a naked male body, and knowing that if they spoke about it, their daughters could lose everything: their place at university, their funding, their sponsorship, all the other networking, whatever opportunities or benefits that come from being on that swimming team. "I just felt that it would be a complete dereliction of duty in those moments of silence if I didn't fill them with 'he's a man'," remembers Kellie-Jay.

It was sort of thrilling. She felt almost euphoric. Like the boy who shouts that the emperor has no clothes; she's the one who calls it when most people are a silent part of the crowd. "I guess my role, if I have any role, my role is to be the person that will actually say, I can see the emperor's penis quite clearly." That can give courage to other people, as it did for Riley Gaines, one of the students who raced Lia Thomas at that swim meet. Riley has said that hearing Kellie-Jay at the NCAAs showed her it was not so hard to call Thomas what he is: a man. Riley Gaines has gone on to become a high-profile campaigner for protecting women's sport in the USA, with over a million followers on social media. Riley says, "She's my role model! The word fearless gets tossed around a lot, but Kellie-Jay Keen is the embodiment of it."

Just below Kellie-Jay in the stand there was someone who was clearly a transactivist, clapping and cheering for Thomas. This person, face covered by a Covid mask, turned and looked up at Kellie-Jay, who started a conversation about Thomas, saying, "Are you saying his body is the same as the other girls in the pool? Are you saying he doesn't have male advantage? I'm a woman and that's not a woman." It was only as they were talking that Kellie-Jay saw past the beard and the voice deepened by testosterone and thought maybe this person was a trans-identifying woman so she said, "Have you got ovaries?" It was clear that the activist was presenting as a man so just asking, "Are you a man or a woman?" wouldn't answer the real question. The campaigner didn't answer her question and said, "Can I ask you a question? Are you a biologist?" To which Kellie-Jay, sounding exasperated, replied, "Oh my god, don't be ridiculous. I'm not a vet but I know what a dog is!"

The whole interaction was filmed by Madeleine Kearns, a US-based Scottish journalist. She did a quick edit and posted it and it went viral, getting tens of millions of views on TikTok and Twitter. From a local mall, Kellie-Jay got herself a T-shirt with "I'm not a vet but I know what a dog is" embossed on it.

At the swimming venue the next day, she, Beth and Madeleine ran into a trans-identifying man called Dawn Ennis in a corridor. The tiled background is why people thought Kellie-Jay had challenged him in a women's bathroom. A sports journalist formerly called Don, he was there to report on the championship. Kellie-Jay felt a visceral response when she saw a woman saying thank you to him. She describes it as a feeling of, "That's a man who invades our spaces. I don't want to thank that man for anything."

She jumped in and introduced herself and asked whether he used women's spaces. He wouldn't answer directly. He just said, "I'm a woman," and that no one had ever objected to his presence. In the video, Dawn Ennis seems to tower over Kellie-Jay. What woman would challenge him? Well, here was one, all five feet two inches of her. When he interrupted her she went, "Ah ah ah!" and wagged a finger at him, like warning a naughty child. She kept pushing until Dawn turned to Beth, who was filming, and said, "I would ask you to please call off your dog."

Beth was livid, saying, "That was way out of line." Kellie-Jay was calm. "I beg your pardon," she said. "As a mother, I am asking you – do not use female spaces. It makes women and girls very uncomfortable."

"As a mother," Dawn Ennis began, but first Beth and then Kellie-Jay cut across him. "You did not birth your children," Beth said, sounding really angry. "You are not a mother." Kellie-Jay's was more of a quiet fury. "How dare you," she said. "You are not a mother."

Madeleine Kearns filmed and reported this encounter too. The clips were shared by big US commentators with huge followings, people like Ben Shapiro and Matt Walsh, and Kellie-Jay was invited onto Tucker Carlson's show on *Fox News*, though she was home by the time it happened so the appearance was online. It wasn't great that these were all right wing commentators, but no one else wanted to cover the story. Also annoying was that any commercial benefit from these viral videos went to the people who shared them, which wasn't Kellie-Jay because she was banned from Twitter.

The NCAA trip is pure Kellie-Jay. There was a breaking-the-silence moment in the main pool arena, when she shouted, "He's a man." And there was what she calls a "really living-by-my-sword moment where I don't just say to people that you can say these things, but I say them."

What you don't see on the viral videos is what happens next. Security turned up and told Kellie-Jay and Beth to leave. Dawn Ennis wasn't asked, just the women. And that was the end of their trip.

Later that year, she did a US tour of Let Women Speak, starting on the west coast in Hollywood and then up to San Francisco. She was supposed to go to Portland but there was a man there who put up a Go Fund Me page to buy weapons to attack her. Even Kellie-Jay thought maybe it would be better to leave that city off the itinerary. She doesn't go looking for trouble, it just finds her. There were events in Seattle, Chicago, Austin, Miami, Oklahoma, Philadelphia and New York City. She also went to Loudoun County, where a girl had been raped in a school toilet by a trans-identifying boy, but the girl's father was the one the police went after. It was mostly hostile. In Austin, Texas, her supporters had banners saying, 'No child is born in the wrong body' and 'Let Women Speak'. They faced off against trans rights protestors in hoods and masks banging cowbells and blowing horns and sirens. Their banners said 'Fascists love transphobes' and 'Terfs Fuck Off'.

It may surprise you to know that mostly Kellie-Jay travels on her own. Her husband and two younger children went with her to the US west coast, but when they went home she was on her own. At each location, she meets up with women who've planned the event on their home turf. They handle the logistics, hire a sound system and a couple of security guards, and liaise with the local police. Some events, like at Oklahoma, happened because women there were desperate for her to come. Often women are quite emotional about meeting her, wanting to tell their stories, which is what Let Women Speak lets them do, but also wanting to thank her for her courage, and for giving them courage too. Although there could be transactivists and a lot of noise and hostility, she wasn't worried about her security on those USA trips, other than with the madman in Portland.

All the same, her family weren't thrilled about her doing all this, especially the two younger children. They all fully supported her, and still do, but they wish she didn't need to do it.

Kellie-Jay at Let Women Speak in Hyde Park, London, 2023

Photo courtesy of Fiona McAnena

Let Women Speak Down Under

Back in 2016, Kellie-Jay had heard the story of a girl in school, somewhere in New Zealand, who'd had to deal with a boy in the girls' changing rooms. This boy was claiming a trans identity. The girl had tried to avoid confrontation by using a private cubicle but the boy had followed her in. When she complained, she was suspended from school. Kellie-Jay felt that just because these places were so far away, she wouldn't neglect them.

With the help of women in Australia and New Zealand who were vetted and guided by experienced UK volunteers, she planned a series of events for March 2023. She wanted to reach women all over Australia, not just in the cities of Sydney, Melbourne and Canberra in the south east corner but going up to Brisbane in Queensland, all the way to Perth on the west coast, down to Adelaide in South Australia and over to Hobart in Tasmania. She travelled on her own, meeting up with the local organisers, with logistics support back in the UK. In each location, she hired two or three burly men as bodyguards. A couple of times, local police met her off the plane and walked with her through the airport. It wasn't intimidating. They were friendly and seemed quite helpful, a sort of escort. But the tour itself was not so comfortable, and not just because of her polyester jump suits in the Australian heat.

The Australia plan was seven cities in ten days, then on to Auckland and Wellington in New Zealand. At each event, Kellie-Jay would open by saying she and the women were taking back the public square, and that they would say things that needed to be said, like women don't have penises, while a couple of security guys and sometimes police officers stood around looking bemused. Then women came up one at a time and said whatever they wanted to say. In her closing speech, Kellie-Jay would call out her catchphrase, "I never lose," to much cheering and applause. Every event was live-streamed and filmed for the Let Women Speak website.

At the first two rallies, in Sydney and Brisbane, there were a few dozen women and some protestors chanting and waving their baby blue and pink trans flags. Both the numbers of supporters and the opposition grew as the tour went on. Protestors chanted, "Posie Parker you can't hide, you've got Nazis on your side," but in Sydney and Brisbane the police kept them well away. They were close enough in Perth to hear the chant of "Posie you're not welcome here," but the women were undeterred.

Things ramped up in Melbourne. It started calmly with a couple of hundred supporters and a noisy group of protesters held back behind a line of police. Kellie-Jay met up with Moira Deeming, a Liberal member of the Parliament of Victoria, at the state parliament building. She filmed as the two of them and her two private security guys walked around from the back of the building to the wide steps at the front which Moira had booked for the event.

She was told that there were some men dressed all in black sporting masks out there too. This sounded like a description of Antifa and she wasn't surprised because men often turn up to barrack at her events. As she came onto the steps, she was more interested in the women who were there to meet her. On the video you can see her welcoming the legendary feminist academic Sheila Jeffreys, who has been writing and talking about this issue for years and was visiting Australia. Then a woman in her 60s came up to her and said, "We've never met but I'm related to you. I'm your husband's cousin."

Kellie-Jay opened the event with her usual rabble-rousing speech which included shouting to the protestors, "Women don't have penises!" There were transactivists all around, but also a strong police presence. She and others saw the activists hitting the police horses. The protestors were only 50 metres away, behind a police cordon, making so much noise, banging on metal saucepan lids, blowing whistles and chanting, that anyone towards the back of the Let Women Speak rally struggled to hear the speeches. Kellie-Jay recalls a red-haired woman called Alexis who started off very quietly and then made what Kellie-Jay describes as perhaps the best speech that's ever been given at any Let Women Speak rally.

The activists kept pressing against the police line to get closer. A couple of times, one or two got through to the front, even trying to wrestle the microphone away from the woman who was speaking at the time. It may have been the same activist who assaulted a woman in the crowd. The victim was pushed to the ground and needed hospital treatment for a suspected fracture.

Then a weird thing happened. The men in black, the supposed Antifa people, seemed to be marched off in single file by the police, not in an aggressive way, but in an orderly way as if they were working together. It was already confusing because there were two crowds of these men in black, one on each side of where the Let Women Speak crowd was, in front of the parliament steps. Plus there was another protest group, a civil liberties crowd protesting against lockdown. But this Antifa-style group marched off together, seemingly escorted by the police, and then performed the Nazi salute, on the steps. The civil liberties people were in between so they weren't that close but lots of people saw it. Antifa is short for anti-fascist, so a Nazi salute was the last thing anyone expected. There was no plan to condemn Nazis because it just wasn't remotely on the agenda beforehand. When it did happen, Kellie-Jay's position was that it was nothing to do with Let Women Speak, so why would she even need to comment on it.

After a couple of hours, the police said it was too dangerous to continue and that the event had to finish early. But later that day she saw news reports claiming the men in black were Nazis and that she had known or even invited them. Moira Deeming had spoken at the event, reading a message from a Muslim friend and constituent who was too afraid to attend. She was summoned to a meeting with her party's leadership, then suspended from the party.

Other politicians and Australian media variously accused Kellie-Jay and Angie Jones, a local campaigner who had helped organise the day, of being white supremacists and neo-Nazis, because of these masked, black-clad young men who'd turned up uninvited. Maybe those men were looking for a confrontation with the transactivists. That has happened elsewhere. She also feels that if someone planned to discredit Let Women Speak, this would be a great way to do it. While she was still in Australia, Kellie-Jay issued a statement saying, "They're absolutely not associated with me whatsoever. I absolutely abhor anything to do with Nazis." But the damage was done. The hostile opposition really ramped up. In Hobart, she was physically assaulted. Despite the security around her, young men managed to land a few kicks and punches. The women who went to the Let Women Speak events faced hostility and risked assault themselves.

Some of the allegations were so outrageous that eventually both Angie Jones and Kellie-Jay felt they had to issue proceedings for defamation. The leader of the Liberal Party in the state of Victoria, John Pesutto, had accused them of having "known links with Nazis, Nazi sympathisers, far-right extremists, white supremacists." A UK newspaper, *The Independent*, said Kellie-Jay had staged a mass Nazi salute. After receiving a letter from her solicitors, they conceded it was untrue and apologised.

A year later and after considerable expense, John Pesutto also backed down. His statement in May 2024 opened with this:

> Kellie-Jay Keen and Angela Jones are passionate women's rights activists with long histories of advocacy in Australia and internationally. I agree with them that genuine community concerns regarding women's safety and access to single-sex spaces, services and sport warrant meaningful public discussion.

For Angie, the fall-out from this one day continues. The rally itself had been tough. She was down patrolling the boundary to watch for protesters breaking through the police line, though she knew that all she could do if that happened was to get to the front and shout, 'Run!' Being on the front line all day was traumatic, with men shouting and threatening violence, some drawing their finger across their throat at her.

Then she was named and shamed on television by senior politicians. No one interviewed her to hear her side of the story. She received thousands of threats of assault, of rape, of accusations that, "You don't deserve to have children. Your kids should be taken away from you."

Her life changed. Former friends shunned her. People didn't want to be seen with her. She's been shouted at and chased by men calling her a Nazi, to the point where she no longer feels safe on the streets of Melbourne. It's affected her children, who don't understand. Why is Mum so upset? Why is Mum on the phone all the time? Why does Mum have to go to court? Why is Mum on TV? All she did was volunteer to help organise a rally about women's rights. "I centre women in my politics. I'm a vegan. How many feminist vegans are in the Nazis? It was just ridiculous."

Angie was already several years into the fight to regain women's rights. She'd known trans-identifying people her whole life, transsexuals who she understood as gay men with internalised homophobia. When her former father-in-law had declared he was a woman, she thought something wasn't right. A few years later, she heard about autogynephilia[20] from feminists on Facebook, and the penny dropped. She started speaking up about it then, and, just like Kellie-Jay, got kicked out of social media groups. She was a lefty too, and she was also involved with a women's domestic violence programme. A man identifying as non-binary took offence and Angie was booted out of the programme.

She had made a conscious decision to fight this battle in her own name because then your position has integrity. "If you're a real person, and you put your real name and your real face out there, then you really believe in what you're saying." But for years she felt like

20 Autogynephilia is defined as a male's propensity to be sexually aroused by the thought of himself as a female. It is the paraphilia that is theorised to underlie transvestism and some forms of male-to-female (MtF) transsexualism. It is described in this academic paper by transsexual Anne Lawrence <https://pubmed.ncbi.nlm.nih.gov/22005209/>.

she was the only Aussie 'terf' on Twitter. The big change was in 2019 when Maya Forstater retweeted a post of Angie's. As she remembers:

> ... after that, all these UK terfs came onto my Twitter. And it all just took off from there because once I got the UK terfs, then the Aussies could find each other because they all knew who Kellie-Jay Keen was and Magdalen Berns. And so we all found each other through the Terf Island terfs.

Kellie-Jay's 2023 visit was hugely important because they thought, after years of being ignored by the media, they would finally get some coverage. They never imagined it would go the way it did. Kellie-Jay went on to New Zealand to continue her tour, and, says Angie, "Moira and I were in the witches' cauldron with the water bubbling around us." It was life-changing, in the most distressing way. And yet Angie says, "I'd do it all again tomorrow. This might be the thing that peaks Australia. It certainly took it from a right-wing view into the mainstream."

Two months after the Melbourne rally, Moira Deeming was expelled from her political party. She filed legal proceedings for defamation which John Pesutto defended. The case finally came to court in September 2024. It seemed odd that he had withdrawn his criticism of Kellie-Jay and Angie but stood by his criticism and suspension of Moira for associating with them. With the protection of the witness stand he was able to repeat his worst slurs against Kellie-Jay and Angie. His side referred to Angie having tweeted, "Nazis and women want to get rid of paedo filth. Why don't you?" She had posted that in response to being accused of Nazis agreeing with her but the Pesutto team refused to acknowledge the context. As Moira had written in her own defence against expulsion from her party, "Her clear point was that if even Nazis (the worst of the worst) are against paedophiles, why are you not?" Angie says, "I posted one tweet that John Pesutto misrepresented. Absolutely. And it's ruined my life." It felt as if she and Moira were on trial, with no opportunity to defend themselves. Angie says, "I feel guilty about what happened to Kellie-Jay because it was in my city, and I feel devastated that my tweet got Moira in trouble."

The evidence for the case included an agreed detailed account of what happened in Melbourne, which seems to support Kellie-Jay's feeling that the Nazi salute was staged, and that the police allowed it.

The judgment was handed down in December 2024. Moira Deeming won on all counts and was awarded AUD$300,000 in damages. The judge said explicitly that some of John Pesutto's sworn evidence about Moira was untrue. The ruling listed some of the shockingly abusive emails, social media posts and voicemails she'd received, to show the harm caused by his allegations. Angie has experienced similar abuse. Moira's win in court is some vindication for Angie, but it can't wipe out the harm she's suffered. After the judgement, Moira Deeming was reinstated in the Liberal Party and later, John Pesutto lost his leadership of the Party.

"The Police Aren't Coming"

The final part of Kellie-Jay's 2023 antipodean tour was to be two events in New Zealand. Veteran campaigners from the Indigenous women's rights organisation Mana Wāhine Kōrero, together with a lesbian group called LOUT, planned events in Auckland and Wellington. With barely eight weeks between Kellie-Jay announcing she would come until the date of the visit, they scrambled to find suitable venues, get the necessary permissions, book sound, security and fencing, and crowdfund to cover it all. Three weeks beforehand, there were marches for trans rights in the same two cities so Sarah Henderson of Mana Wāhine Kōrero went along to gauge the numbers and see how they were policed. There were a couple of hundred marchers and it was all very peaceful and family-friendly. That was encouraging. The women felt their event would be similar. The women planned a proper Maori welcome for Kellie-Jay, collecting gifts and souvenirs for her and booking party venues for after the rallies.

Then the Melbourne event happened, and the media went wild, calling Kellie-Jay all sorts of slurs. Three Green MPs wrote to the New Zealand immigration minister demanding that her visa be revoked. In response the minister said, "Like many New Zealanders I would prefer it if Parker never set foot in New Zealand. I find many of her views repugnant." He said she had "inflammatory, vile and incorrect world views." Some politicians supported her on the basis of free speech. Those against her argued that she would endanger the Muslim and LGBT communities. A rapid review concluded that there were no grounds to revoke her visa. A last-minute attempt in the New Zealand high court by Kiwi pro-trans campaign groups to force their government to cancel her visa also failed. It's an astonishing level of scrutiny and hostility towards someone who talks about protecting women and girls.

Auckland City Council demanded that extra private security be laid on, which cost almost NZ$10,000. Kellie-Jay paid for that. The security firm booked in Wellington pulled out, citing "a difference in values," so the Auckland security team would go straight on to Wellington with her. Getting sound and fencing people was a challenge. One provider who'd been booked withdrew, saying they would not get any council work if they did the Let Women Speak rally.

As Kellie-Jay boarded the plane in Sydney, one of her team back in the UK, Clare, told her that the hotel in Auckland had just cancelled her booking. It seems that the New Zealand police had called the hotel to let them know who was coming. When she landed in Auckland, an official-looking woman approached her in the line to go through immigration and said, "Come this way." Kellie-Jay thought it was because she had so much luggage – two large trunks and two carry-on bags, enough for a four-week trip.

This woman took her into a room and spent two hours going through her luggage, which by this time was more dirty laundry than anything else. Kellie-Jay asked her why she was being searched, and asked if the woman knew who she was. The woman said she didn't know. Kellie-Jay said, "Do you know there have been two high court actions trying to stop me from coming to New Zealand, and the foreign minister has made comments about me?"

"I don't read the news," said the woman, and carried on rummaging. Kellie-Jay herself was not searched, which made no sense if she was thought to be some sort of threat. It just felt like harassment.

With Clare's help, she found another hotel. In the morning, two notes had been slid under her door. One said, "We know where you are and we know what you are wearing." The other made threats of sexual violence. She called her security people to collect her from the bedroom door. The hotel staff were alerted, and they reviewed the CCTV to identify the culprits. They said they were other hotel guests, and that they had been made to leave. Who knows? It could have been staff. Either way, someone was leaking information about her. Later, she heard that one of the police officers involved in organising security for the rally in Auckland was a well-known transactivist.

The Auckland rally was in a large public space called Albert Park, with all the standard arrangements in place: permit obtained, police briefed, local women as stewards in high visibility jackets, and six private security guards, more than usual. Kellie-Jay arrived at 11 a.m. with Tania Sturt, one of the local organisers, to see a crowd that was already amped up against her, chanting, "Fuck off Nazi, go home." Later, the New Zealand women found out that the police were told in advance that there could be 2,000 protesters. But this information was not shared with the event team.

They made their way to the rotunda, a sort of bandstand where the amplification equipment was set up ready for her and then other women to speak. But the protestors were so noisy, and so close, that there was no chance of being heard over the cacophony of sirens, whistles and clanging saucepans. Instead of two groups held apart by police in a central no man's land, the protesters were right there, while the police stood back on the periphery. The intensity of the mob was terrifying. To another organiser, Di Landy, it felt as if "nothing short of barbed wire and the military would have held them back."

Then a man lunged at her and threw something at her and Tania. Her first thought was, "Oh god he's ruined my hair!" She was annoyed. She was already filming the crowd on her phone so she kept filming. The photographer she'd hired to document the tour took a photo of her, spattered in red sauce, holding up her phone. It turned out to be tomato juice, but people thought it was tomato soup. There is a subliminal association between Marilyn Monroe and Campbell's tomato soup because of the Andy Warhol pictures of both, so maybe that's the reason. Then she spotted one of the reporters in the crowd and shouted at them, "This is you! You've done this." She felt that the media had whipped it all up.

Kellie-Jay at Let Women Speak Auckland, New Zealand, 2023

Photo courtesy of Adam Baines

Then things got really bad. The crowd started breaking down the barriers and coming in from all sides. There was jostling and roaring and it felt out of control. The private security people tried to send someone out to get the police. She thought the police would arrive any minute, but then the security guard said to her, "The police aren't coming. They're not coming."

She was aghast. "They're not coming?"

"No, but we're going to get you out," her guys said. "You're going to stand in the middle. We're going to link arms around you. We're going to push through the crowd."

Half a dozen Let Women Speak stewards in high visibility jackets, all women, and three burly guys who were the paid security surrounded her. They started pushing slowly through the crowd in a group. Then the crowd surged and she was pushed sideways, almost knocked off her feet:

> And I'm relatively near a wall, like the rotunda. And I'm thinking, they push much more, I'm crushed. And if I go more than 45 degrees, if I go too far, and my feet have left the ground, I can't stand. If I get to the floor, I'm never going to get up. It's game over. I've got to stand up, and I've got to put one foot in front of the other.

The group kept surging with Kellie-Jay looking tiny in the middle with her hair all messed up, covered in red juice. She says she knew what she had to do, but the enormity didn't really hit her for quite some time. There's footage where she's saying, "Mind, mind, mind," because she thought someone was going to fall over. She was sure that anyone who fell wouldn't be able to get up again:

> And I did think, oh, my kids are going to be so cross if I die. If I don't get back up, and I come here to do this thing, not even anything to do with my children, then they lose me.

All this was being livestreamed. Kellie-Jay didn't know that her husband was at home in the UK watching it on Facebook Live. People were writing, "Oh, my God! Oh, my God! Is she dead? Is she dead?" Fortunately, her children were not watching.

Angie Jones was watching it live in Melbourne. "I thought, they're going to kill her." She says watching it was like when there's an accident in Formula One motor racing, when you're waiting to see the driver get out of the car. "It felt like that through the whole time, that was just so traumatic. I felt responsible because it was my city that led to all this."

They met police officers after they'd pushed most of the way through the crowd to the edge of the park. The crowds were coming after them, but she and a bodyguard were bundled into a police car. Inside the car, she said to the guard, "I thought they were going to crush us to death." Protestors surrounded the car, and she was afraid they were going to tip it over or smash the windows, but the police got them out. Even then, she was still game for the tour to continue. She said to her security, "Do you think they'll be this bad in Wellington?" He replied, "We're not going to Wellington."

They were taken to a police station. By then, the police must have realised that someone on their side had leaked her movements, because they made it clear that no one should be told where she was. That she was there was kept to the commanding officer and the two officers on guard outside the room in the station. From there, she was transferred to the airport under armed guard. Her security had to go to her hotel and pack up her belongings and meet her there. The police with her were friendly. The female officer told her that the changing and showering areas at the newly-built police station were unisex, just a couple of curtains. Male officers were saying, "We're going to see your tits." The woman told her that her male colleagues thought it was all a joke, not realising that for women that's a genuine fear.

Kellie-Jay received armed protection through the airport and onto a flight home. The plane stopped over in Dubai on the way, a place she says she never wanted to go to, because she dislikes that women have to cover up "as if we're sinful." But as the enormity of what had happened at the rally hit her, she felt safer there than in New Zealand.

She found out afterwards that a 70-year-old woman had been punched in the face by a young man who called himself non-binary.

There was video footage of the incident and he was charged, but ultimately he got off without a conviction.

Once Kellie-Jay had left the park, the crowd surged forward. The women left behind had to run the gauntlet of the protestors to get out, helped by male friends and family who'd come along in support. The protestors were screaming and spitting at them, jostling and pouring water on them. A few were thumped. One got her eye socket broken. Di Landy says, "That told us in no uncertain terms, there's no help here for you." It was traumatic but the media coverage helped raise awareness among ordinary Kiwis. Anyone who saw that terrifying footage had to wonder what was going on. Di feels that Kellie-Jay's visit to Auckland is now synonymous with male violence against women. Politicians still had little to say about it but at least they started to be asked, "What is a woman?"

Auckland police received dozens of complaints from attendees and many more from online viewers. An official investigation concluded that a flawed risk assessment, based on inconsistent and incomplete information, led to inadequate planning and resourcing, and that on the day, commanders did not properly respond to unfolding events by deploying additional staff to protect Let Women Speak supporters. An officer told the investigation that after Kellie-Jay had left:

> There were people yelling abuse, essentially standing over people and yelling abuse at them and pointing fingers and megaphones in faces and I was thinking this is getting too much ... I had to direct staff to go in and identify Let Women Speak people and individually get them out ... I didn't know who was who until I saw counter-protestors basically following them around and just abusing them ... Could not negotiate with the counter-protestors. They just would not listen to police at all. It went from a peaceful protest to full blown hatred.

A man attending the Let Women Speak rally told the investigation:

> I told my wife to grab my belt and I led her out ... We went through the crowd ... On the way out there were fists being thrown, we were kicked, punched, spat at, we got liquids poured over us ... I just barged through.

He went back through the crowd to the rotunda to help other women to leave. He said they were trapped in the rotunda, "petrified and in tears."

In a footnote, the investigation report says, "The gender identity views expressed by speakers attending Let Women Speak events are widely regarded as being discriminatory and harmful to the transgender community." There is no comment about the views of anyone else.

JK Rowling tweeted that there had been "repellent scenes" in which "a mob assaulted women speaking up for their rights." She said, "Your men's rights activists showed the world exactly who they are."

It took Kellie-Jay a long time to process what had happened. She talked about it on one of her livestreams, many months later. "It's the first time I really felt myself break, and I thought I might cry."

It did give her an iconic photo though. It looks like she's taking a selfie but she was filming the crowd. She likes how defiant she looks. "If I want to be immodest, which I think we've both established that I am, it totally encapsulated what that moment felt like for me, which was like, yeah, you can do whatever you like. I'm still standing."

This woman is tough. She came home and carried on. Monthly events in London, and then a European tour to Vienna and Geneva in 2023, and in 2024, Madrid.

She did Belfast and Dublin too. She does her live broadcasts from her home office. Every week there's Terf Talk Tuesday, plus whatever else Kellie-Jay feels needs saying. People tune in from all over the world, usually several thousand. Among her supporters she has superstar status. When people hear she is coming to their town they get in touch offering to meet her at the airport and have her stay in their homes. That can't happen because of the security risk, for her and for them. Her chief events planner, Iris, has always taken a lead, planning her route in and out for each event, but she wants the police to step up more now, because the threat is real.

In Dublin, a well-known English transactivist was waiting for her when she got out of the car at an event. A core member of the Let Women Speak volunteer team, Jo, shouted to the police, "That man's dangerous!" and they moved him away. He has come to London Let Women Speak events, too. In Sheffield in September 2024, a very tall chap ran up and threw tomato soup over her head, then ran away. A couple of people ran after him yelling, and he ran straight into two police officers. He was convicted of assault, fined and ordered to pay compensation. It probably won't be the last time that happens.

You'd think women would be intimidated, but Kellie-Jay's supporters are hardened to the swearing, shouting transactivists. Others have seen worse in their own lives. One woman said, "My husband broke my nose three times. This is nothing."

There have been so many brushes with police that Kellie-Jay is not quite sure if she's been interviewed four or five times. After charges were dropped over the whole castration thing, she was reported by Susie Green again, this time for showing on her livestream a framed photo of her, captioned, 'Children's champion'. Kellie-Jay was also arrested in Leeds for having a meeting during the pandemic lockdowns in 2020. The most recent was when an English police officer went to her house and accused her of being "untoward about paedophiles." Being untoward is not a crime, whatever it means. She thinks he meant that she had accused someone of being a paedophile. Sussex police interviewed her as well, after a rally in Brighton in September 2022. They turned up six months later and said she'd called someone a lesbophobe. That time, she got herself a tough solicitor. He did not come cheap, but she was taking no chances. His advice, as before, was "no comment."

Activists have posted information online about Kellie-Jay's children and where they go to school. There was a website about her, so she reported that to the police. When they came to see her they just said, more or less, that if she said 'bad' things, what did she expect? As far as she knows, nothing was done. After New Zealand she got big security gates at home.

Party Of Women

In 2024, Kellie-Jay registered a political party called Party Of Women (POW). The UK already has a party purporting to advocate for women: the Women's Equality Party. But like so many other women's organisations, it decided that women included men who say they are women. The Party Of Women's website says it was founded to make sure that people can safely say that no woman has a penis, no man has a vagina, there is no such thing as 'non-binary', and 'transitioning' children is abuse.

As a single-issue party its manifesto is very simple. It lists a series of concerns and proposes three solutions. The concerns are:

- Men who claim to be women are in female-only spaces.
- Children are being indoctrinated into this nonsensical ideology at school in Personal, Social, Health and Economic education (PSHE), as well as the entire curriculum.
- Female language is being erased and diluted. The National Health Service (NHS) refers to birthing persons, chest feeders, cervix havers, menstruators or vagina havers.
- Women's sport is being given away to mediocre men who pretend to be us.
- Women are not able to speak freely about our concerns in our places of work, within the NHS, to our children's schools, and in all areas of our public and private life without fear of intimidation or punishment.
- Single-sex spaces and services are vanishing in care, hospitals, and schools, and even on Girl Guides residential trips!

The proposed solutions:

- Repeal the *Gender Recognition Act 2004*. This act created the legal fiction that allows men to be recognised as women.

- Remove the protected characteristic of 'gender reassignment' in the *Equality Act*. This is often used to discriminate against women.
- Restore all government institutions and services to reality based, impartial and professional establishments.

Kellie-Jay called for women to stand as candidates for her party, first in local elections in May 2024 and then in the UK general election in July when they had 16 candidates including Julia Long and Kellie-Jay herself. There was no expectation of winning seats. The goal was to get the issues discussed in hustings and in the media during the election campaign. It's hard to say that any one campaign was the one that made the difference, but there's no doubt that the issue of the erosion of other people's rights by trans demands got onto the agenda at that election.

Kellie-Jay keeps going because, she says:

> It's more important to be right than to be liked, and it's more important to be able to speak than be liked. I am the woman throughout my life that if something is happening, I'm the one that will say it. I don't want to spare people's feelings when they're wrong.

Her actions inspire others. In January 2019, a group of women calling themselves Resisters United went out in the night across the UK and dressed dozens of female statues with Adult Human Female T-shirts.[21] The following year, when a new statue of the British feminist campaigner Mary Wollstonecraft was unveiled to great fanfare in London, she soon had an Adult Human Female T-shirt on, too. That was Julia Long's work. A woman was asked to leave a pub in the north of England for wearing an Adult Human Female T-shirt. The next month 20 women went to that pub together. They bought their drinks, sat down and took their coats off to reveal that they were all wearing the same T-shirt. Journalist Sanchez Manning went with

21 The gallery of photos is at <https://resistersunited.org/>.

them to report on it. When they challenged the bar staff to say, "Why haven't you thrown us out?" they got no answer. They stayed.

It's become a worldwide campaign. Adult Human Female T-shirts and stickers are everywhere. A Canadian campaigner known as Billboard Chris put up an "I heart JK Rowling" billboard in his hometown, Vancouver, in 2020, just like the one in Edinburgh, and as in Edinburgh, it was removed the very next day. That only encouraged him to put billboards up all over North America. For her involvement with the Vancouver billboard, a nurse called Amy Hamm was reported to, and investigated, by her professional body, and found guilty of unprofessional conduct. Women in Kellie-Jay-style jumpsuits and blonde wigs campaigned on the streets of San Francisco, calling themselves a 'Pocket full of Posies'. Kellie-Jay has been refused a new visa for Australia but that has not dampened support for her there.

Let Women Speak events continue in the UK, and every month more women venture up to the microphone, many saying they don't like speaking in public, but they have to do this. Or they say, "I've never told anyone this before, but I can't keep quiet any longer." Campaigning groups inspired by Let Women Speak have sprung up all over the UK, often because Kellie-Jay has held an event in their town.

Every time Kellie-Jay goes abroad, women turn out to thank her. Every time a woman wears an Adult Human Female T-shirt or badge, she's asserting her right to define herself. Kellie-Jay is helping us all to hold the line, as she says she will. She doesn't think what she calls "this madness" will end any time soon, but she says she will not stop until it does. As she likes to say at the end of her rallies, "I never lose."

Kellie-Jay at Let Women Speak, January 2025

Photo courtesy of an anonymous supporter

4

Maya Forstater

MAYA FORSTATER HAS ALWAYS BEEN AN INDEPENDENT thinker. She is not afraid to articulate and defend her own opinion, even if she is in a minority of one. It was that very trait that got her a job with the policy thinktank, the Center for Global Development (CGD), and which later lost her that job.

Back when she was just another working mother, with children in primary school, she was already a keen tweeter and blogger. She dared to write a post on her blog about the *Charlie Hebdo* attack in 2015, when 11 people were killed at the office of the satirical French magazine for representing and parodying the prophet Mohammed. Many people were afraid to say anything about it, still less to defend the free-speech rights of the journalists. Maya questioned in her post whether children in school should really be instructed to write "PBUH" (peace be upon him) after "Mohammed" in religious education. In a post that now seems uncannily prescient, she wrote:

> Too often, religious education seems to confuse respect for people with respect for ideas, and in this case goes as far as requiring all students to demonstrate obedience to some of them ... Handling Muhammed with extreme care in schools is motivated by concern for respect but instead reinforces prejudice – reflecting a 'better safe than sorry' view that sees all Muslims as extremist, intolerant people who might take offence easily. Further, it encourages

> students to get used to seeing freedom of expression and academic rigour as things that should be casually discarded in the face of any imagined potential for offence-taking.

She'd got into her first feminist activism via Mumsnet in 2012. She worked part time in the esoteric world of international development policy, on issues such as international tax and climate finance. Mumsnet was nothing to do with work. Like so many other women, she says she "came for the nappies, stayed for the feminism." She had two sons, and she was annoyed by how toy shops separated everything by sex. The toys, the packaging, the aisles the toys were in, were all labelled and colour-coded for either girls or boys. It seemed mad, regressive, and potentially harmful to be telling children what they should play with based on their sex. If all the construction toys are called boys' toys, what does that say to boys who don't like construction or girls who do? It was a topic of conversation in the Mumsnet feminist talk boards, and a few of them decided to start a campaign. They didn't know each other in real life, only through Mumsnet.

They called it Let Toys Be Toys, created Facebook and Twitter accounts and set up a petition calling on retailers to stop promoting toys as only for girls or only for boys. They wanted to publicise the worst offenders in reinforcing sexist stereotypes to children. They crowdsourced the information by asking people to visit and report back on their local toyshops, using a survey Maya set up. Then Let Toys Be Toys rated how the shops were doing and posted the results on social media.

It went big on Twitter. In the first couple of weeks of the campaign, BBC Breakfast got in touch with the group via Twitter to ask if someone would come and talk about it on the sofa. There were six of them in the group but the others didn't want to do it, so Maya said she would. She was put up in a hotel overnight so she could do the early morning appearance live in the BBC studios in Manchester. That was her first media experience, and her only one for a while.

She wasn't looking for attention. It was an early instance of what she calls "the trouble I get myself into when I'm a bit bored at work."

The women attracted some haters on Twitter, men replying to the Let Toys Be Toys account saying they were sexist. It was quite intense but short-lived and the hate wasn't personalised, so it didn't bother them. The campaign had some positive impact. Retailers took down the signs for boys' toys and girls' toys. But the toys and the packaging are still very pink and blue. It's still a problem.

Maya became less involved in Let Toys Be Toys as her boys got older, and she wasn't on Mumsnet much for a while because she was busy. But when she became interested in sex and gender in 2017, she went back to Mumsnet.

The first thing that pricked her consciousness was when a journalist called Jenni Murray was 'cancelled'. Jenni had presented *Woman's Hour*, a daily radio programme on the BBC, for many years, and she was something of a national treasure. She got into trouble for comments she had made about men who identified as transgender women. She'd written an article in *The Sunday Times* which was headlined 'Jenni Murray: Be trans, be proud – but don't call yourself a "real woman"'.

It is sub-editors, not the journalists themselves, who write the headlines. Jenni had written that everyone should be respected and protected from bullying and violence equally, listing "transsexuals, transvestites, gays, lesbians and those of us who hold to the sex and sexual preference assumed at birth." She'd quoted some high-profile trans-identifying men, including India Willoughby, to illustrate how they seemed to think being a woman was mostly about choosing what to wear and shaving your legs. "I know that in writing this article I am entering into the most controversial and, at times, vicious, vulgar and threatening debate of our day," wrote Jenni. "I'm diving headfirst into deep and dangerous waters." You bet.

The piece was greeted by "a chorus of protest – and some support" as *The Guardian* put it. That month, students protested when Jenni spoke at the Oxford Literary Festival. There was much worse to come – cancellations and restrictions on what she could cover on *Woman's Hour*, which eventually led to her leaving the BBC in 2020. What Maya was seeing in 2017 was mainstream media coverage of the social media abuse, the name-calling and threats. She read a couple of articles in *The Guardian* about the furore and was baffled. She thought that Jenni Murray seemed like a good person; surely not controversial. She found *The Sunday Times* piece in which Jenni said a transwoman is a transwoman and deserves to be respected as a transwoman. "I couldn't understand how she could be condemned for that."

Maya started noticing more things on Twitter about the topic. She set up a private list there so that she could follow the issue, calling it Peak Trans, the term people used on Mumsnet to mean realising that transgender issues were a problem for other people, especially women. Doing it as a private list meant that other people couldn't see what she was following. She knew this topic was toxic and dangerous because of what happened to Jenni Murray and, soon after, Maria MacLachlan. Also she didn't really know what she thought yet, and didn't want to say anything until she'd sorted that out.

She found a blog by a campaigning woman with the pen name Lily Maynard and stayed up until 3 a.m. reading Lily's account of how her daughter thought she was a boy, and how she finally got over it.[22] For about a year, Maya kept reading and thinking, but didn't say anything publicly. She says it was like one of those magic vision pictures that flips between two different things:

> My understanding just flipped. It was a change of perspective, and then I was seeing the issue as male violence against women, and also that people who are saying this is a problem are not bad people. Everyone is pointing at them saying nazis, bigots, these are outdated views, you shouldn't hold these views, and at the same time I was seeing that the problem they are raising is male violence against women and the people who are raising it are not bad people.

---

22 Lily Maynard's site <www.lilymaynard.com> also has accounts of many of the early meetings and events.

The other big wake-up call was the assault on Maria MacLachlan at Speakers' Corner (see Chapter 3). On social media, trans activists were saying that a woman had got a poor young girl in a headlock. There was some confusing video footage but if you watch it a few times you realise that the poor young girl is actually a six-foot-tall young man and his dispute was with a small 60-year-old woman:

> The trans position was, you have to call that person she, she's a model, she's a poor young woman ... but you know what this is. This is male violence. I haven't experienced it myself but I know men are stronger.

Maya knew what she thought but she didn't have the courage yet to tweet about it.

Working at CGD

Maya got her job with CGD through being outspoken on Twitter, and because of her curiosity, her rigour and her willingness to challenge. CGD is a charity and an economic think tank, established in the USA with a European office in a lovely building in Westminster. Back in 2014, when Maya was a consultant and researcher working in international development, she had spotted a major flaw in a paper published by CGD.

It was about international trade in commodities between developed and developing countries. The paper claimed that "if Zambia had received the price for its copper that Switzerland declared on re-exporting the exact same copper, then Zambia's GDP would have nearly doubled." She instinctively felt this must be wrong and she said so on Twitter, getting into a back-and-forth with senior people from CGD. After figuring out why the claim was false, she published a blogpost with the reasoning on her personal blog. She was right and they were wrong. They withdrew the paper, which was a very big deal for them. It had never happened before.

The CGD people called Maya, wanting to meet her, and that led to a consultancy offer and later a contract.

CGD sounds like a good place to work if you are interested in international development. Their stated approach was:

> CGD does not take institutional positions, and fellows are encouraged to follow their interests and reach their own conclusions – provided they can back these up with evidence and clear argumentation.

What a great place for a curious researcher who wasn't afraid of upsetting people when something needed to be said.

In the summer of 2015, Maya published her first paper for CGD, again taking issue with previous positions taken by CGD people. Some people might have thought it wise to be conciliatory, but Maya is a truth-seeker. She's also not that sensitive to office politics, as we will see later. In any case, she was encouraged by senior colleagues not to worry about disagreeing with received wisdom, or to be intimidated by personal attacks, so long as she could back up what she wrote with clear argument and evidence.

She became informally part of the team, when late the following year she was appointed a Visiting Fellow with a one-year contract, renewable for up to three years. Although she wasn't a permanent member of staff, she had a CGD email address and business cards and she was listed on their website. She was doing well for them, helping them get noticed in the area of international taxation and making inroads with the World Bank and the US Treasury. She was known in CGD's parent office in Washington DC, partly because of the earlier drama around causing their own paper to be withdrawn, and also for being critical and argumentative on social media about non-governmental organisations such as Oxfam promoting wishful thinking on international tax policy. She was invited to give talks at prestigious places like the World Bank and the International Monetary Fund. That was very good for CGD's reputation.

"I Wanted to Stand Up"

Maya's first careful comments about the sex and gender issue on social media were in response to other people's posts.

In the summer of 2018, when the UK government was running its public consultation on the *Gender Recognition Act, The Economist* published an article looking at the different approaches to people who identified as transgender around the world. An ex-CGD colleague who was now at the World Bank posted it on Facebook, saying how terrible it was that the UK was behind on best practice. Maya replied, saying that international best practice wasn't all it was cracked up to be and that there were other issues to consider. It was the kind of thing she might say about tax and climate finance, her topics in the world of international development where she worked. It was also a typically CGD thing to say that the statement was not backed up by evidence.

On that Facebook post, there was a three-way chat between her, the person who had posted the original comment and another CGD colleague. This was her first in-work conversation about the issue; he posted the article and she replied. She thought it was a good exchange, typical of CGD, where they discussed and disagreed in a civilised way, often in public on social media. CGD was the place where you could do that. She liked working there because it wasn't politically partisan and there were no institutional positions. And, after all, she got the job there by daring to debate and disagree on social media. When, later, she was accused by CGD of bringing the toxic issue to work, this first instance where someone else had initiated the conversation was not mentioned.

Her first mention of it on Twitter was also a reply to someone else. A friend of Maya's, a female academic who writes about women and gender, had posted a multiple-choice question about definitions around gender, sex and sexual orientation and whether sex is a spectrum. Maya replied and there was a bit of chat on Twitter. Then the academic deleted her part of the discussion but "that broke the dam for me."

She began to post about sex and gender issues alongside her existing tweets on tax and international development. At first she reposted mainstream media stories, like that of the male sex offender Karen White in a women's prison in England. There was also the Aimee Challoner story, which was being followed on Mumsnet. Aimee was a young trans-identifying man in the Green Party whose father was his election agent and who was celebrated as a transwoman in politics. Then the father was jailed for violent sex crimes against a child. Maya noticed this was reported in most mainstream media but not in *The Guardian*, and she was frustrated by that. She had about 2000 followers at the time. Normally these people would argue with her about tax or whatever, but on this topic there was no engagement, no likes, no comment. There was just no response.

Maya's first in-person action was at Westminster Magistrates' Court in support of Venice Allan and Linda Bellos. She had heard on social media that these two women, whom she didn't know, were being sued by a trans-identifying man in a private prosecution. She decided she wanted to stand up and be counted. There was to be a protest outside the court in support of the women. Maya took a couple of hours off before work and went there.

A few weeks before, she'd sent off to Fair Play For Women for their information pack on the *Gender Recognition Act* and the risks of self-ID so she brought the leaflets along to hand out. She went to the protest on her own, not being connected in the protest world, but she recognised Kellie-Jay Keen. Maya had watched her video, 'Cognitive Dissonance, Gaslighting and Fuckwits', about a feminist meeting she'd gone to in Glastonbury where everyone was asked their pronouns. Maya was impressed by her, and seeing her in the flesh she thought, "She is so small and brave!" Maya got a picture of herself in front of the 'Woman Adult Human Female' banner and put it in the header of her Twitter bio.

Maya went on to the CGD office late morning. It was quite usual for people to go to marches on issues such as Brexit, climate change and the anti-Trump women's march and then to discuss this in the office. Maya mentioned in the shared office she was sitting in, and in the staff Slack channel (an intranet chatroom), that she'd just been to this protest about Linda and Venice, and that there was a consultation going on. She said if anyone wanted to talk to her about it please do. There was a bit of conversation in the office and with one young man on Slack who wanted a chat about it. Mostly, they disagreed with her in a friendly CGD kind of way, before they all got on with their work.

She said in the Slack post that she had a booklet if anyone was interested to read more, and she left it on the edge of the desk she was working at. When she left the office that evening, she accidentally left it behind along with a banana that had also been in her bag. The office was hot desking so it wasn't her desk, and she didn't go to the office every day. "When I came back, the booklet was still there and the banana was black. I was embarrassed about the banana. It was antisocial of me! I threw the banana away and put the booklet in my bag and thought nothing of it." There was supposed to be a clean desk policy but it wasn't that strict so she wasn't concerned. She didn't think anyone would even have noticed, apart from the banana.

She posted a careful four-post thread about the proposals to reform the *Gender Recognition Act*, linking to an online version of the same Fair Play for Women booklet, saying it was important and people should engage in the democratic process. She felt that's what she was doing by drawing attention to it and linking to content she thought was relevant and important, like Fair Play For Women's guide to responding to the consultation.

A week later she came across Pips Bunce. His employer Credit Suisse tweeted:

> Congratulations to Pips Bunce on being listed on the Top 100 Female Executives list in the 2018 @HeroesinB @FT champion of #WomeninBusiness #FTHERoes18

along with a split picture of a man in a suit and the same man in a pink dress and a wig. Women tweeted that it was insulting to women to give an award for women in business to a man who is a part-time cross-dresser.

In *The Times* it was reported:

> Philip Bunce, who is married with two grown-up children, typically spends half his time as Philip and half as his female alter ego, Pippa. He says he is 'gender fluid' and 'non-binary'.[23]

In previous interviews, Bunce had described waiting until he was "very established" and "quite senior" at the investment bank before starting to cross-dress at work. There were discussions on Mumsnet about how insulting this was to women.

Maya's boss at CGD, Owen, had pledged, years before, that if invited to speak on an all-male panel, a 'manel', he would decline and recommend a woman be invited instead. This had become known as the 'Owen Barder Pledge' and he had set up a website where other men could sign up to it. Maya had attended an internal meeting at CGD in early 2018 to promote gender equality where this pledge had been discussed, although it wasn't CGD policy.

Seeing Pips Bunce, she tweeted:

> I've got a Q for my male twitter friends who have pledged not to appear on all male panels – if u were invited on a panel w Pip Bunce – one of FT's top 100 female champions of women in biz & another guy would u say yes or call the organisers & say sorry i don't do #manels?

This triggered some Twitter chat that ran on for over a week, with people from the international development world discussing the definition of woman, and in what circumstances people should view, or be compelled to act as if they view, a male person as a woman.

23 <https://www.thetimes.com/article/anger-over-women-s-business-honour-for-cross-dressing-banker-h0gv3l7nw> 22 September 2018.

One woman asked, "Maya, are you saying that transwomen are not women? I'm a bit confused ..." Maya replied:

> Yes I think that male people are not women. I don't think being a woman/female is a matter of identity or womanly feelings. It is biology. People of either sex should not be constrained (or discriminated against) if they don't conform to traditional gender expectations.

She also tweeted:

> Yes people should of course be able to define their identity any way they like. But other people are not compelled to accept it as relating to any material reality. It is not possible to identify into the sex: woman. But you can identity your gender as woman (or whatever) ...

Looking back on these tweets, Maya says:

> All of that time I thought I was safe. I knew people like Professor Kathleen Stock at Sussex University were being harassed but I thought the place where I worked didn't have that culture. And then I was at home and I got an email from a guy in HR called Luke in Washington DC. Saying, 'about your tweets'.

The email said, we ask our staff and fellows to use inclusive language. It asked her to put a disclaimer on her Twitter posts saying these were her personal views. That was normal for CGD too. She showed the email to her boss in London, Owen, and said, what shall I do? Owen had been in Washington and it seemed he had talked to Luke, CGD's head of HR, and he knew there was consternation about it in DC. He advised her to talk to Luke and tell him about the issue. Maya emailed Luke back explaining that this was a live policy issue in the UK, not culture wars. She sent him an article by Kathleen Stock from *The Conversation*. She confirmed that she would put an "all views my own" disclaimer on her Twitter bio, which she did.

She thought no more about it. There had been complaints to CGD about her before, about her work on international tax, so this was nothing new. People from outside, in the development sector, had emailed, objecting to her positions on development issues, asking why CGD employed this 'right-wing person'. In response to these complaints, her boss had stood up for her. As a former member of the Labour Party, Maya had rolled her eyes at the political tribalism and the accusation that disagreement must put you on the right wing. CGD was all about going where the evidence takes you. It was known for this, and for not following the herd, even if the conclusions were contrary to mainstream opinion. Some years before, a CGD person had pulled apart the fondly-held idea that micro-loans were a panacea to turn poor people into entrepreneurs and pull them out of poverty. The idea of micro-loans as a way out of poverty was a big deal in the development sector, backed by the World Bank, and the CGD person had gathered evidence to test the theory. So a bit of pushback about the *Gender Recognition Act* should have been water off a duck's back for CGD.

Maya had been to the Washington office a few times and knew people there. She'd been invited to meet a senior official at the US Treasury, to speak at the International Monetary Fund and to directors of the World Bank because of her contrarian streak and her original thinking. But she didn't realise quite how different the political climate was on the sex and gender issue in the USA. Nor did she have any idea, at this stage, about the kerfuffle she was causing at CGD's head office in Washington DC. She knew the sex and gender thing wasn't why they'd hired her, but her individuality and fearless challenge was. She knew it was controversial but it was being covered as a public policy issue in *The Economist*, which lay on the coffee table in reception at the office. That seemed to make it a suitable topic for work. She thought, great. "If *The Economist* can talk about it then so can I."

When you are in trouble at work, there are two layers to the story. There's the layer you are experiencing in real time. Then there is the stuff you don't know about, what is being said about you, the meetings and emails you're not privy to. When Maya brought her legal case, after she left CGD, she got the disclosure from the other side. That's when she found out that she had been the subject of intense scrutiny at CGD head office in Washington DC.

She was fortunate that because CGD was international, with a big time zone difference between the two offices, things happened on email and left a record. Phone calls do not leave an evidence trail. At the time, she was aware of only those communications she was directly involved in, some emails and a few conversations with the new Europe office boss, an American called Mark Plant who took over because Owen was leaving. Mark was a guy in his 60s, with no real interest in this topic, but Maya was sure he knew what a woman is. What she didn't realise was that he could see more of the US political climate that she was naively unaware of, and that he was looped in to frantic discussions among senior CGD people about her tweeting.

Maya, oblivious, wanted to do more. Tweeting more about it would be one thing she could do, with her careful disclaimer that these were personal views. She was very involved with the Scout Association so she dug into their transgender inclusion policy and started an email exchange with the Scouts. This would go on for months and eventually blow up into a major problem for her. She posted on her local mums' Facebook group too. Mainly the reaction was people accusing her of being a transphobe but a few women liked her post and four of them met up in a pub. They became a local activist group that is now part of the Women's Rights Network.

She started working up a long article with a friend about what self-ID might mean in the international development sector. She thought it might work on the CGD blog, which hosted thought pieces from staffers about a wide range of topics relevant to the sector, so she sent it round for a few colleagues to comment on, which was the standard thing to do. Her boss Owen made a few comments and suggested she sent it to the US HR guy, Luke, the one who had emailed her asking for the disclaimer on her Twitter account. What happened next was odd and troubling. Instead of giving comments, he replied saying he had sent it to others for their input. This was a bit worrying, because it was just a blog post, not an official CGD publication, and this was not the usual way of dealing with blog posts.

Then she received a meeting request from Amanda Glassman, the chief operating officer of CGD and for a while CGD Europe CEO too. It was for a "check-in call" which they did online as Amanda was based in Washington, though they had met in person when Maya had been over there. The call lasted barely 20 minutes and covered a few topics. Amanda said CGD didn't have an appetite to get involved with the sex and gender issue, so it would be better for Maya not to push to get her post published on CGD's website. The tone was friendly and informal. Maya didn't think it was an official corporate message. Amanda did say, "Is this really the hill you want to die on"? But even that sounded rhetorical. Maya didn't take it personally but as a clear message this wasn't a topic for inside work. Fine. She knew it was a sensitive subject so she accepted that decision and carried on working on the article, intending to post it somewhere else.

Amanda followed up on the discussion later the same day by sending Maya an American article about Paige Abendroth, a person who "flipped back between male and female several times in her life."[24] Maya replied to Amanda with her draft blog post. Much later, when the legal case was up and running, she would discover that Amanda had already seen it. A couple of weeks after that, Amanda sent her an article from *The New York Times* by Anne Fausto-Sterling, entitled 'Why Sex is Not Binary' with the comment, "The complexity is more than cultural. It's biological too." Maya replied to her with her thoughts. This felt like a normal CGD intellectual discussion.

The request to meet with Amanda had arrived on a Friday, scheduling the call for the Monday. Over that weekend, Maya posted a photograph of herself wearing a new T-shirt she'd ordered online from Standing For Women which had just arrived. It was black, with

---

24 NPR *Invisibilia: The Power of Categories*. Transcript at <https://www.npr.org/transcripts/384104070>.

the dictionary definition of woman ("adult human female") printed on it in white. She also linked to a short video by the campaign group Fair Play For Women warning of the dangers of self-ID.

All this time she was working on CGD projects and on grant applications. Much of the organisation's work was funded by grant-making foundations which took an interest in international development. Some of Maya's work at CGD had been funded by the Ford Foundation, established with Ford Motor Company family money. The next aim was to get a grant from the Gates Foundation, set up by Bill and Melinda Gates, to fund a big project which would include a workstream led by Maya. If this was confirmed, she would be brought onto CGD staff as a Fellow.

Meanwhile, her second year as a Visiting Fellow was ending and she expected it to be renewed, pending confirmation of grant funding to make her role permanent. The feedback on the work was good, and all the signs were positive. Or so she thought. She had no idea how much they were talking about all of this until afterwards. To her, it was just odd words here and there, no big deal. But she thinks now, "It's also me being a bit oblivious. Not having an instinct for self-preservation and not being a corporate animal." At the time she just thought, "There's this interesting thing and I want to write about it, I'm being robust, it's all with footnotes, read Kathleen Stock and you'll see." She totally underestimated the heat being generated in the DC office.

Things Fall Apart

Maya was asking about her job status, but suddenly her new boss in Europe, Mark Plant, was too busy to meet with her. She didn't worry. She was involved in a few projects which were going well and working with CGD colleagues on getting funding from elsewhere. The Visiting Fellowship officially ran out in October but the Gates Foundation grant was close to being confirmed which would mean she would join the staff. Everything seemed on track. She started work on a topic that would be part of the Gates-funded project.

Then a hammer blow. At a team lunch in mid-November, in front of about 25 CGD staff and guests, Mark announced that the Gates grant had been approved. The lunch started with Mark sharing this news and getting a round of applause and congratulations. Maya felt humiliated. Everyone knew she had been working on getting this funding, but Mark did not mention her. She felt it must be obvious to those present that this was news to her too. People on the staff team looked at her and she flushed and welled up, but as there were external guests no one said anything. Then they went round the table with everyone introducing themselves. She was in shock, but held it together and said something like, "I'm Maya Forstater, and I'm just happy to hear the news."

After lunch she finally got the meeting with Mark that he had been putting off for a month. He told her that CGD had changed its mind and did not want to employ her on staff, but that she could instead stay on as a Visiting Fellow for another year and then be a "non-resident fellow" and be paid under a consultancy contract. Maya says that Mark made it clear it was "because of your tweets."

This was absolutely crushing. She had been working with CGD since 2017 on developing this project, and now, just as the grant was agreed, she had been humiliated in front of her colleagues and then told that she would have no future with the organisation.

Mark told her that she had antagonised key personnel in Washington by tweeting about sex and gender (he did not say who, and she had no idea) and that these relationships were irrevocably broken. He suggested that she just get on and do the Gates project on a half-time basis, on a consultancy contract, and not try to fundraise further or develop other projects at CGD, but to do other work outside instead.

She was gutted but felt she had no choice. She felt cheated, ashamed, and foolish for having trusted the process and the culture of the organisation. But she couldn't afford to walk away. She was the main breadwinner in her household. She felt it would be hard to get other work in the development sector, because how would she explain why she had left CGD after winning the grant from the Gates Foundation? She tried to put on a brave face to be able to carry on and not be seen as a problem. She said that she hoped they would now get the renewal of the Visiting Fellowship sorted before Christmas.

A couple of weeks later, she went to the staff Christmas party. What a trooper.

In December, Mark told her that her Visiting Fellowship hadn't yet been renewed and that he had saved it from being refused altogether by proposing a process in the European office to investigate and address the issues of intellectual freedom and social media policy. But she would not be involved in that process. All she could do was wait anxiously. She had a stressful and worried Christmas, with her consulting contract with CGD running out on 31 December.

She hadn't stopped worrying about self-ID in the UK, though. She set up a separate, anonymous Twitter account called @2010 Equality and used that to share thoughts and articles about the issues.

A Secret Trial

Some months before, CGD had contracted a US group called Quantum Impact to run diversity training across its Washington and London offices. The London date was mid-January 2019. Maya still didn't know her status and she felt uncomfortable about going in to the office so she emailed Mark:

> Having this thing hanging over me all through Christmas and now into the new year is making me feel anxious, precarious and unable to plan for the year ahead.
>
> I cannot tell people that I am going to continue as a visiting fellow at CGD, or that I won't, or why I am uncertain about it. I do not know if I will be doing the Gates-funded project or if I should be looking for other work. I do not know what has been said about me in Washington. I do not know what the 'process' is, or when

> it will be decided what the process is. I do not know what its aim, scope and subject matter is. (Is it concerned with specific tweets from October, or other social media posts, or that I continue to hold the view that [there] is a biological class of women, which does not include men with gender dysphoria?) I do not know if it is a disciplinary process – to determine whether I have undertaken misconduct prohibited by the policy under harassment 'generating, receiving, or forwarding any message that might be taken as offensive to any protected group' or some other kind of process. I do not know when I might be told the answers to any of these questions.
>
> I do not know whether it is appropriate for me to attend the training session on January 15 to participate in a general discussion on the Anti Harassment and Bullying policy, as I am not sure whether the 'process' that I am facing is an investigation of misconduct in respect of the policy.

He told her to come to the training, and that Quantum Impact (QI) had been asked to review her case. She thought this meant using it as an example to help develop a policy for CGD on academic freedom and freedom of expression. Only much later did she understand that they had been asked to pass judgment on her social media activity. It may not have helped her that she found fault with the material presented by the two people from QI at the diversity training. They had a section on definitions which used 'gender identity' but not sex. She helpfully pointed out that 'sex' is a protected characteristic under the *Equality Act 2010*, and that this is different from 'gender identity'. Then they asked the attendees to divide into two groups, "people who identify as women" and "people who identify as men." You can probably guess what Maya had to say about that.

Knowing that these two trainers had been asked to look at her case, Maya spoke to them in the lunch break. It didn't go well. She tried to explain the policy and social dilemmas around the sex and gender issue in the UK, like the fact that lesbians were being called bigots for calling themselves same-sex attracted and rejecting transwomen with penises. One of the QI trainers agreed that of course everyone should be able to choose who they have sex with, but "maybe your friends could come up with a different word for their identity than lesbian, because that includes transwomen."

Undeterred, Maya pushed on with active CGD project work, still waiting for some confirmation of her status for the coming year.

Meanwhile, unbeknownst to her, QI proposed writing two reports on her, one "deliberately vague" for her to see and a confidential one for senior CGD eyes only which would include more evidence and detailed recommendations.

This second report was eventually disclosed to her legal team many months later. In it, the QI people wrote:

> Maya is arguing that transgender women should be treated differently from cisgender women based on the physical characteristics that they were born with (and may or may not still have).

No issue there, you might think, given that 'transgender women' are male, but they clearly found it reprehensible that anyone would hold such an opinion.

The report said that "it sounds like Maya may have been handing out pamphlets in the office for a rally on the issue of protecting single-sex spaces." This must have been a reference to the Fair Play For Women booklet she'd left on the desk after going to the demonstration for Venice and Linda. Maya didn't get a chance to dispute this because they hadn't talked to her for the report as she had expected them to. They had at least grasped something of her character when they advised against trying to talk to her about any of this, writing:

> Based on Maya's depth of knowledge of this topic we believe it would be highly counter-productive to discuss any specific tweets or comments and engage in discussion of whether, or why or how specific comments are disrespectful, contribute to a hostile work environment or are offensive to co-workers.

> She has people in her online community who have been reprimanded at work for making similar comments. Maya believes society is wrong and that her colleagues were wrongly reprimanded.

They referred to three female academics: Kathleen Stock, Rosa Freedman and Eva Poen. They quoted a letter that had been published responding to and criticising Stock's article in *The Conversation*, the article Maya had sent to Luke in HR. They said they agreed with all the points in the letter as criticisms of Stock and which applied to Maya's draft blog post too:

> We think that it makes a number of claims that are inherently transphobic, and that are not backed by any evidence. For instance, the article asserts that transwomen are not women ('Transwomen are not biologically female.')

They even reported back on the lunchtime conversation during the diversity training, saying she had made "explicit statements about people's genitalia, etc." and suggesting this was a breach of CGD's policy on sexual harassment.

Their conclusion was that: "Argument itself is offensive. Maya's main argument that transgender women are not women is baseline offensive because it seeks to eliminate the existence of a group of people."

No debate.

Maya didn't see any of this. She saw the other report, much shorter and vaguer, but still shocking. It said that her draft blog post:

> ... used disrespectful and offensive language including verbiage that suggested that a group of individuals has not existed in history, and language crafted to induce fear against a marginalized community. Such language stands in opposition to CGD's values of for [sic] a non-hostile, fear-free and inclusive workplace.

The report featured lots of her tweets and articles she had shared in support of what she thought was a perfectly reasonable position:

> All the way through, I've been like, Here's this reasonable thing. Here's this reasonable thing. Here's this reasonable thing. And all those things were turned back on me. For them, the very fact of saying these reasonable things is the offensive act.

Getting the QI report was a low point, like the lunch where Mark announced the Gates money. Says Maya:

> I was like, What the fuck? Because up to then I'd been dealing with Mark Plant, who didn't know anything about the issue, wasn't desperately interested, but was sane, and was trying to do right by me. And then I got this report that was nuts.
>
> There was the world falling out from under your feet, thinking you were in this organisation, that it was robust and evidence-based and collegiate and all of these things, and then getting this absolute Kafka-esque report.

The suggestion that her actions – raising the policy issue and mentioning the protest she'd attended – were not acceptable at CGD made no sense to her. This did not feel like the organisation where she had worked for the past three years. She emailed her response to the QI report to her CGD overlords. Nothing. At the next meeting with Mark, she made some suggestions about how she would keep the sex and gender issues away from her CGD work. To her shock and dismay, at the end of the meeting, when she thought it was all agreed, he told her she should forget the idea of being a Visiting Fellow and just be a consultant. She left the meeting and the building so that no one would see her cry.

Was there a dawning realisation? Did she think, maybe this isn't the right place for me? No, for a couple of reasons. She had put so much into making a name for herself on the tax issue, persuading the funders, having fights with people, getting recognition, and getting published. She'd been controversial because of her views on tax in the development sector and they'd overcome that and won the Gates money. She had invested so much. She didn't want to give up.

The other reason was that CGD was supposed to be a place where evidence and reason prevailed. She knew that most people that she was talking to, whether they agreed or disagreed on the sex and gender issue, thought she should be able to express her views. It wasn't even as if people were complaining about her. Friends inside the organisation had been telling her to back off, just to avoid trouble. Not that she was wrong, but just to protect herself. But she still thought she could bring it round because she was only being reasonable. She thought the QI report was illiterate, based on identitarian arguments, while the organisation she knew was robust and careful.

She asked to speak to the head of CGD, Masood Ahmed. Then she was accidentally copied in on an email from Masood's PA to Mark. It said:

> Hi Mark – I am scheduling a call for Masood with Maya later this week. Ellen's asked me to reach out to you to please provide talking points to Masood re: the decision before he speaks with her. Thanks.

This really worried her. She asked Mark if this meant a decision had already been made. He said Masood had decided not to pursue the option of visiting fellow and that he wanted to explain his reasoning to her. But why would Masood need talking points if he was explaining his own reasoning? She sent an icy email to both men:

> The mis-sent email at least gave me an honest view into the decision process. If a person needs to be given talking points after the fact in order to explain their reasoning then that suggests it is not their reasoning. I do not want second hand talking points and I do not trust verbal communication anymore. Everything that has been said to me verbally has been later withdrawn: that if CGD got the Gates Foundation grant I would be employed as a staff member to work on the project. Then that offer was rescinded and I was told I could continue as a Visiting Fellow. Then that offer became uncertain and I was told that the decision was in the hands of the Senior Policy Group and that if I wanted them to consider it

> I should write to them in my own words explaining how I propose to keep a separation between my work at CGD and my wish to continue to express an opinion on women's sex-based rights. When I did this some other decision-making process came into play and the decision was taken out of the hands of the SPG.
>
> This untransparent process has gone on for three months now, with people writing reports about me, and talking about me in meetings to which I have had no input or visibility. I would appreciate a clear response from the decision makers, whoever they are, about the decision that they have made.

And that was when she didn't know the half of it.

The call with Masood Ahmed resolved nothing. He burbled about how:

> … CGD policy on this is that we recognise the right of people to self-identify their sex and gender and we sort of respect those people for whatever sex / gender they identify themselves, and I understand there is an active argument about this in the UK, but I think it's become an issue where your position on it has led to quite a lot of distress amongst other staff.

For that reason her Visiting Fellowship would not be renewed.

She said that she was happy to accept anyone's self-identity in social terms but "I don't think CGD can unilaterally say we don't recognise the protected characteristic of sex in the *Equality Act*, because you know that's the law." She said she couldn't see how she could do the Gates-funded work if she were not part of the CGD team. He told her to take some time to think about it. He then emailed to confirm that she was no longer a Visiting Fellow and that her CGD email account would be closed one week later. He finished by writing, "Thank you for your contribution to CGD and CGD-Europe's work over the last two and a half years."

That felt terminal. She thought she was meant to be thinking about it but this email seemed to be goodbye. Shocked, she sent an email to all CGD staff the next day headed "Dear colleagues – on leaving CGD" in which she expressed sadness at leaving and set out the reasons for her departure. She wrote:

> I am leaving by the same route I came in: being argumentative on Twitter and unwilling to stay quiet about 'The Emperor's New Clothes' in service of a progressive movement. The issue at hand is nothing to do with being an outspoken woman about tax but being outspoken about being a woman.

The long painful process of trying to keep her job was over. Another one was about to begin.

Maya Forstater made her first public speech about losing her job at a Woman's Place event in 2019 where Meghan Murphy also spoke

Photo courtesy of Lily Maynard

A Public Trial

A few days later, on 8 March 2019, International Women's Day, she posted the blog post on Twitter, saying, "I've lost my job at @cgdev over this."

A couple of lawyers got in touch. One pointed out the risks of pursuing litigation, something Maya was acutely aware of because her father, a film producer, had been involved in a long-running case against Monty Python. "He won the case but he lost his shirt." Mark Forstater had helped to produce the film *Monty Python and the Holy Grail in* 1973. When it was made into a musical called *Spamalot,* he demanded his share of royalties. He won a seven-year battle but the cost left him living in a bedsit and terrified about bringing "disaster on myself and my family." The lesson for Maya and her sister was, whatever you do, never sue.

The other lawyer, Anya Palmer, was a lot more bullish. Anya had spent eight years working at Stonewall in its infancy in the 1990s when its focus was still on gay rights. Working on test cases there had got her interested in law and she'd left to become a barrister specialising in employment law. She had been following the trans issue for years, in various closed chat groups.

Through one of these groups she was invited to participate in a consultation meeting on GRA reform at the Government Equalities Office. This was in August 2018 during the public consultation. This was the round table that Stephanie Davies-Arai of Transgender Trend wasn't invited to. It was a big meeting, with maybe 20 women representing different women's groups, among them Nicola Williams, Helen Saxby (Stephanie's twin sister), and Karen Ingala Smith who ran Nia, a women's charity providing services for women and girls who have been subjected to sexual and domestic violence and abuse. Like them, Anya felt hostility from the civil servants, sitting there stony-faced. The mood was not good. Anya says:

> Pretty much the entire room was very angry that women had not been listened to as part of this consultation. They'd done a big

> LGBT survey but they hadn't done any surveys of women. They weren't interested in what women had to say.

After the meeting the women went off to a pub and stayed there until closing time. Anya was fired up. She decided she would throw herself into this fight.

She started thinking about how this could be an issue of discrimination. She says it just hit her between the eyes one day. "I just thought, oh, belief discrimination." She started looking for a claimant but six months later still hadn't found one. Then a lawyer friend mentioned that this woman had lost her job as a Visiting Fellow at a think tank and might need advice. Anya contacted Maya on Twitter direct messaging. Maya hadn't thought about bringing a case, thinking that as a consultant of sorts she didn't have employment rights. That, and her father's miserable experience of litigation. Anya didn't put pressure on her, but she did explain why she thought Maya had a case.

Maya hesitated because she was hoping to take her share of the Gates funding and do the project work somewhere else. She had a contact at Sussex University who seemed keen at first but soon told her she was considered "too controversial." Then she understood there was no rescuing this work. She had nothing to lose. She told Anya she wanted to do it. Anya could see she would be a brilliant claimant:

> She was very articulate. She was very competent, and intelligent, and personable, and people would like her. You do want a test case, ideally, with someone who's robust, who can handle what's going to be thrown at them. And the facts of her case were very strong.

They worked together to lodge the claim with the employment tribunal as soon as possible. There is a three-month time limit on what you can bring up in a case and you have to get the judge's agreement to bring up things that happened before then, so every day counts. They submitted the claim eight days after Anya first sent her a direct message on Twitter. They still had not met in person.

Anya did this for no fee, but they both knew that wasn't sustainable. Anya suggested crowdfunding, and they got that up and running within weeks. Maya also needed a solicitor to act for her. The first one they'd lined up had to turn her away because the LGBT network at her firm complained. Then they found Peter Daly, who became a core member of the team.

Maya's story was reported by Andrew Gilligan at *The Sunday Times*, who'd covered Nicola's work on prisons (see Chapter 2). The friend with whom Maya had developed her blog post tweeted this out, prompting a response from CGD people. Amanda Glassman emailed him to say:

> Maya was offered a follow-on contract after her consulting contract expired which she declined. Her affiliation as visiting fellow (which is more honorific) expired and we did not renew. She took down tweets which were explicit about people's genitals and related [matters]. They were vulgar and disrespectful. This is just inaccurate.

Another email to Maya's friend said:

> She is suing CGD, which constrains what I can say publicly, which is why I am communicating to you privately that she is lying. The person whose claims you trusted when writing your own statement on this subject does not deserve your trust.

Maya was livid. These were private emails defaming her, and she had no right of reply. She did not know, but could safely assume, that other people in the sector were getting similar messages about her. One ex-colleague who had been contacted by three different CGD people told her, "I've told them I don't want anything to do with it. I'm going to stop tweeting about this (at least until your case is heard). Cowed."

She knew then that she was finished in the development sector. She stopped going to meetings and conferences. She did not know who had been told what about her, but she saw enough to know that CGD had utterly trashed her reputation. Formerly supportive contacts were now cold. Legal action seemed like the only option. The only way out was through.

She consulted her husband, but her mind was already made up:

> I said the stupidest thing I've ever said, which was, 'I'll keep the stress away from you'. I thought this could be a thing that didn't affect our life in such a big way. And I said, I'll give you updates as and when. It won't take over our lives. It won't cost us anything. My poor husband.

The crowdfunder was the first high-profile crowdfunder for someone who'd lost their livelihood because of beliefs about sex and gender. Maya sat at home in her pyjamas and watched it going up and up, watched the comments coming in and watched it going mad on Twitter and Mumsnet. She had worried they wouldn't reach the initial target but they shot through that to the stretch target. It was the antidote to those awful moments at CGD. Maya says, "It felt like you're jumping off a cliff and then hundreds of arms are catching you."

The crowdfunder was shared by big names like Martina Navratilova. Maya thought, "Right, CGD. You don't know it yet but you've bitten off more than you can chew." It sent a big message that people were behind her, that she had support.

That covered legal fees, and Maya got some project work from a previous boss and mentor now working at the United Nations who stood by her. The case was listed for a preliminary hearing in November, which in the legal world was considered quick. The first stage was to determine whether Maya's beliefs qualified for protection from discrimination under the *Equality Act*. Only if she cleared this hurdle could she pursue her claim that CGD had discriminated against her because of her beliefs. Only then would the actions of CGD be under scrutiny. This first stage was all about her and her beliefs.

The criteria to qualify as a protected philosophical belief in UK law are known as the Grainger test after the legal case that sets them out, based on case law on the European Convention on Human Rights. There are five:

1. It is genuinely held.
2. It is a belief and not an opinion or viewpoint based on the present state of information available.
3. It is a belief as to a weighty and substantial aspect of human life and behaviour.
4. It demonstrates cogency, seriousness, cohesion, and importance.
5. It is worthy of respect in a democratic society, is not incompatible with human dignity and does not conflict with the fundamental rights of others.

Maya wrote her belief witness statement in which she set out her "gender-critical belief" as follows:

a. 'Sex' is a material reality which should not be conflated with 'gender' or 'gender identity'.
b. Being female is an immutable biological fact, not a feeling or an identity.
c. Sex matters.
d. In particular it is important to be able to talk about sex in order to take action against the discrimination, violence and oppression that still affect women and girls because they were born female.

The statement detailed how this met the five criteria of the Grainger test with Maya's usual rigour and carefully-referenced evidence base.[25]

Scouting for Trouble

The focus was on Maya's beliefs so her witness statement was not much about CGD or work at all. For example, there was this short statement about when she had raised her concerns about self-ID in the Scouts, where she was very involved:

25 <https://www.forstater.com/on-the-question-of-belief/>.

> As a Scout Leader I have raised the issue of whether the Scout Association's transgender policy is in line with safeguarding and inclusion of all children, contributed to a review of the policy and I have also raised the issue with the CEO of the Youth Hostels Association. After posting about this issue on a scouting forum on Facebook and in a discussion on Twitter, I was subject to abusive comments, and I was put under investigation following a complaint from one of the men who led the comments.

When her younger son had wanted to join the Scouts, years before, Maya was told there was a huge waiting list and the only way in was to volunteer. Her husband had done all the football coaching so it was her turn. She became an assistant Scout leader and she loved it. She freely admits to being very bad at maps and knowing nothing about knots, but she loved all the other stuff – camping, crafts, fires, cooking. It was fun. When her son had finished with Scouts she stayed on as a Cub Scout Leader. In her local group it was three men and her. That was a good reflection of Scouts membership, which was about 75% boys, 25% girls.

In October 2018, one of her actions had been to write to Scouts head office about their policy on transgender participation, which she thought was riddled with safeguarding failures. The Scouts wrote back, and eventually Maya went for a meeting at Scouts headquarters. It took months but the policy was amended and improved. Maya was in touch with Stephanie Davies-Arai and she wrote it up for the Transgender Trend website as a positive story about how they had listened and improved. It appeared in May 2019, after she had left CGD.

She was in a big group of Scout leaders on Facebook called 1st Facebook Scouts, where people shared recipes and games and knots, Scouty stuff. She posted her Transgender Trend article about getting the policy changed. It was positive about the Scouts, but it led to her first pile-on. A dozen people joined in, calling her a bigot, scum and transphobe. One wrote, "You're killing trans children. How dare you?" A Scout leader in Scotland called Gregor Murray posted,

"Your guidance will leave children dead." One of those posting was someone called Monica, who later made news as the trans-identifying man who became a Girlguiding leader despite posting selfies online dressed as a dominatrix and wielding a crop.

The group had men and women members, and she was getting strong negative reactions from all these people who were Scout leaders like her. She was shocked, but also concerned that raising a safeguarding issue would trigger such a response. She sent screenshots to Scouts HQ. They said they were disappointed that she had published an article without consulting them. About the abuse, they said she could complain about each of those Scout leaders individually to their districts. This was hopeless, and anyway not the point she was raising. She was trying to show them a possible safeguarding failure and a response to it that they should be concerned about, not object to individuals' rudeness online. It felt like they had learned nothing.

When Maya posted her Transgender Trend article on Twitter, Gregor Murray replied and they had an exchange. Gregor was a bearded chap and Maya called him "he," forgetting that Gregor's Twitter bio stated a preference for they/ them pronouns. For this misgendering offence, Gregor reported Maya to the Scouts. His complaints came to her district leader, a volunteer who didn't know what to make of it. Maya felt bad for causing all this work, and dragging her district leader into it, especially when Gregor put in a complaint about her as well. The Scouts' investigation of his complaint against Maya dragged on for two years. The process is the punishment.

All of this was outside work and invisible to anyone connected with CGD but she put it in her evidence bundle as she had been told to include all examples of expressing the 'gender-critical belief' to illustrate her commitment to the reality of sex and its implication for child safeguarding. She didn't imagine it would be used against her.

Before the hearing the two sides exchanged witness statements. Maya was perplexed to see a statement from someone called Clair

Quentin, an academic whom she knew from the tax world as David Quentin who was apparently now non-binary. They'd spoken at the same conferences and had some disagreements on Twitter about tax policy but he did not work at CGD. Clair Quentin's statement included the bizarre claim that there was a paramilitary wing of the gender-critical movement and that when Maya had tweeted about Pips Bunce she was really tweeting about Clair.

Maya quickly put together a response, showing tweets in which he had taken things that she'd said out of context and implied that she was a Nazi and a bigot. These dated from after she had left CGD so couldn't be relevant to her case against them or their reasons for not employing her. The point was to show that Clair Quentin had an agenda. Like the Scouts complaint from Gregor Murray, this would also be used against her.

Maya visited the employment tribunal in central London in advance so she'd be familiar with it when her turn came. Usually there are a handful of people watching a tribunal: a friend, a law student or two. On the first day of her hearing in November 2019, the small public gallery was full. She made brownies for her supporters. A few women live-tweeted and there was a running commentary on Mumsnet. It was like a prototype of Tribunal Tweets, the citizen journalist group set up in 2022 to cover these sorts of cases. The judge, James Tayler, seemed like a very nice man. As the place filled up, he kept jumping up and getting chairs for the growing crowd of women.

After that it did not go well. When Maya was giving evidence, it felt as if she, not CGD, was on trial. The judge himself started cross-examining her. Pronouns and 'misgendering' had not been any part of the issue at CGD, where there were no trans colleagues or clients as far as Maya knew, but the judge got fixated on the harm that you might do by not using someone's preferred pronouns. Maya had said in a CGD email that she would respect anyone's pronouns. She saw it as being something like religion. "I'm not going to pick a fight with somebody's religion at work, but I'm also not going to profess to share it."

When James Tayler raised a hypothetical discussion about how Maya would introduce a new teacher who was a 'trans woman' to the children if she worked in a school, Anya knew things were way off track. This had nothing to do with whether Maya's belief was protected in law.

Maya ad-libbed, saying she might say, "This is Mrs X, they are a trans woman, they are male." She would respect that X identifies as a trans woman but she wouldn't pretend that made him a woman; she would clarify that he was male. She explained that she believes it is wrong to lie to children about sex. She said you can make a distinction between what people want to be referred to and reality and find a way to do that. It was clear that the judge didn't like that at all. He asked if she would still say X was male if X had a gender recognition certificate. Then he asked if X would be lying if X said "I am a woman." Yes, said Maya. This line of inquiry went on and on, the judge asking three different versions of the question and getting the same answer every time. He clearly didn't like what Maya was saying.

In her closing submissions, Anya said, "Gregor Murray may identify as non-binary, but he's still a man." She felt she needed to address it because even though she thought it was self-evident the judge didn't seem to think so. She recalls that "James was looking at me as I was saying this and shaking his head. And I never had anything quite like that. This really was flat-eartherey to me."

At that point, Anya knew that they had lost.

A month later, the verdict came. James Tayler judged that Maya's belief failed the Grainger test on point 5: it was not worthy of respect in a democratic society (WORIADS). He seemed to believe that misgendering was so offensive that it was intolerable. He cited what she had written to the Scout Association in response to Gregor Murray's complaint:

> If I was to come across Murray or any other male in the women's changing showers or toilets at scout camp I would have no hesitation in referring to that person as 'he', whatever their professed gender identity, removing myself and supporting other women to remove themselves and in reporting the incident.

Judge Tayler called this an "absolutist" view of sex and cited it as evidence she "would refer to a person by the sex she considered appropriate even if it violates their dignity and/or creates an intimidating, hostile, degrading, humiliating or offensive environment." He chided her for not "seeking to accommodate Gregor Murray's legitimate wishes." He cited Maya's own tweets, which she had included in her response to the Clair Quentin witness statement, as evidence of her being hateful and a bigot. In his judgment he wrote, "The Claimant's position is that even if a trans woman has a Gender Recognition Certificate, she cannot honestly describe herself as a woman. That belief is not worthy of respect in a democratic society."

Maya was shocked. "When I got the judgment, it was like when a rape victim goes to court and the judge says, but what was she wearing?" She had lost her job. This seemed to suggest it was her own fault. If that wasn't bad enough, she felt she had let everyone down. The ruling meant that all those who believed that sex was real, immutable and sometimes important were not worthy of respect in a democratic society. Trans rights activists made a little meme of it with a rainbow, "You're not worthy of respect in a democratic society." Any time Maya posted on Twitter, someone would post the meme at her.

It was a miserable time. "I felt shame. I had taken people's money. I lost." The loss at the employment tribunal meant Maya could not bring a case against CGD, because the basis for discrimination, her gender-critical beliefs, had been deemed not to be covered by the *Equality Act*. Anya's big idea had been tried and had failed, for now at least.

JK Arrives

With her legal team, Maya had prepared a good news press release and a bad news one. They issued the bad news one and started thinking about whether to appeal. Anya's view was that the judgment was clearly wrong and they should appeal. Maya and her husband needed to think about whether they could go through it all again. Then someone sent Maya a screenshot of a tweet by JK Rowling. She thought it was a joke, because they'd had a running gag that JK Rowling was watching. When someone put a large donation into the crowdfunder, they'd joked, oh that's JK Rowling! But it was just a joke. When she got this picture she thought, he's trying to cheer me up. "And then I looked on Twitter and it was going mad."

The tweet said,

> Dress however you please.
> Call yourself whatever you like.
> Sleep with any consenting adult who'll have you.
> Live your best life in peace and security.
> But force women out of their jobs for stating that sex is real?
> #IStandWithMaya #ThisIsNotADrill[26]

JK Rowling had millions of followers. Maya was suddenly famous. The next day, there were journalists on her doorstep. Finally her story was in all the national media, even *The Guardian.* It was reported in the USA and Australia. She hadn't decided to appeal but it felt now that the decision was out of her hands. How everything ramped up was unnerving. She went from a small band of Mumsnet denizens supporting her and a few haters to a lot more supporters and a lot more hate. Plenty of hate was being directed at JK Rowling, too. But Maya had not known this was coming. There was no contact beforehand and no warning.

26 "This is not a drill" was a quote from a tweet by Professor Kathleen Stock about the emergency facing women, whose rights were under threat.

Maya at Platform 9¾ in Kings Cross station, London, Jan 2020

Photo courtesy of Maya Forstater

Maya reflects:

> She didn't know me. She didn't know whether I could cope. I guess I'd put myself out there by doing it in the first place. I'd raised money. I'm sure she'd donated. People had a stake in it. But at the same time, her magic wand is powerful, and she waved it over my family. I felt quite happy about that, but my husband felt less sure. And it meant the decision about the appeal was made. I don't think I would have made a different decision about the appeal, but the thing didn't belong to us."

The appeal was on. It had to be filed within six weeks of the judgment, and it had to state reasons for believing the original ruling was wrong. Anya decided they should get a Queen's Counsel in, a legal heavyweight. She would continue to do most of the work as Junior Counsel. She and Maya chose Ben Cooper QC. There was plenty to pick at in Judge Tayler's judgment, some of it infuriating.

Of Maya's belief that sex is biological and immutable he had written "she has come to this belief recently," even though Maya had been clear in court that she had grown up with this belief and held it all her life.

He had cited the Equal Treatment Bench Book, which at that stage Anya had never heard of. The Equal Treatment Bench Book is guidance for judges on how to run a hearing with diversity issues, making allowances and accommodations according to need. It is not a guide to the law. Worse than that, he brought it into his judgment but he hadn't said that he was considering it, so Anya had no opportunity to address it during the case. That meant it was wrong that he relied on it in his judgment.

But Ben said, let that go. He helped them focus. Ben is a master at taking potentially complex legal issues and making them seem straightforward and perfectly clear. He traced the history of how the law has treated sex and gender to show that Maya's views were entirely right in law. If that was not worthy of respect in a democratic society, then much of English law wasn't either.

He also showed how it was wrong to consider the Twitter exchange with Gregor Murray because the hearing was only to consider whether Maya's beliefs qualified for protection under the *Equality Act*, not whether anyone was offended by them. Plus, the tribunal went too far when it sat in judgment on her for those tweets on the basis that they might amount to harassment in certain cases. Ben pointed out that Maya, in law, could not be harassing Gregor Murray when she said on Twitter that Gregor Murray is a man, because she was not in any kind of relationship with him that was covered by the *Equality Act*.

The tribunal had made the mistake of getting into questions of manifestation when it should have just been: What are the beliefs and do they meet the Grainger test? If CGD wanted to argue that her manifestation of her beliefs was a problem, that was for them to do in the next round, where the details of her case would be heard. Even then it couldn't be the Gregor Murray stuff because that all happened after she left CGD.

The Employment Appeal Tribunal, presided over by its president, Mr Justice Choudhury, heard the appeal in April 2021. This time there were no witnesses giving evidence and being cross-examined. It was just the barristers arguing that Judge James Tayler had got it wrong as a matter of law on his ruling that Maya's beliefs were not protected. She felt she was in very good hands with Ben arguing her case but it was frustrating to watch them discussing her and to have no say.

CGD had the same barrister as before, Jane Russell. She argued that a core component of Maya's belief was to cause trans people enormous pain by misgendering them. This seemed, yet again, to prioritise the thoughts and feelings of trans-identifying people over Maya's.

Jane Russell also argued that the leading case in UK case law, Corbett v Corbett, which is invariably referred to for guidance on the meaning of sex in law, was out of date. You don't have to be a barrister to see that you can't say a previous court decision should be ignored just because it was a while ago. There is no sell-by date on court decisions. Unless it is overturned or superseded by new law, it stands. Saying the law is behind the times is a classic trans activist argument but not one an experienced barrister would normally try. She also quoted a judgment from a European court, which she read out in French, to the bemusement of those present. Mr Justice Choudhury is from Glasgow.

There were also barristers for the intervenors. These are organisations not involved in the case which are given permission to intervene and submit legal points if they can show they have something important and relevant to contribute. Both intervenors were on Maya's side. One of the two, Karon Monaghan QC, representing the Equality and Human Rights Commission, ventured to suggest that Mr Justice Choudhury himself had erred in a previous judgment about the manifestation of belief as opposed to the belief itself. Stonewall had also applied to intervene but had been refused permission.

The appeal lasted two days. Then they had to wait for the result.

We Need an Organisation

Maya was still working part time as a self-employed consultant on the UN project run by her previous mentor. The work was also in international development, in a field adjacent to CGD. It was awkward. She didn't want to bring the issue into her new working life, but felt she had to explain that she was that person who had launched a case, about whom awful things were being said. She felt she had to warn people in case they googled her and got another version. The work was useful but her heart wasn't in it. That lasted a year, until the pandemic put an end to it. Planned work on an international conference dried up. The UK government gave self-employed workers income support so that, like millions of others, Maya could claim lost earnings. It also gave her a bit of head space to think about what she would do next.

Anya was ahead of her. She had been thinking for a few months that a new organisation was needed, one that would reassert the importance of sex as opposed to gender. The established women's rights groups in the UK, like the Fawcett Society, and even the Women's Equality Party, had accepted self-ID, in effect making women, the constituency for whom they campaigned, a mixed-sex group. Anya had been supportive when Kate Harris and Bev Jackson co-founded the LGB Alliance in 2019 as an antidote to Stonewall. But she felt there was a need for an organisation that was for everyone, not just women or gay people. She shared her thinking with a lawyer friend, Rebecca Bull, who suggested the name 'Sex Matters'.

This was when the Scottish Government was moving forward with self-ID. Anya was in touch with Lucy Hunter Blackburn of the Scottish policy group Murray Blackburn Mackenzie. The day after the first employment tribunal ruling, when Judge Tayler ruled that Maya's beliefs were not WORIADS, Anya went to Edinburgh to meet the women leading the resistance there. On the train up from London, she was getting messages and seeing posts on social media with suggestions for grounds of appeal, which is not something that normally happens to a lawyer. Then Maya sent her the JK Rowling post. Neither of them knew then that Jo Rowling had been feeling this way for quite a while but had kept quiet because of someone close to her. But now she had reached the point where, as she later explained, "I had to say something."

In Edinburgh, the Murray Blackburn Mackenzie women took Anya to lunch and to meet some members of the Scottish parliament, and suggested she come back the following month with some lawyer friends. The next month, Anya, Rebecca and Maya went to see the Scottish women again. They talked all the way there on the train about Anya's idea for an organisation, Anya proposing that Maya should start it. A few weeks later Covid hit, forcing everyone home. Maya started a new blog on single-sex services and opened a folder she called "project lockdown." With Anya and Rebecca she began working out what it would take to set up a new organisation.

They recruited board members over Zoom meetings: Rebecca plus academics Michael Biggs and Emma Hilton. By the autumn they were ready. They registered Sex Matters as a company. You can see the origins of its manifesto in the email Maya sent to Mark at CGD in December 2018, months before she knew she was going to lose her job:

> As I mentioned I would like to be able to make the case that this is a policy issue around the world that people and institutions should be able to talk about clearly. If women's rights and transgender people's rights matter, we need to be able to talk about them.
>
> Arguing that it is offensive to talk about women as a sex I think is not a defensible place to draw the line (since this is current law in the UK, US and most other places, and is in CEDAW etc. ...). It is totalitarian for an ideology to make it impossible for people to discuss the law.

So Sex Matters was about everyone's human rights, and about being able to address issues where sex matters in the law, in policy and in life. During 2020 and into 2021, in parallel with working on the employment tribunal appeal, they worked up this new organisation. Shortly before launch, Anya suggested they bring in Naomi Cunningham, another barrister. At that point it was just Maya putting the website together with a web designer.

Sex Matters' first action was to submit evidence to the Women and Equalities Committee in parliament, which yet again was looking at transgender rights, even though its proposals for amending the *Gender Recognition Act* to self-identification had been rejected by the government. A few donors funded a Sex Matters website and the first month of Maya's salary so she could focus entirely on this. Maya had met Helen Joyce, who had taken a sabbatical from her job at *The Economist* to write a book about the rise of transgenderism and its impact on laws, policies and rights. Helen suggested launching with tiers of support, like podcasts do with bronze, silver and gold subscribers, to raise money to fund the organisation. Sex Matters was ready to launch in June 2021, just as the Employment Appeal Tribunal judgment came.

The first time Maya and Helen met, London, March 2019

Photo courtesy of Maya Forstater

R-E-S-P-E-C-T!

The judgment was issued on 10 June 2021 and given privately to both sides three days beforehand. The verdict was on page three of 61 pages of careful reasoning and legal references:

> The vulnerability of many trans persons is something we bear very much in mind. This case, however, is not about whether greater protection ought to be accorded to trans persons under the EqA [*Equality Act 2010*], the *Gender Recognition Act 2004* or otherwise, such legislative steps being a matter for Parliament and not for the court. This appeal is about the much narrower issue of whether the claimant's belief as to the immutability of sex is one that amounts to a philosophical belief under section 10 of the EqA. For the reasons we set out below, we have come to the conclusion that it does. That does not mean, however, that those with gender-critical beliefs can

> indiscriminately and gratuitously refer to trans persons in terms other than they would wish. Such conduct could, depending on the circumstances, amount to harassment of, or discrimination against, a trans person.

The first part of this statement represented a total victory, clearing the way for Maya to pursue her case against CGD. The last two sentences would be widely quoted and misrepresented by trans rights activists to claim otherwise. They were echoed in a sentence in the judge's conclusion, where he wrote, "This judgment does not mean that those with gender-critical beliefs can 'misgender' trans persons with impunity." This has been used by activists to make people believe that misgendering is a crime.

The judgment cited chunks of the ruling given a couple of years before in a case brought by Harry Miller, founder of a campaign group called Fair Cop, against the police for his treatment over supposedly 'transphobic' posts on social media. It was Harry who had sent Maya a screenshot of the tweet on what later became known on Terf Island as JK Rowling Day or Terfmas.

Mr Justice Choudhury accepted Ben Cooper's point that, not only were Maya's beliefs widely held, they were entirely consistent with the law of the land so could hardly be deemed beyond the pale. He took issue with how James Tayler had called Maya's views "absolutist," pointing out that any firmly held belief could be called absolutist, and that did not mean it was not a protected belief. If it meant that Maya's behaviour was totally uncompromising, he pointed out that the Tayler judgment itself had acknowledged that she'd said she would usually use preferred pronouns. Judge Tayler had not disputed that her misgendering of Gregor Murray was unintentional.

The ruling has more general significance. It says, "there is nothing in the [*Gender Recognition] Act* that requires a person acting in any private capacity to refer to a person's acquired gender or to refrain from referring to a person's gender before it became the acquired gender." In the UK, as elsewhere, many people think it is not just unkind or offensive but possibly unlawful to admit to the evidence of your own eyes and refer to a man as such when you know he wants to be known as a woman or a transwoman. Here's the President of the Employment Appeal Tribunal, a very senior judge, saying that is not so. Later he says, "The effect of section 9 of the GRA is not to erase memories of a person's gender before the acquired gender or to impose recognition of the acquired gender in private, non-legal contexts."

As for Karon Monaghan's assertion that Mr Justice Choudhury had made a mistake in an earlier ruling, he wrote in the judgment that he agreed with her.

The win mattered not just for Maya but for everyone sharing her views. In the end, it was actually good to lose at the first stage employment tribunal and then win at the Appeal Tribunal, because in the UK that sets a legal precedent. That means others can refer to it and rely on it for their own protection.

Some people have said it is daft that the reality of sex is now somehow classified as a belief. They are wrong in two ways. First, this is not about what's true but about what is recognised in law as the basis for a discrimination claim. You can't claim discrimination just because you said something true and got fired. It has to pass all five parts of the Grainger test. And second, the protected 'gender-critical' belief is more than the simple facts of biology. It's that *sex matters* and that it is important to be able to talk about sex in order to take action against the discrimination, violence and oppression that still affect women and girls because they were born female. That is what is protected in law.

Maya used the time when she knew about the appeal judgment but couldn't divulge it yet to make a little video, a photo montage of lots of brave campaigning women who'd defended women's and children's rights against the overreach of trans activist demands, set to the Aretha Franklin song, *Respect*. Among those featured were

Stephanie Davies-Arai, Nicola Williams and Kellie-Jay Keen. It was a rousing call to arms and a wonderful way to announce her win.

A few days after the judgment was announced, she went out for lunch with Anya, Helen Joyce and Helen's agent Caroline in still pandemic-empty London. She felt like they'd achieved something amazing but there was no ticker-tape parade. "I wanted to shout, and there was no one to shout to." How surprising, then, when the chief executive of Stonewall walked by. In her exuberance, Maya wanted to take a photo but Anya discouraged her.

The Scout Association Apologises

Gregor Murray's complaint to the Scouts about Maya calling him "he" on Twitter was still going on. After the Employment Tribunal judgment in 2019, the Scout Association quoted Judge Tayler's argument to justify their treatment of her and say that she was perhaps not fit to be a Scout Leader. When that judgment was overturned in the Employment Appeal Tribunal in June 2021, the Scout Association took no notice. They appointed a trustee to investigate. He wrote a report accusing Maya of bringing Scouts into disrepute, saying that she could have been suspended as a Scout Leader.

Even faced with this hostility from the very top of the organisation, Maya stood her ground and demanded to be treated fairly. In December 2021, the Scout Association issued an apology saying:

> The evidence that you provided in response to the complaint to demonstrate that it was vexatious was not considered at the appropriate time by the Scout Association. If it had been, the complaint may well have been found to have been vexatious.
>
> In any case it is clear you did not deliberately misgender the complainant in order to cause harm and did not spread lies and misinformation about them, as alleged in their complaint about you.

> The Scout Association therefore apologises for the experience you have encountered through this process which has gone on for over two years.
>
> The Scout Association recognizes that it is unlawful to harass or discriminate against someone on the basis of a protected characteristic under the Equality Act 2010, and will seek to ensure that its complaints process operates without fear or favour in relation to all of the protected characteristics under the Equality Act 2010.

Maya wrote on her personal blog: "I have accepted the apology. But I have left Scouts this year, as the organisation made it a hostile environment. I loved being a Cub Scout Leader, but I couldn't stay."

Merits and Remedy

The way was finally clear for Maya's case against CGD for discrimination, harassment and victimisation to be heard. The 'merits' hearing would consider the events leading to her exit from CGD and the behaviour of everyone involved. Ben would stay on the legal team with Anya. Getting the evidence together was a monumental task. There is supposed to be full disclosure of all the relevant emails, meeting minutes and so on so that there can be an agreed set of facts about what happened. The legal argument is then about whether this was lawful or not.

But as an experienced discrimination lawyer, Anya could tell from what she was seeing that there was lots missing. "It's detective work. You think, well, how does this person know this? There must be more. And then you just keep asking questions. You keep prodding and stuff unravels." Eventually, she had to threaten an application to the tribunal to force the proper disclosure, and then suddenly a whole new tranche of CGD emails appeared.

These newly-disclosed email exchanges showed that the CGD people had decided quite early on to channel the funding away from

Maya's post to make it look as if there was no funded post to give her. The only thing that they were arguing over, and they were arguing for quite a while, was what crumbs they would give Maya instead. The employment contract that they'd promised would come with the Gates grant was not going to happen.

At the time, Maya didn't know this. She had thought that if she could just keep her advocacy on sex and gender separate from work it would be okay. From what Luke in HR and then Mark in London were saying to her, it did seem like that would be enough. By the time her team got disclosure for the full tribunal hearing, it was more than two years since she had left, and three years since the start of the trouble at work with her social media posts, but when she saw all the emails about her, rather than to her, she was shocked. Somebody in CGD USA whom she had never met wanted her out almost as soon as she started talking about sex and gender. That person pushed and pushed, saying the company must distance itself from Maya. Gradually, everyone else came on board with that.

Last to cave in was her newish London boss, Mark, who she says tried to save her job. In disclosure, she saw an email sent just after her departure in which he wrote to senior colleagues:

> Maya did everything we asked of her and agreed to moderate her behavior and did so. There was no negotiation to find a way forward. Management decided it didn't want to renew her appointment as a senior fellow. For transparency management should say why. The only thing Maya was intransigent on was her views.

The abuse she was getting on social media was at times hard to take. People would say libellous things about her, but Maya took Anya's counsel and ignored them. It was also frustrating that trans rights activists were claiming on social media that her EAT win meant her belief was protected but manifesting it was not. This is clearly nonsense, because how would anyone know what beliefs you hold if you don't express them? The CGD legal strategy took a similar approach. They had to accept the Choudhury ruling, so they tried to draw the line about what it was acceptable to say when expressing those views as close to zero as possible.

Owen Barder, who by then had left CGD, and who was well respected in the international development world, would occasionally post, challenging the smear on social media that Maya had harassed a transgender colleague. Maya says, "I was so grateful to him for that. He is fundamentally a decent man and it was quite brave of him even to do that."

The merits hearing was listed for two weeks in March and April 2022. By that time, Sex Matters was up and running. Maya would be in Westminster at least one or two days a week, just like when she was working at CGD, whose offices were close to Parliament. Before the EAT ruling, every time she came out of the Tube station and walked down across the front of Parliament and down that road, she was nervous about bumping into CGD people, which she sometimes did.

After she won the EAT, she stopped being nervous. "I felt like, I'm here. I've won, whatever happens now. I've worked and I've won this thing." People would come up to her, at conferences, in the street sometimes and on tubes, and say, "I said your name, it saved my job." That's huge. "I'd come out of the Tube station and feel like I'm here and I'm worthy of respect in a democratic society."

Back in court the barristers for CGD did their best to suggest she wasn't. The cross-examination was brutal, but also at times ludicrous. Maya was a model claimant in Anya's opinion – cool, calm, collected and rational. Not emotional, unlikely to break down in tears, fearless and full of fight. Nothing was going to stop her. She'd thought about the issues for a year before expressing them in public. By the time of this hearing in March 2022, she'd been thinking about them for years. She was sure of her ground. As the QI report about her in early 2019 had said, "Based on Maya's depth of knowledge of this topic we believe it would be highly counter-productive to discuss any specific tweets or comments and engage in discussion." You could almost feel sorry for the barrister for CGD who had to do exactly that.

Maya gave evidence for two days. Counsel for CGD, Olivia Dobbie, may have wished she could have heeded QI's words and avoided the discussion with Maya. After spending almost a day trying to show that Maya wasn't really employed by CGD at all, prompting the judge to say, "The claimant has already said she is not an employment lawyer," Olivia Dobbie questioned Maya about the Fair Play For Women leaflet she'd left on an office desk. Based on Tribunal Tweets' reporting on the hearing in real time and notes taken by Anya at the time, it went like this:

OD: The opening page we see in bold "female rights are under attack and the government is robbing women of their rights." It's written in very dramatic language.

MF: Yes, it's written in campaigning language.

OD: It's not a neutral document and it's advancing an agenda. So it's not neutral.

MF: I agree, it's advancing a particular point of view and it's not neutral.

OD: We see it takes a very firm stance and opposes the proposals.

MF: Yes, it's a campaigning document.

OD: It says one of the ideas is self-ID which will lead to the end of women's spaces ... but it wouldn't have any bearing on the exceptions in the *Equality Act* would it?

MF: It would in relation to women in prisons.

OD: But it didn't touch on the *Equality Act* at all.

MF: This legislation is still being proposed in Scotland, and the Equality and Human Rights Commission has stated that it will have an impact.

OD: It basically means a small proportion of transwomen can get a GRC and it wouldn't impact on anything else because of the *Equality Act*.

MF: You can disagree but it's respectable to advance the argument, as I do, that changing the definition of sex of a male to be that of a female will impact women's rights.

OD: But it wouldn't have affected the *Equality Act* would it?

MF: The *Equality Act* uses the words men and women, male and female for sex and if those are defined in other laws to mean self-defined gender then it becomes harder to understand and implement the Equality Act.

Olivia Dobbie read out parts of the Fair Play For Women pamphlet, trying to point out its flaws. Yet again she made the error against which QI had warned.

OD: That distinction between transsexual and transgender is false isn't it?

MF: No, that is the distinction currently made by the GRA and that was debated in Parliament.

OD: So you think to be transsexual you have to have surgery on your genitals ... the distinction isn't defined anywhere in law.

MF: Transgender isn't defined anywhere in law, transsexual is the word used.

OD: Socially language has moved on, the word transsexual is offensive.

MF: It's the word used in law, I don't see it as offensive, some people don't identify as transsexual, many people do.

OD: The judges' handbook [Equal Treatment Bench Book] states transsexual is an outdated term.

MF: I don't think the Equal Treatment Bench Book can define what is and isn't language we are allowed to use. Transsexual remains the word used in the *Equality Act.*

OD: We can see for each question in the proposal the pamphlet is saying how to vote.

MF: It wasn't a vote, it was a consultation.

OD reads more from the pamphlet.

OD: Why is it suggesting transwomen are dangerous to the child?

MF: The expectation is that a transwoman is male.

OD: So you think men are a danger to children?

MF: Safeguarding needs to consider risk and sex is a clear factor in risk, 98% of sexual assaults are by men and people need to be able to say what they're experiencing. Safeguarding children is about them being able to state the truth about what they have experienced. They need to know what male and female is and be able to speak truthfully about their experience.

OD: You're saying it's a safeguarding matter that transwomen are with children.

MF: No it's a safeguarding matter to tell children that they can't tell the truth.

Over the two days she was quizzed about Pips Bunce, the banker whom she'd described as a part-time cross-dresser in a Twitter exchange about manels; about Clair Quentin, the non-binary tax expert who had given evidence against her for the belief hearing; and about a tweet where she'd mentioned Stefoknee, a middle-aged man who claimed to be a six-year-old girl. Gregor Murray wasn't raised because that happened after she had left CGD.

Olivia Dobbie tried to say that calling Pips Bunce a part-time cross-dresser was offensive. Maya pointed out that this was taken from his own description. The barrister pushed her to acknowledge that her tweet saying men cannot be pregnant could be offensive.

MF: I think people can find anything offensive.

OD: A transwoman did complain didn't she?

MF: No, not a transwoman. I understand Clair Quentin is non-binary and didn't complain.

OD: Clair works in tax policy doesn't she?

MF: They.

About the manels debate, Olivia Dobbie put to her that it is completely inappropriate to expect someone to prove their gender to take part in a panel. Maya replied, how do you know if you have a mixed panel if you can't ask them how they identify? In the gender identity world you can't go by their observed sex. You'd have to ask them how they identify.

Olivia Dobbie challenged tweets that she said likened being trans to being anorexic.

MF: I'm saying that feelings about a person's body that don't have a basis in material reality can still be serious.

OD: Here you are likening trans people to psychiatric illness.

MF: I'm likening gender dysphoria which has been classified as a psychiatric illness and is treated in the NHS with other psychiatric conditions.

OD: Gender dysphoria is not a psychiatric illness.

MF: I don't know if the classification has changed but it is assessed and treated by doctors.

OD: Not to cure them but to assist them to align more closely.

MF: I'm not a psychiatrist.

OD then draws differences between anorexia and gender dysphoria.

MF: They're both things that affect people's wellbeing and their health.

Of course the question of whether transwomen are men or women had to be discussed.

MF: I said I would respect their self-definition of their gender identity and had no desire to be rude to people.

OD: You also have been told it's offensive to say transwomen are men and that a woman is an adult human female.

OD: This blog argues strongly against recognising trans women as women, that's the tone.

MF: It argues that we need to have the debate and to be clear about the categories.

OD: It argues to separate trans women from women.

MF: Yes, the distinction between male people and female people, to understand what the policy impacts would be on those two groups.

OD: And when you say male people you mean transwomen.

MF: It means anyone who is male, which includes male people who identify as transwomen.

Olivia Dobbie took issue with the Fair Play For Women film against self-ID which Maya had tweeted early on, claiming it said more trans people would lead to more sexual assault. Maya explained patiently, yet again, that it was about providing male-free space to ensure privacy, dignity and safety for female people.

Olivia Dobbie challenged Maya for expressing her views at work, saying, "So you think it's a right at work to try and persuade people at work you're right?"

Maya said, "I think I have the same right to talk about my understanding of the word sex as anyone else."

Throughout her cross-examination, Maya seemed calm and quietly sure of her ground. Depending on your world view, she was reasonable and convincing, or she was as intransigent as ever.

Without Identity a Body Is Just a Corpse

Then it was Ben's turn to cross-examine the CGD witnesses. His job was to prove that Maya had been treated differently from other CGD people, not because of how she'd expressed her beliefs but because she had expressed them at all.

There were some technical hurdles to be cleared. Ben had to show that Maya was entitled to the legal protections of an employee; that the US and Europe parts of CGD operated as one and the same; that the proposed pathway for Maya – securing grant funding and then being confirmed on staff – was not uncommon.

The first witness was Luke Easley from HR. Ben dealt with the technical issues, and then established that there was no written policy, no corporate position or any guidance at all about social media activity. He quoted an email from another CGD person in which they pointed out that it was inconsistent to ask Maya to put a disclaimer on her social media saying these were not CGD's views because other staffers who had tweeted about manels, one for and one against, had not been asked to do this.

Luke comes across as rather thoughtless when he says he only skimmed the Kathleen Stock article Maya had sent, and that he didn't really understand that there was a difference between sex and gender identity, nor that believing in material reality was a philosophical belief. He said he'd focused more on the "reality" bit and not on "material." He also delivered the classic line, "A body without a brain or feeling is just a corpse."

BC: We have a tweet saying, so if a load of people stopped identifying as women they could get paid more, stop being harassed. Do you understand the point the claimant is making?

LE: I'm not sure I do, this ties my mind in knots. I keep telling you her belief is confusing to me quite frankly, she is couching these in academic arguments but that's not how I view it, it's really offensive.

BC: This may be the problem Mr Easley, you are approaching your whole critique of the claimant from your own assumptions and prejudices about what her belief is. Is your point that the claimant must not express her belief that sex is a biological reality which can't be changed by gender identity because if she says that she is questioning someone else's gender identity?

LE: Yes that's my view.

BC: So when the claimant says gender identity does not change material reality, you find it offensive because she's denying other people's reality?

LE: Yes, I don't believe that someone can be the arbiter of someone else's reality.

BC: You equate identity with reality – the claimant's whole argument is that the two things are different, and perhaps that's why it just doesn't compute for you.

LE: My material reality is a manifestation of my internal reality, I don't have the two like this, a body without a brain or feeling is just a corpse.

Luke had difficulty with the social media discussion of Rachel Dolezal, the American who falsely claimed she was black. He said

Maya should not have brought up Rachel Dolezal. Ben pointed out that she had not, the other tweeter had. Well, Luke persisted, she shouldn't have referred to Rachel Dolezal. He also insisted that Maya had crossed a line by referring to Pips Bunce as a cross-dresser even though *The Times* newspaper had done the same.

Next up was the chief operating officer, Amanda Glassman, who had asked Maya, "Is this the hill you want to die on?" (I think we all now know the answer.) Ben asked Amanda about a story in *Pink News,* an online LGBT news website, about a letter sent to her and Masood Ahmed, CGD's president, after Maya's win at the EAT by CGD staff.

This letter, which 85 CGD staff had signed, had stung Maya, because it claimed that most CGD people agreed that she was bigoted and intolerant. It said they believed the original tribunal findings had been correct, that Maya's views could cause harm to trans people, and it urged CGD to appeal. The *Pink News* story quoted CGD's Director of Communications saying that, "Masood and Amanda were grateful to receive the letter, which they felt was thoughtfully framed and considerate and in the best spirit of CGD's culture."

In court Amanda defended the letter, saying she still agreed that Maya's core belief was not worthy of respect. Since the EAT had ruled that it was, she simultaneously had to claim that the problem was how Maya had expressed it, not the belief itself, but it wasn't convincing. She got into a terrible tangle, with the judge pushing her to answer the question whether there was any way Maya could express her belief that they wouldn't deem offensive. She danced around Ben's questions about whether Maya was correct to have a strong expectation of a permanent role linked to the Gates funding, to the point where he said, "You are sounding as if you're trying to finesse a lie."

She admitted she had not seen the disputed Fair Play For Women campaign leaflet until after Maya had left, but she said the campaign video had portrayed self-ID as sinister, the evil red hand of trans women coming to take women's rights. Her take on manels was that it was unacceptable to ask someone their sex.

Maya's London boss, Mark Plant, sounded hapless in cross-examination, as if he'd been a step behind the Washington crew pushing to get Maya out. He tried to defend the organisation's new position, post the EAT ruling, that it wasn't Maya's beliefs that were a problem but how she expressed them, but he failed. Ben asked how anyone would know from the QI reports what Maya could and could not say. There was a long pause before Mark replied, "It would be difficult to know that."

He sounded a bit shifty when they discussed the email Maya had seen from Masood Ahmed asking for "talking points" for his meeting with her. Ben reiterated Maya's observation that if Masood had made the decision he wouldn't need talking points from anyone else. And how would Mark provide them if he didn't know the reasons for the decision? Mark said it was what he would say if in Masood's shoes.

Mark looked particularly foolish when he seemed unable to grasp that saying 99% of convicted sex offenders are men is not the same as saying all men are sex offenders, or that transwomen are sex offenders. Ben tried hard to explain. He was patient and careful but Mark just couldn't get it.

He had written in emails that he didn't understand the issue that so enervated the Washington people until someone suggested substituting the word "gay" for "trans", and then he understood. But in court he acknowledged that he understood that this was not an attack on trans people but a defence of women's rights, and that both the CGD people in the US and the QI consultants had misunderstood this.

The final witness was the big boss himself, Masood Ahmed. He had a bad start. Olivia Dobbie asked him to confirm that he'd based his understanding of Maya's belief on various things she had written, on tweets, and on the Fair Play For Women video and leaflet.

Ben pounced: "Did I understand from your answer to Miss Dobbie that you took your understanding of the claimant's beliefs from, in particular, the video and pamphlet that the claimant didn't write?" Like Amanda, Masood had to claim that he had always agreed that Maya's beliefs were WORIADS as the EAT had determined they were, but that she had held other beliefs, not written down anywhere, which were not. Ben was ruthless, saying, "I'm giving you an opportunity to come clean. This is revealing of the tendency to spin and obfuscate."

The judge joined in, saying to Masood, "You seem to be saying that you personally have always thought these beliefs are WORIADS. So it follows that when the argument was put forward on the respondents' behalf that they are not WORIADS you personally disagreed?" Masood insisted it was how Maya had expressed her beliefs, that the CGD people had thought there was more going on that wasn't WORIADS. Ben pinned him down on that, since there was nothing in the real-time events that referred to how Maya expressed her views. It was all about her position on sex and gender. He accused Masood of giving a less than truthful account and of rewriting history in his witness statement.

In his summing up, Ben said that CGD's grounds of resistance, which is their written defence, had given an account of why Maya was not hired "in terms which I have established are not true." He said there had been "fatal duplicity" by CGD, and many examples, especially from Masood Ahmed, of disingenuousness, spinning and duplicity.

The victimisation claim was about whether CGD had treated Maya badly because she had filed a claim. In equality law, the employer can't punish people for trying to uphold their own rights if they genuinely feel they've been discriminated against. Ben was able to show that Maya had been on the CGD website as an alumna, as was usual for ex-employees, but that after she filed her claim she was removed. A month later, CGD had a new policy saying no ex-employees feature on their site. A couple of weeks later, everyone who was classified as an ex-employee was removed. It was crystal clear from the chronology that this was done retrospectively, on a pretence that Maya had not been removed because of her claim. Ben went in hard to suggest that CGD had lied in its written response to Maya's claim when it stated it had always had that policy.

This case was the first time the campaigning issues against sex self-ID had been explored in a UK court. Witnesses couldn't avoid questions like, Why is it offensive to say that allowing men to self-identify as women will make it harder for service providers to maintain single-sex spaces? Or that it could increase the risk of sexual assault? Or simply that women will be concerned about their privacy?

Maya's posts and tweets were all about the impact on women, but the CGD responses were always about trans. In emails disclosed as part of the case, one CGD person had written that Maya's tweets were "dumb and transphobic" and that it was clear she "hasn't done gender studies." Another had written that anybody with gender-critical views should not be employed, because that is "transphobic."

Vindication

The verdict came on 6 July 2022. Maya won her claims for direct discrimination and victimisation. This was huge. But it still wasn't over. There would be one more hearing, to determine what remedy should be made. This would be the fourth round of court activity, the third for which she had to provide a witness statement and face cross-examination. She was concerned about raising money for legal fees yet again. She could take comfort from knowing she had established an important precedent with her win at the Employment Appeal Tribunal which gave legal protection to anyone treated unfairly for gender-critical beliefs. She was already hearing from people who had cited it at work.

In this final hearing, in March 2023, counsel for CGD tried to minimise the compensation by claiming she would never have been employed as a senior fellow anyway because she didn't have a PhD, and that she'd planned to set up Sex Matters so she hadn't suffered

Naomi Cunningham and Maya celebrate her win, July 2023

Photo courtesy of Maya Forstater

Shelley Charlesworth, Eileen Gallagher (LGB Alliance),
Stephanie Davies-Arai, Maya Forstater and Kate Harris (LGB Alliance)
outside the court after Maya's win in 2023

Photo courtesy of Maya Forstater

a financial loss. The tribunal didn't buy it. In the remedy judgment, CGD was ordered to pay Maya compensation of £91,500 for loss of earnings, injury to feelings and aggravated damages, with an additional £14,900 as interest.

Despite the harshness of the judgment against CGD, which questioned the reliability of their evidence, and the significant compensation awarded to Maya, activists tried to say it was a partial win because she didn't win on every part of her claim. That is failure to understand how claims work. It's not unusual in a discrimination case to put in more than one basis for the claim, giving a legal back-up if the primary basis fails. Winning on direct discrimination and victimisation, as Maya did, was the best possible outcome.

Cries of, "Sue them! We'll support you!" are not uncommon on social media. Maya had a strong case and it took four hearings and three court appearances, starting when she filed her claim in March 2019 and finally concluding in June 2023. As her father had told her, litigation is not for the faint-hearted. Amid the many ugly things said about her by trans rights activists, faint-hearted was never on the list. Her win has helped other people, some to win in court, some to avoid going there. But erroneous beliefs about the law, and policies built on centring people with transgender identities at the expense of everyone else, are so embedded that there is a lot more to do.

By the time the case was resolved, Sex Matters was established as a significant voice in the UK. In early 2022, Helen Joyce joined Sex Matters, initially on sabbatical from *The Economist* and then permanently. The Sex Matters team has had a significant impact, raising awareness and understanding of the need to resolve conflicts arising from trans demands and their impact on other people's rights.

In 2023, Sex Matters succeeded in getting over 100,000 signatures from people in the UK supporting a petition to clarify the meaning of sex in the *Equality Act*. This led to a parliamentary debate in Westminster. Another significant achievement was the report written for Sex Matters by Matilda Gosling about the chilling effect of transgender ideology in the women's sector. It showed how women seeking refuge from domestic violence or care after sexual assault could no longer count on those services being male-free, even though most staff said that was what they wanted too. That report was cited in the UK Supreme Court in the case of For Women Scotland against the Scottish Government in November 2024.

There can be no doubt that the issue of sex and gender is now on the political and social agenda in the UK. It was significant in the 2024 UK general election. No debate is no longer an option. Our beliefs are worthy of respect in a democratic society and cannot be silenced.

Sex Matters was awarded charitable status in early 2024.

Ben Cooper KC represented the new charity in intervening in the case of For Women Scotland at the Supreme Court, about the question of the definition of sex in the *Equality Act*.

When that case was heard, in November 2024, five years after Maya had first been questioned about her belief in the employment tribunal, the President of the Supreme Court thanked Sex Matters for its contribution to its deliberations, saying the judges had found it "very helpful." Then it was a matter of waiting for the judgment, expected to take some months.

Maya is optimistic that we are winning on sex and gender, but troubled that our institutions could be so easily overrun by an idea that is so obviously harmful, particularly to women and children. Like Stephanie, she says she was naïve at the start, believing that sensible conversations would be possible, and thinking there were sound organisations staffed by decent people who would engage and respond. Like Kellie-Jay and Nic, she thought that if the facts were out there, if people knew what was going on, there would be change. Now they know it was never that simple.

Maya's case was an important tipping point. The first step is being able to name the problem. People are less afraid now to talk about the policy capture by stealth, and the harmful consequences that must

Maya Forstater with Helen Joyce and Ben Cooper KC, London 2022

Photo courtesy of Karen Varley

be recognised and resolved. There will be more such tipping points. Each time someone wins a case, it's a ladder in this protracted game of snakes and ladders. Maya feels there has been a shift. But, she says:

> We can't win this case by case. We can't ask people to be outrageously brave, to put their jobs and home and family life on the line. We need to see policy-makers and regulators and judges and all the rest get back to doing their jobs based on reality.

How long will that take? She thinks it will be the rest of her career. But she clearly has no regrets. She says she's met fantastic people, and she's had a lot of fun.

> Everyone thinks, what would I have done, in whatever period of history. They look back and think they'd have stood up. But most people don't, because of their job or their family. And I've met the ones who have.
>
> Losing my job was the most important thing I've ever done. Founding Sex Matters was the second. I'll do this work until it's done.

5

What Next for Terf Island?

WHEN POLITICAL POWER IN THE UK CHANGED HANDS FROM Conservative to Labour in the 2024 general election, many of us were worried that the gains made in the past couple of years could be lost. The so-called reform of the *Gender Recognition Act* in 2018 was one of the few policy areas in which the Labour opposition had happily endorsed and supported the Conservative government's proposals. They held onto it as official policy long after the Conservatives had reversed course. The Conservative election manifesto pledged to "Protect female-only spaces and competitiveness in sport by making clear that sex means biological sex in the *Equality Act*." While welcome, many people wondered why they hadn't done it already.

In contrast, the Labour manifesto said:

> We will also modernise, simplify, and reform the intrusive and outdated gender recognition law to a new process. We will remove indignities for trans people who deserve recognition and acceptance; whilst retaining the need for a diagnosis of gender dysphoria from a specialist doctor, enabling access to the healthcare pathway.

This is a step back from self-ID, but not much different in practice. Needing only one doctor to approve an application would amount to self-ID. There are plenty of pro-transition activist doctors making good money out of prescribing cross-sex hormones seemingly on demand.

The UK's *Equality Act 2010*, which provides the legal basis for single-sex services, spaces and sport, was the work of the previous Labour government. Its primary purpose is to oppose discrimination against people on the basis of one of nine protected characteristics. These include sex, sexual orientation and gender reassignment as separate characteristics. It also allows exceptions – lawful discrimination – where it is proportionate in order to achieve a legitimate aim. These exceptions are permitted by the *Equality Act*, while other legislation applying to workplaces and schools stipulates that they must be provided.

Single-sex facilities, services and sport were never seen as controversial. It's obvious that it is not discriminatory in the negative sense of that word to offer male-only and female-only services. We encounter them every day. Every toilet and changing room in every gym, school, shop and office with a sign up saying 'men' and 'women' is in effect invoking that provision of the *Equality Act*. It means they are not breaking the law when people of the other sex are told they may not enter. This is normal for everyone's privacy, dignity and peace of mind.

The Labour Party manifesto said, "Labour is proud of our *Equality Act* and the rights and protections it affords women; we will continue to support the implementation of its single-sex exceptions." But it's hard to see how. Trans activists have been pushing for years the idea that any decent person accepts a trans-identifying person as the opposite sex. That to do otherwise is considered hateful, bigoted, selfish, harmful to the trans person, and, in effect, accuses them of being predatory.

Trans-centric lobby groups have for years promoted a flawed interpretation of the law, claiming that 'gender reassignment' gave a person the right to be treated as the other sex in all circumstances. Few politicians have pushed back. This is separate from the *Gender Recognition Act*, which has enabled a small number of trans-identifying people to get a new birth certificate. It is in effect self-ID without the paperwork. The original simplicity of the single-sex exceptions has been totally undermined by the widespread belief that it is bigoted not to see a trans-identifying person as the sex they claim to be, and unlawful to exclude a trans-identifying person from the facilities of their claimed sex. If you can see he's a man, try harder.

Labour also said, "So-called conversion therapy is abuse – there is no other word for it – so Labour will finally deliver a full trans-inclusive ban on conversion practices, while protecting the freedom for people to explore their sexual orientation and gender identity." Again, it's hard to see how both parts of this pledge can be kept.

Given their manifesto statements, the arrival of the Labour government did not provide reassurance. Yes, they also said "Women's equality will be at the heart of our missions." But this is a government led by a prime minister who has said that some women have a penis.

The first big test was whether they would defend the Cass Review. A pro-trans group had launched a court action, a judicial review, of the Conservative government's decision to put an immediate and temporary ban on puberty blockers as a treatment for gender identity issues in children. The new Labour government defended this in court. That was a big relief. This was the responsibility of the Department of Health and it has gone further to cement the ban and close loopholes.

There is other unfinished business from the previous government, like guidance for schools on how to manage gender-questioning children. Yes, that thing the Equality and Human Rights Commission tried to do in 2018. Transgender Trend published its approach back then, but in early 2025, there is still no official guidance. That falls under a different department, Education. The Conservative government spent years working and reworking draft guidance which was published for a public consultation that closed in March 2024. Perhaps something will be published in 2025. Meanwhile, schools are uncertain how to deal with the safeguarding issues that arise when children claim to be the other sex.

The threat of a 'trans-inclusive' ban on conversion therapy remains, as does simplification of the GRA. In both cases, these legal changes would cement custom and practice which are already widespread. It is already challenging for therapists to explore rather than affirm a transgender identity because of the Memorandum of Understanding adopted by their professional bodies. Despite this, a UK group called Just Therapy has launched a directory of therapists who do not reflexively affirm.

Sport is perhaps the area where most progress has been made. In the past few years, there have been reversals of self-ID policies in sport at the international level and many more in the UK, even when their international federation continues to allow male competitors in women's categories. There has been progress in prisons policy too, though it is still riddled with compromise. Having allowed trans-identification to overrule sex in all cases, the rollback is tentative and partial, as if it is somehow unreasonable to restore single-sex provision. Some policy reviews in sport seem to approach this as a tussle over territory by two sides – women and 'transwomen' – so that the solution is not informed by simple facts about biological reality but is instead a negotiated – or imposed – settlement.

It is progress, all the same. Maybe it is easier in rules-based situations like sport and prisons. Workplaces, universities, theatres, and many more places still operate as if a man who says he is a woman must be affirmed immediately and any fall-out for women is irrelevant. Consequently, there are several legal cases for discrimination citing the *Equality Act*. One is a women's rape counselling service where 'women' includes men who say they are women, even though there are trans-only and men-only services available. There is more than one ongoing case of a nurse in the National Health Service having to share the women's changing rooms with a man who says he is a woman. Whether these men genuinely believe they are women is impossible to assess. Whether they have had medical intervention or sought a gender recognition certificate is, arguably, irrelevant since the women see and hear them as male, in some cases experiencing behaviour that is stereotypically male.

Maya Forstater's Employment Appeal Tribunal win provided the legal precedent for several other women to take legal action against their employers, winning without exception. But this is a hard and expensive road. They should not have to do it. It is likely that even though other people will have been able to cite the Forstater ruling to defend their position, the chilling effect remains for many more.

The Supreme Court Judgment

On 16 April 2025, there was a seismic shift in the UK. The Supreme Court decreed that the meaning of 'sex' in the *Equality Act 2010* is biological sex. For the purposes of this Act, which is about preventing discrimination and permitting positive action for under-represented groups, the category 'woman' does not include men who have obtained a gender recognition certificate saying they are women.

Since 2018, a campaign group called For Women Scotland has opposed the Scottish Government's attempts to bring in sex self-ID. A major strand of this was a legal challenge to a law passed by the Scottish parliament called the *Gender Representation on Public Boards (Scotland) Act 2018*, intended to increase female representation. But 'woman' was defined in the Act as anyone who lived as a woman. For Women Scotland challenged the legality of this definition, supported by a crowdfunder. They lost the first hearing but won on appeal in 2022.

The Scottish government was forced to revise the definition to drop self-ID, but it swiftly decreed that 'woman' would include holders of a gender recognition certificate saying they were female. This meant that men who legally changed their 'gender' would count towards the goal of increasing female representation on public boards.

For its opponents, the *Public Boards Act* wasn't really the point. Accepting this definition would mean that having a gender recognition certificate conferred women's rights on men who took the trouble to get one. This completely flew in the face of claims that a gender recognition certificate was a personal and private matter. It meant that a gender recognition certificate was in effect a passport into the other sex's spaces and services.

For Women Scotland launched a fresh legal challenge in 2022. Again it lost the first round in court, and again it appealed. This time, it lost on appeal too, in 2023. Losing is painful and dispiriting, and expensive, having to pay the other side's costs as well as your own. The three directors of For Women Scotland, Trina Budge, Marion Calder and Susan Smith, had put endless hours of their own time into the fight. Pushing on was no small thing, but they bravely decided to seek permission to take the case to the UK Supreme Court, the highest court in the land.

Leave to appeal was granted, and they raised yet more money to fund the legal team, continuing to work unpaid themselves.

The case was heard in November 2024. For Women Scotland's case was backed up by interventions from Sex Matters and from Scottish Lesbians, The Lesbian Project and LGB Alliance working together. The Equality and Human Rights Commission intervened to say the Scottish Government's interpretation of 'woman' in the *Equality Act* was correct but caused problems. Amnesty International UK also got involved to say, in effect, that 'trans women are women'.

Judgment was given on 16 April 2025. No one knew in advance what the decision was. We sat in court to hear the Deputy President of the Supreme Court, Lord Hodge, say that it was their "unanimous decision" that the meaning must be biological sex. He went through the areas of the *Equality Act* where sex matters, and showed that it had to mean reality, not a private government-issued certificate.

As the decision was read out, Marion and Susan were sobbing silently with relief and joy. We had been warned by the clerk of the court to be silent while the judges were present, but the moment they left, there was a spontaneous burst of applause. Trina was in Edinburgh with a group watching the livestream of the reading.

Hearing the "unanimous decision" bit, their cheers largely drowned out the rest of Lord Hodge's 17-minute statement.

Marion Calder and Susan Smith of For Women Scotland
after the Supreme Court judgment, 16 April 2025
Photo courtesy of Fiona McAnena

There was a huge media presence outside the court. The judgment was the UK's top news story for two days, covered right across the media. It was reported internationally as well.

The vibe shift is palpable. One police force, which was facing a legal challenge from Sex Matters for its policy of allowing male officers with a gender recognition certificate to perform intimate searches on women, immediately announced that the policy was suspended and that searching would be based on biological sex.

The Supreme Court ruling cannot be appealed. It gives us the best possible shield, and sword, with which to fight on: to reestablish the common understanding that sex matters in law and in life; to regain the rights women have lost; and to protect children, gay men and lesbians, and vulnerable adults, from the harms of gender ideology.

A Round-up of Groups and Campaigners

It is a risky business deciding whose story to tell, who to mention and who to leave out. In *Terf Island* I have told the stories which I believe have been central to the UK becoming a beacon of resistance to gender identity ideology. As a result, it is ahead of other English-speaking countries on restoring sex-based provisions.

Political changes can lead to revolutions, as we have seen in the USA in 2025, but this does not always translate into practical change. For each of the main UK political parties there is a women-centred campaign group, usually an unofficial one set up because the official women's network has changed its definition of woman to include men who say they are women. After years of work in the face of considerable resistance, usually, but not only, from their parties' LGBT networks, these women-centred groups seem to be gaining traction. They have played a crucial, though largely unseen, role in shifting mainstream political policy away from self-ID.

Conservatives for Women shifted the Conservative government. Labour Women's Declaration did essential work to move Labour policy while they were in opposition and is now gaining influence in Westminster. Liberal Voice for Women won a battle for recognition by its party, the Liberal Democrats, which acknowledged in 2025 that it must not discriminate against the group for its legally-protected beliefs, those about the reality and importance of sex. This legal protection comes straight from the Forstater case. By contrast,

Green Party Women used to be its party's officially-recognised women's group, but when sex-realist women got control of it, it was 'disaffiliated' because of its promotion of 'gender-critical views'. Without groups like these, I believe resistance in other countries will be marginalised and politicised.

Political party banners at FiLiA, October 2021
Photo courtesy of Karen Varley

A growing, maturing movement naturally spawns more specialist groups, by sector and target group, and we've seen that in the UK. I've listed some of them below. There are also dozens of other campaigns and groups around the world pushing for sex realism and opposing the harmful effects of gender ideology.

The sex and gender threat to women's rights has led to the creation of new feminist groups like Women's Rights Network, Scottish Feminist Network, and several smaller groups. Wales has Merched Cymru.

Groups like LGB Alliance and Gay Men's Network were set up by same-sex attracted people who felt that established groups like Stonewall no longer represent them. LGB Alliance was seen as such a threat that when they were granted charitable status, a consortium of LGBT groups, led by Mermaids, brought a legal challenge against the Charity Commission. The claim failed, but not before taking up the best part of two years and a lot of LGB Alliance's time, money and emotional energy. On the upside, Susie Green was out of Mermaids at the end of it.

Kate Harris and Bev Jackson at LGB Alliance conference

Photo courtesy of Eleanor Bentall

Bayswater Support Group and Our Duty are led by parents of trans-identifying children to provide support to parents and to work towards removing gender ideology from education and healthcare.

Safe Schools Alliance was set up by a group of mothers worried about how safeguarding in schools is totally undermined when gender ideology gets into school policies and lessons.

In the medical and therapeutic world there's CAN-SG and Thoughtful Therapists as well as international groups like Genspect and SEGM.

Some of the pioneers have stepped back in 2024: Woman's Place UK, which started public meetings in 2017, announced its closure, as did Keep Prisons Single Sex, which ran from 2020.

Other pioneers fight on. Two of the most effective early groups, featured in the book, *The Women Who Wouldn't Wheesht,* are For Women Scotland and Murray Blackburn Mackenzie, each run by an impressive trio of women working for the cause without pay since 2018.

That same year, Sheila Jeffreys was a co-founder (with Heather Brunskell-Evans and Bernadette O'Malley) of what is now Women's Declaration International, which has tens of thousands of signatories in support of women's sex-based rights and many international chapters. In Ireland, the Countess group started in 2019. Across Europe there are groups like Spain's Contra el Borrado de las Mujeres (Against the Erasure of Women). Keep Prisons Single Sex and Women's Rights Network groups have spread beyond the UK.

There were a few early grassroots campaigns that burned brightly during the critical run-up to the GRA consultation.

Venice Allan started a jokey social media campaign about the antics of 'Sticker Woman', whose 'Women don't have penises' stickers often popped up in unexpected places. This prompted an LGBT newspaper *Pink News* headline, 'Anti-trans vandals are plastering vile "women don't have penises" stickers around London.' The article reported how "Trans campaigners have criticised 'anti-trans bigots' after a number of 'disgusting' phallus-shaped stickers – carrying the phrase 'women don't have penises' – were found across London, including on Stonewall's office building." Naughty Sticker Woman! Penis stickers have found their way to Australia – they've been seen in Brisbane, where the local Women's Liberation Group are active sticker feminists.

The artwork for the 'Women don't have penises' sticker was shared, and a woman from a group calling themselves Liverpool ReSisters ordered some online. Unfortunately, she got inches and centimetres mixed up so when the stickers arrived they were tiny. Undeterred, she paddled out to sticker one of the Antony Gormley statues on Crosby beach, near Liverpool. These are life-size human figures cast from the artist's own body. So they definitely do have that male appendage,

Montage of protest stickers and flyers from 2018 onwards

Photo courtesy of Fiona McAnena

and that's where she put her sticker. Some of the statues are quite far out and are covered by the tide. Knowing one tiny sticker was never going to be seen, she took a photo and shared it on the Liverpool ReSisters social media.

The newspapers reported this exploit by claiming all 100 statues had been stickered, and quoting outraged transactivist groups and the mayor of Liverpool, who was equally appalled. He posted online about loving Liverpool's trans residents and the LGBT community, but said nothing about the message on the sticker and the issue it raised. The police said they were investigating to see if a crime had been committed, but no more was heard of that. This mayor, now former mayor, subsequently found himself under police investigation. In 2025, he was charged with criminal offences relating to his time in public office.

Liverpool ReSisters inspired other ReSisters groups around the country, leading to the 2019 stealth-dressing of statues in Adult Human Female T-shirts.

And there was Man Friday, inspired by a comment on Mumsnet, which ran a year-long campaign during 2018. The Man Friday website encouraged women to "identify as a man and take part in random acts of manliness on Fridays." They suggested such manly behaviour as manspreading on public transport, mansplaining, walking in straight lines and letting others weave their way around you, or using men's changing rooms in stores that allowed self-ID.

A major focus was the row over Kenwood Ladies' Pond, a beloved women-only outdoor swimming pool on Hampstead Heath in London. The local authority which ran the pond had changed the rules so that it was open to anyone who identified as a woman. There is also a mixed pond and a men's pond on Hampstead Heath so women were furious, especially as the pond is used by Orthodox Jewish women. A woman on Mumsnet said she was going to identify as a man, to show how absurd it was. That inspired a thread about how Mumsnetters and other opponents of sex self-identification could take action in an organised way. And that became Man Friday, led by Hannah Clarke and Amy Desir.

Women turned up at the Men's Pond in the summer of 2018 wearing obviously fake beards (and their own swimsuits) and claiming the right to identify as a man and swim there. At first, the men using the pond were furious at the intrusion, but when the women explained their reason, they were mostly sympathetic. On the first occasion, the police arrived and escorted the women out. They said that some of the men were getting so irate that there were fears of a breach of the peace, and also that one man had complained about the media taking photos in the changing room. The police did admit that the women were perhaps the most polite protesters they'd ever encountered.[27]

The stunt generated good media coverage, but also a highly critical response from pro-trans campaigners. They said the women

27 <https://lilymaynard.com/yes-but-today-is-monday-swimming-in-the-mens-pond-on-hampstead-heath/>.

were transphobic for pretending to be trans – missing the point that self-identification means anyone can do exactly that. A few weeks later, an unknown caller made a bomb threat to a Woman's Place UK meeting, saying it was "in retaliation" for this action.

At its peak, there were around 200 women – or 'men' – taking part in Man Friday-inspired direct action across the UK, before the group retired their beards at the end of the year. Their activism is probably what pushed the City of London Corporation to run a public consultation on the policy in that summer of 2018, though it wasn't widely advertised. There wasn't even anything at the ponds to say it was happening until the Man Friday women posted their own signs publicising it.

They also met with Corporation officials early on to object to how the consultation survey was written. They pointed out that it conflated sex and gender all the way through, and that it failed to mention that sex was a protected characteristic in the *Equality Act*. They felt that its questions were heavily skewed in favour of maintaining the self-ID policy, the one which the Corporation had already adopted and enacted. In due course, the policy was indeed maintained after the consultation results were analysed – though almost half the responses were discarded because they came from people who didn't accept the premise that transwomen were women and transmen were men.

In the USA, Women's Liberation Front, WoLF, has been around since 2013 and has not yielded to pressure to be trans-inclusive. More recently, the trans-identifying male swimmer Lia Thomas (formerly William Thomas) becoming an NCAA (National Collegiate Athletic Association) women's champion in 2022 was the catalyst for the creation of ICONS (Independent Council on Women's Sport), which has rapidly become a significant force in opposing men in women's sports. ICONS was set up by Kim Jones, the mother of one of Thomas's opponents, and Marshi Smith, a former NCAA swimming champion. ICONS works closely with former college athletes like swimmer Riley Gaines who competed against Lia Thomas.

A small number of retired athletes with media careers like Sharron Davies in the UK and Martina Navratilova in the USA have been tireless in using their profiles to advocate for women and girls for several years. Both have endured much abuse as a result, and Sharron has lost income, but their commitment has not wavered. They have been joined by other former elite athletes like Mara Yamauchi and Tracy Edwards but it is still a shamefully small roster. Among men, Olympic gold medallists Daley Thompson and his friend Sebastian Coe stand out for their support. Behind closed doors, many people working in sport, whether competing, retired or commentating, acknowledge that they know it is wrong to let men into women's events. It seems that only when these people no longer fear that speaking the truth could cost them their livelihoods will they say so in public.

There has been huge collateral damage, some of it very public, as exemplified by the brilliant comedy writer Graham Linehan, who spoke up for women and children, and as a result lost his career and his marriage.

There are numerous legal cases in the UK, most brought by women denied male-free facilities at work or facing men in women's sport. The USA has multiple litigants on both sides of the issue, particularly on sport and on medical treatment, or mistreatment. The case of Giggle v Tickle in Australia, in which business owner Sall Grover is opposing a trans-identifying man's demands to access a women-only app, has gained worldwide attention. That case is on its way to the Australian Supreme Court. Also in Australia, the Lesbian Action Group based in Melbourne is appealing a ruling that it may not exclude men who identify as lesbians, an issue also raised in the UK Supreme Court in November 2024 in the case brought by For Women Scotland.

The suppression of free speech that goes with the promotion of transgender ideology and demands has fuelled another type of activist group. Fair Cop was co-founded by Harry Miller who was told to 'check his thinking' by a police officer who visited his workplace and recorded his jokey tweets about transgenderism as a Non Crime Hate Incident. He won a legal action in the High Court against the police for this. In court the judge said he understood that 'terf' was "a derogatory term used by those who seek to deplatform those who hold different views." This case was the beginning of Fair Cop's campaign to force the police to do their job "without fear or favour," as they are supposed to do.

There's also the Free Speech Union, a membership organisation that helps people protect their legal right to speak about contentious issues without losing their jobs. They have dealt with thousands of cases since they started in 2020, with gender-critical or trans-related commentary being the single biggest issue they encounter. Most never become public, because the Free Speech Union legal team helps people defend their position with their employer. But there are also high-profile cases like that of Linzi Smith, the football fan who was banned from attending matches at the club she supported, because she had posted on social media that she objected to men in women's sport, and that gender affirmation in schools was counter to NHS advice and was anti-safeguarding.

The rise in employment tribunals and court cases relating to gender ideology has also spawned a new type of citizen reporting, in which volunteers attend hearings and report live on social media, usually by posting on Twitter, now X. Tribunal Tweets was set up to do this in 2020 and has reported dozens of cases.

They are all doing their bit to protect everyone's rights, to ensure that the demands of one group cannot be permitted to override the needs and trash the rights of everyone else. It is still not easy work but it is no longer as lonely, difficult, risky or exhausting as it was.

Early campaigners like Stephanie Davies-Arai, Nicola Williams, Kellie-Jay Keen and Maya Forstater are generally pleased that others have joined the fray and that the burden is now shared across so many brilliant campaigners, even if they don't always agree on campaign tactics. But memories can be short. As the movement has grown, I have met women who have no idea what went on before they got involved. Understandably, they are inclined to give all the credit to the campaigners they can see now. I wrote this book because I wanted to make sure that the work of these courageous women was recorded, acknowledged and remembered. Without them, there would be no Terf Island.

RECOMMENDED READING

Gender Hurts: A Feminist Analysis of the Politics of Transgenderism by Sheila Jeffreys (2014)

Transgender Children and Young People: Born in Your Own Body edited by Heather Brunskell-Evans and Michele Moore (2018)

Inventing Transgender Children and Young People edited by Heather Brunskell-Evans and Michele Moore (2019)

Lesbians at Ground Zero: How Transgenderism Is Queering the Lesbian Body by Angela Wild (2019)

The Politicization of Mumsnet by Sarah Pedersen (2020)

Trans: When Ideology Meets Reality by Helen Joyce (2021)

Material Girls : Why Reality Matters for Feminism by Kathleen Stock (2021)

Transgender Body Politics by Heather Brunskell-Evans (2021)

Feminism for Women: The Real Route to Liberation by Julie Bindel (2021)

Time to Think: The Inside Story of the Collapse of the Tavistock's Gender Service for Children by Hannah Barnes (2023)

Unfair Play: The Battle for Women's Sport by Sharron Davies MBE (2023)

Defending Women's Spaces by Karen Ingala Smith (2023)

Hags: The Demonisation of Middle-aged Women by Victoria Smith (2023)

The Women Who Wouldn't Wheesht edited by Susan Dalgety and Lucy Hunter Blackburn (2024)

Hounded: Women, Harms and the Gender Wars by Jenny Lindsay (2024)

ACKNOWLEDGEMENTS

INTERVIEWING STEPHANIE DAVIES-ARAI, NICOLA WILLIAMS, Kellie-Jay Keen and Maya Forstater was a pleasure, and I owe them huge gratitude. I could not have written the book without the precious time that these warrior women spent talking to me.

The same goes for Venice Allan and Julia Long, and many others who helped me get the story straight or shared their experiences, among them Jo-Ann Atkins, Keira Bell, Michael Biggs, Julie Bindel, Heather Brunskell-Evans, James Caspian, Shelley Charlesworth, Susan Evans, Anya Palmer, Rachel Rooney, Susan Smith, Helen Steel and Janice Turner in the UK, Kara Dansky in the USA, Angie Jones in Australia, and Sarah Anderson and Di Landy in New Zealand. Other women prefer not to be named.

I am grateful to everyone who hunted through their photos for me – several of those above plus Marion Calder, Karen Varley, Nicole Jones, Bryndis Blackadder and Lily Maynard. Lily also gave me permission to use her description of Stephanie's and Helen's childhood. My thanks to Eleanor Bentall, Adam Baines and Pamela Garfield-Jaeger for letting me use their photos, and to Nicole Jones for my author photo.

Big thanks to Helen Joyce for, among many things, that meeting in Pret that helped me clear a blockage at a critical time when I was not sure I could do this.

I appreciate my shadowy agent who doesn't want any credit but who started this whole thing years ago when he approached Nic Williams. She is too modest to write her story so I took it on. His feedback on my early efforts helped me find my writing voice. "The bin is your friend." Thanks Piers.

I approached Susan and Renate of Spinifex Press as a complete stranger at FiLiA in Glasgow in 2023. I was delighted when they expressed an interest, and buoyed by their encouragement as the book took shape. My thanks to them and to Pauline, Deb, Helen and the rest of the Spinifex Press Team for editing, cover design and beautiful layout including the photos.

Joan Smith, Jenny Lindsay and Ursula Doyle generously gave me the benefit of their experience in publishing.

My mum was a great terf and I'm sorry she's not here to see this. My siblings are equally feisty and supportive, as are my children. Most of all I am lucky to have my number one fan and terf-ally, whose belief in me never faltered.

INDEX

Page numbers in **bold** refer to photographs

Other books published by Spinifex Press

Gender Identity: Lies and Dangers

Laura Lecuona

From Mexican philosopher and critic comes a book that is essential reading for the urgently needed conversation we need to have about whose interests are being served with the advancement of transgender ideology and what this means for women's sex-based rights.

ISBN 9781925950908 ebook available

On the Meaning of Sex: Thoughts about the New Definition of Woman

Kajsa Ekis Ekman

Translated by Kristina Mäki

Swedish feminist and Marxist Kajsa Ekis Ekman shows how biological determinism is back – but minus the biology. A brilliant examination of the intellectually incoherent and antifeminist character of gender identity theory.

ISBN 9781925950663 ebook available

Detransition: Beyond Before and After

Max Robinson

In this brave and thoughtful book, Max Robinson goes beyond the 'before' and 'after' of the transition she underwent and takes us through the processes that led her, first to transition in an attempt to get relief from her distress, and then to detransition as she discovered feminist thought and community.

ISBN 9781925950403 ebook available

Transgender Body Politics

Heather Brunskell-Evans

At a time when enlightened attitudes are championed by the mainstream, philosopher and activist Heather Brunskell-Evans shows how, in plain view under the guise of liberalism, a regressive men's rights movement is posing a massive threat to the human rights of women and children everywhere.

ISBN 9781925950229 ebook available

If you would like to know more about Spinifex Press, write to us for a free catalogue, visit our website or email us for further information on how to subscribe to our monthly newsletter.

Spinifex Press
PO Box 105
Mission Beach QLD 4852
Australia

www.spinifexpress.com.au
women@spinifexpress.com.au